150

S0-BYY-584

THE CHALLENGE OF CHANCE

THE CHALLENGE

OF CHANCE

*A Mass Experiment In Telepathy
and Its Unexpected Outcome*

ALISTER HARDY
ROBERT HARVIE
ARTHUR KOESTLER

VINTAGE BOOKS
A DIVISION OF RANDOM HOUSE
NEW YORK

FIRST VINTAGE BOOKS EDITION, March 1975

Part One and Part Two © The Religious Experience
Unit 1973
Part Three and Part Four © Arthur Koestler 1973

Library of Congress Cataloging in Publication Data

Hardy, Sir Alister Clavering.
  The challenge of chance.

  Includes bibliographical references.
  1. Thought–transference—Case studies. 2. Chance—
Case studies. I. Harvie, Robert, joint author.
II. Koestler, Arthur, 1905–   joint author.
III. Title.
[BF1171.H28 1975]   133.8   74–16462
ISBN 0–394–71393–1

CONTENTS

PART ONE

Telepathy or not—or what?

INTRODUCTION

Alister Hardy

Again and again in the history of science investigators have set out to study some particular problem and then found that their researches had led them to something very different from what they were looking for—something quite unexpected. This book is based upon just such a happening; or "is it?," as the saying goes, for some may maintain that what we have found may indeed be related to the nature of our original quest. It is certainly a puzzle. Whatever the consensus of opinion may be as to the true nature of our results, we believe that one way or another they are likely to tell us something new about the queer universe in which we find ourselves. But I must begin at the beginning.

It all goes back to my interest in telepathy, one which I have had for very many years, in fact ever since I had what appeared to be a remarkable demonstration of this alleged phenomenon when I was a very young man some fifty-six years ago. In order to explain the object of the experiments from which the present work arose and the reasons for their particular design, I must, as an introduction, say a little about the development of the study of telepathy since the days when systematic research into its possible reality began. I would also like to say in this introduction just why I think the subject of telepathy is such an important one, important for the understanding of the very nature of ourselves, for it was this conviction that led to the setting up of the experiments in question.

First of all, however, let me relate the particular example I have just referred to, for there can be no doubt that it has colored my whole approach to the subject of telepathy and made me from that day on an interested follower of any research attempting to establish its existence. I quote from the account I gave in the *Proceedings of the Society for Psychical Research* (vol. 50, pp. 105–7, 1953):

They [my experiences] took place during the First World War. For a time I was in a Cyclist Battalion stationed on the Lincolnshire coast where there lived a Mrs. Wedgwood who was very kind in entertaining some of the officers of the regiment. Sir Oliver Lodge's book *Raymond* had just been published, and after we had been discussing it she confessed that she herself had been an amateur medium. She was, I understood, the widow of a Mr. Arthur Wedgwood who, with his brother Hensleigh Wedgwood, was much interested in spiritualism towards the end of the last century. She then very occasionally, by holding objects, claimed to be able to "see" and describe people she had never seen before. Once, by holding a letter she gave a reasonable but not very exact description of my mother who was then alive. I mention this without attaching much value to it only as an introduction to the two cases I consider so important, but in passing I may just say that her description of the path along which my mother and I had so often walked together was much more striking than that of my mother herself.

Mrs. Wedgwood from earlier talks knew that my brother was an engineering student and that he was a prisoner-of-war in Germany. One Sunday afternoon I went up to her house, to tea. With one or two others I had been trying some table-tilting seances with her—without getting anything but quite meaningless messages spelt out—and that afternoon after tea we sat down at the table. A moment or two after I had put my hands on the table next to hers—I cannot remember now whether they touched hers or not—she suddenly said, "Oh, I can see your brother in Germany quite clearly." (I am not reporting her exact words, but as nearly as possible the gist of them.) "I can see him in a little room in his prison camp with a camp bed, he is sitting at a table drawing what I think must be some engineering plan; on a large sheet of white paper I see him painting what seem to be squares and oblongs of red and blue." Actually she had described exactly what I had been doing myself all that afternoon and no one else knew I had been doing it. Our colonel had a great interest in military history and was giving the officers a series of lectures on Monday evenings on various campaigns. He knew I was quick at drawing and he had asked me to make a map for him to illustrate his next talk on the Franco-Prussian War. He didn't know how I was going to do it; it was only that afternoon that I had the idea of cutting out squares and oblongs of card painted red and blue to represent the various units of infantry, cavalry and artillery of the two sides so that he could move them about on pins to their different positions as the lecture proceeded. It was an obvious thing to do, but he had only asked me to prepare a large map of the area. I spent the greater part of the afternoon—in my rather bare room in my billet with a camp-bed in it—looking at the large white map and moving the red and blue cards about following a description of the campaign and making pencil marks where they should be at different stages. After I had finished I put the cards away, rolled up the map, and went straight off on my bicycle to tea with Mrs. Wedgwood: I am absolutely certain that no one could have told her before I went what I had been doing. I would find it difficult to believe that the correspondence of her description of what she thought my brother was doing and what I myself had actually been doing all afternoon was mere coincidence; with another case of almost the same kind I am convinced that coincidence cannot explain it.

The second case was a year later. I was now attached to the Royal Engineers as a camouflage officer and was attending a special course at the school set up in Kensington Gardens under Solomon J. Solomon, R.A. Mrs. Wedgwood came to stay in London whilst I was there and I went out to dinner with her. The case is remarkably like the other one. That afternoon at the school we were doing experiments in dazzle effects. I had taken a large sheet of white cardboard and then painted it all over with a most vivid pink distemper. I was then going to cut it up into all sorts of shapes to use in our experiments, but I found it took much longer to dry than I had expected so that I had it in front of me and kept looking at it to see if it was ready for some considerable time before I actually cut it up. Again I am quite certain that no one could have told Mrs. Wedgwood what I had been doing, for no one at the camouflage school knew her or knew that I was going out to dinner with her. I had not sat down at the dinner table with her for more than a moment or two when she suddenly said, "Oh, what have you been doing? I see a large pink square on the table in front of you."

There is no need to emphasize how alike the two cases are; I will only add that I know I have a good visual memory and that color and shape make a strong impression on me. It was not as if Mrs. Wedgwood frequently made statements as to what she thought I, or people connected with me, had been doing and that these particular cases just described were the only two correct ones. The only other occasion I believe when she made such a statement to me was the one concerning my mother that I have already referred to.

There can be no doubt that this made a tremendous impression on me. From that time on I must admit that I was myself, in my heart of hearts, convinced that telepathy was real; at the same time I knew that my account was not scientifically good evidence and could not convince others. It was one more example of the vast number of such cases of spontaneous telepathy reported in the files of the Society for Psychical Research. The psychologists will say (and indeed have said) that it is evidence of my pleasure in telling a good story; all I can say is that what I have recorded has been for me as real an observation as any that I have ever made in the field of natural history. Before leaving the account, however, I should, I think, draw attention to an expression that I used and to make my point I have now introduced italics: in regard to the first instance I wrote "I would find it difficult to believe that . . . [it] . . . was mere *coincidence*; with another case of almost the same kind I am convinced that *coincidence* cannot explain it." It never occurred to me when I wrote that, or indeed until quite recently, that the word or idea of "coincidence" might imply anything more than mere chance; now, however, I cannot be so sure, but that again is just what our book is about, and I am bound to say that I am still puzzled. We can hardly expect that what we are writing will solve the question, but we may I think hope that the evidence we shall present, both experimental and anecdotal, will make a contribution towards its eventual solution in the future.

Whilst there have been such disconcerting results in the experiments which we are on the way to discuss, I want, before going any further, to assure the reader that, quite apart from these unexpected findings, I am still convinced, on account of the evidence which comes from a number of experiments by others, of the existence of what I call "real" telepathy; these experiments we shall refer to later, for they seem to come under quite a different category. I feel I should make this quite clear before going on, as I shall now do, to explain just why I regard the study of telepathy as so particularly important.

I think there can be no doubt that if telepathy could be demonstrated experimentally in such a way that the results would be fully accepted by the scientific world—in fact to become a part of true science—then it must have profound philosophical consequences. Not only would it influence the course of academic philosophy, but it would, I believe, have a considerable impact upon thought in the fields of both religion and science. I venture to think that it would have in this century an effect similar in magnitude to that which the acceptance of evolution theory had in the last.

If we can get cast-iron evidence that one mind can communicate with another by other than physical means, it will at once bring about a revolution in present-day ideas of the mind–brain relationship. It would at once lend plausibility to the possibility that the influence which religious people feel when they say they are in touch with what seems to them to be some transcendental element—a power that affects their lives, whether they call it God or not—may be something within the same field as extrasensory telepathic communication. Could it perhaps be, to put it at its very lowest, that the element that is at the back of all religion might be some extrasensory shared spiritual experience; perhaps some source of spiritual "know-how" which may be tapped by those who may have discovered or learnt the way of making rapport with it—something perhaps like the shared subconscious of Jung? I think myself that it is likely to be something very much greater.

It is premature to speculate; and it is presumptuous to suppose, even if telepathy is thoroughly established within the scientific world, that it may at once present us with the key to so great a mystery. Nevertheless, if it can be shown to be a fact it would be a most important step towards the recognition of the non-material extrasensory world in which the numinous—to use Rudolf Otto's term for the *"mysterium tremendum"* of religion—would appear to lie. I have already indicated elsewhere[1] that I regard religion—and I don't mean institutional religion or theological dogma, but the faculty of religious experience, or spiritual awareness if you like—as a fundamental feature of man's make-up. If this should be neglected or suppressed by a culture which may be based upon a false materialism, then our civilization may indeed be in danger. This is why I regard the study and establishment of telepathy as so tremendously important.

---

[1] Superior figures refer to end-of-part notes.

In the field of science it would be equally revolutionary. When once established as true for man, it could surely not be supposed that such a remarkable faculty of one mind communicating with another by other than normal physical sensory means would be likely to be unique to just one species—man. I astonished many of my colleagues when I introduced this idea into my Presidential Address to the Zoology Section of the British Association at its meeting in Newcastle in 1949. It caused quite a flutter in the dovecot and I was gratified that it led to the holding of a special symposium on paranormal phenomena at the London conference of the Society for Experimental Biology in the following January at which I was kindly invited to be Chairman. It was I believe the first time that any biological society had held such a discussion. At the risk of perhaps being a little technical I think I cannot do better than quote from my British Association address[2] to show the sort of way in which I believe the subject could have important implications in the realm of biology. This is what I said:

There is another matter which I feel it only right to mention if one is not to be intellectually dishonest. There has appeared over the horizon something which many of us do not like to look at. If it is pointed out to us we say: "No, it can't be there, our doctrines say it is impossible." I refer to telepathy—the communication of one mind with another by means other than by the ordinary senses. I believe that no one, who examines the evidence with an unbiased mind, can reject it . . .

It is perhaps unorthodox for a zoologist to introduce such a topic; but I do so for a reason. If telepathy has been established, as I believe it has, then such a revolutionary discovery should make us keep our minds open to the possibility that there may be so much more in living things and their evolution than our science has hitherto led us to expect. Such an idea as I am about to suggest is no doubt highly improbable and would perhaps be better kept locked in a bottom drawer; I mention it however merely as a reminder that perhaps our ideas on evolution may be altered if something akin to telepathy—unconscious no doubt—was found to be a factor in molding the patterns of behavior among members of a species. If there was such a nonconscious group behavior plan, distributed between, and linking, the individuals of the race, we might find ourselves coming back to something like those ideas of subconscious racial memory of Samuel Butler, but on a group rather than an individual basis. It would remove many of the fatal difficulties of his hypothesis. Samuel Butler's ideas were of course the logical development of Lamarck's, but thought of independently. If there was such a group habit and behavior pattern, it might operate through organic selection to modify the course of evolution: working through selection acting on the gene-complex. If this flight of fancy ever proved to be a fact, it would be a wedding of the ideas of Darwin and Mendel on the one hand and of Lamarck and Samuel Butler on the other!

If I appear to be ending in fantasy or in the spirit of harlequinade, I do so only to emphasize my conviction that we fool ourselves if we imagine that our present ideas about life and evolution are more than a tiny fraction of the truth yet to be discovered in the almost endless years ahead. We are but at the threshold of our understanding of living things.

It is interesting that it has been the philosophers, rather than the scientists, who have tended to take telepathy seriously and some are fully convinced by the evidence available. Professor H. H. Price, when he was Wykeham Professor of Logic at Oxford, writing in the *Hibbert Journal*,[3] said: "Telepathy is something which ought not to happen at all, if the Materialistic theory were true. But it does happen. So there must be something seriously wrong with the Materialistic theory, however numerous and imposing the *normal* facts which support it may be." And the late Professor C. D. Broad, who was Knightbridge Professor of Moral Philosophy at Cambridge, makes the same point: "Telepathy . . . is now an experimentally established fact. There is also ample evidence of sporadic telepathic hallucinations in connection with deaths, accidents, illnesses and other causes. . . . Now it is scarcely possible to reconcile with these facts the epiphenomenalist theory of mind and body which is commonly . . . assumed without question by most scientists and many philosophers. These facts are therefore of the utmost philosophical importance."[4]

It was another eminent Cambridge philosopher, Professor Henry Sidgwick, one of the pioneer founders and the first President of the Society for Psychical Research (which I shall now refer to as the S.P.R.), who in his inaugural Address in 1882 said: ". . . it is a scandal that the dispute as to the reality of these phenomena should still be going on, that so many competent witnesses should have declared their belief in them, that so many others should be profoundly interested in having the question determined, and yet that the educated world, as a body, should still be simply in the attitude of incredulity."

Since that date this pioneer Society under a long line of distinguished Presidents has, through its members, carried out investigations with the highest standards of scholarship in this difficult field, and published over a hundred volumes of research: yet until recently the skepticism or indifference of the intellectual world at large has remained practically unchanged, except for one class of phenomena, which I shall mention in a moment.

In the first volume of the *Proceedings of the S.P.R.* there is a list of subjects which it is felt important that the Society should investigate. The first two are given as follows:

1. An examination of the nature and extent of any influence which may be exerted by one mind upon another, apart from any generally recognised mode of perception.

2. The study of hypnotism, and the forms of so-called mesmeric trance, with its alleged insensibility to pain; clairvoyance and other allied phenomena.

There follow a number of other subjects, such as apparitions, disturbances in houses reputed to be haunted, an inquiry into the phenomena of spiritualism and so on. Whilst it is with the first item that we are here concerned, I would like to point out that of all the subjects listed for study in 1882 it is only hypnotism which has so far received general scientific acceptance. This is probably because it was found to have important applications in medical and psychiatric practice. Whilst these phenomena of hypnotism are accepted, I doubt if they are really understood any more than are those in other fields of psychical research.

Once my interest in telepathy was generated by the experience I have related I was led to study the available experimental evidence: this was in the days well before the development of the card-guessing techniques, introduced by Professor Rhine and his followers in the thirties, which have dominated the subject ever since. It is to these earlier experiments that I will now turn, for they very much influenced me in the design of the tests which I shall presently describe. I particularly want to refer to the series of experiments carried out at Liverpool by Mr. Malcolm Guthrie, who was a J.P. and a member of the Council of the then University College, and Mr. James Birchall, a headmaster and Honorary Secretary of the Liverpool Literary and Philosophical Society; these are reported in detail in three papers in the *Proceedings of the S.P.R.*[5] together with a separate account of some of the experiments made under the supervision of Dr. Oliver Lodge (later Sir Oliver) who was then Professor of Physics at the University College.[6] The ones in which I am specially interested are those concerned with the transmission of the impressions of relatively simple drawings and designs, because it is these which have some resemblance to my own former experience. I consider these investigations to be important because they were conducted under conditions of strict supervision and in each

experiment either Mr. Guthrie, Mr. Birchall, Professor
Oliver Lodge or another responsible person acted as agent,
i.e., attempting to transmit the impression, so that unless
we suspect all of these gentlemen of fraud, for they all at
times got positive results, there can be no question of the
successes being due to trickery by the use of some code to
transmit the impression to the percipient as has been shown
to be used by some professional performers. The drawings
were made either in another room or behind a screen and
looked at by the agent in such a way that they could not
have been seen by the percipient, yet the latter was able on
many occasions to draw a remarkably close reproduction of
the design drawn and looked at by the agent. During one
set of six consecutive trials five drawings were correctly
reproduced as shown in the accompanying Figure 1. Whilst
coincidences, as we shall see, may be very remarkable, I do
not think that those five out of six almost exact reproductions can have such an explanation. Several other series of
experiments similar to the Liverpool ones are also recorded
in the early volumes of the *Proceedings of the S.P.R.*

These experiments, if true, would appear to suggest a

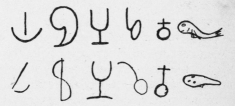

FIGURE 1 Some results from the telepathy experiments conducted by
Guthrie and Birchall at Liverpool under strict control conditions in
1883. A complete consecutive series of six drawings transmitted by
Mr. Guthrie (shown in the upper line) to Miss E. who made the
corresponding drawings shown in the lower line. Traced from the
originals which were reproduced in the *Proceedings of the S.P.R.*
Vol. II, 1884.

type of telepathy—the transference of original patterns of thought from one mind to another—that seems to me to be very different from that supposed to be demonstrated by the card-guessing techniques which as I have said have dominated parapsychology for the last forty years. Why do I think they are so different? I will try to explain.

The great advantage of the card-guessing type of experiments developed by Professor Rhine and his colleagues at Duke University in America, and now repeated in most of the countries of the world, lies in the fact that their results may readily be subjected to quantitative statistical analysis. Whilst these at first sight appeared to provide statistical support for telepathy, I found myself having misgivings. My difficulty was, and still is, that although I am sure that the statistical tests applied to the card experiments are demonstrating card guessing, I cannot be sure that such guessing really shows what I mean by telepathy, i.e., the transference of a thought, *an idea*, from one mind to another without the use of the normal sensory channels. To make my point I must briefly discuss the methods used. Whilst these will be well known to many readers, I will summarize them for the sake of those who are not yet familiar with them.

Instead of ordinary playing cards Rhine and his followers used packs of twenty-five cards, each bearing one of five different symbols: a square, a circle, a cross, a star, or wavy lines; five of each kind of card made up a pack. In an experiment designed to test for possible telepathy one person, called the agent, would go through a shuffled pack looking at each card turned over whilst another person, the recipient, being placed in such a position (in another room or behind a screen, etc.) that it was impossible for him or her to see the cards the agent was looking at, wrote down "cross," "square," "star," etc., according to which card he thought the agent was looking at. At the end of a run it was then seen how many of the guesses were correct. According to probability theory—since there were five of each different kind of card in a pack of twenty-five—one would expect, if the experiment was repeated many times, that, just by *chance*, the average score of correct hits would be 5; now, if a person over several hundred runs scored an average of, say, 7, 8 or 9, then it was assumed that he or she had on a number of occasions received a telepathic impression of the kind of card the agent was looking at.

Why am I doubtful about it being telepathy? It very soon came as a shock to me, when examining the accounts of the experiments, to find that Rhine and others were getting exactly the same kind of results, above chance, with certain subjects guessing the cards being turned over by the agent but without him (the agent) looking at them at all: guessing them by what is called clairvoyance. I may be prejudiced—I expect I am—but I confess I find it much easier to imagine one mind being in touch with another mind—two elements of a similar kind—than to conceive of a mind being able to know what kind of design is on the underside of a card which has never yet been made visible to any living mental system. The former, if true, is certainly marvelous, but the latter looks like magic. Then came precognition which seemed equally difficult to imagine, but was apparently demonstrated by just such similar statistics. Here the subject guesses not the card being looked at or turned over, but the card which will *next* be looked at, or with some subjects the next but one. More recently still has come psychokinesis, the alleged influence of the mind upon falling dice which is once again "seemingly established" by scoring the same sort of above-chance results as may be found in other fields. And there are some people guessing cards who have repeatedly and significantly scored with *below* chance results—i.e., more often wrong than they should be by chance—a curious and difficult matter to explain. Whilst I think many of us have felt uneasy at the similarity of the evidence of these four very different alleged phenomena, it remained for Mr. G. Spencer Brown of Trinity College, Cambridge, to suggest the alternative and simple hypothesis that all this experimental work in so-called telepathy, clairvoyance, precognition and psychokinesis, which depends upon obtaining results above chance, may really be demonstrating some single and very different principle. He believes[7] that it may be something no less fundamental or interesting—but not telepathy or these other curious things—some thing implicit in the very nature and meaning of randomness itself. I am not mathematically competent to pass judgment upon his views.

The difficulty in distinguishing between so-called telepathy and clairvoyance in the card-guessing experiments has recently been well expressed by the Cambridge psychologist Dr. R. H. Thouless when he writes as follows: "We do not indeed know whether these are two different processes or whether they are merely two names we give to the same process under different conditions of operating."[8] And he goes on to say that while it might be better simply to call them both some form of extrasensory perception, even this would be objected to on the ground that it implies that the process *is* some kind of perception. He then suggests that "One may avoid this implication by coining an entirely new term which carries no implications whatever, and say that a *psi*-process is taking place." But then he adds: "If, however, one uses the term 'extrasensory perception,' one is more likely to be generally understood." I see what he means, but we certainly don't understand it, and, as he himself indicates, we don't know that it *is* perception at all.

Since we cannot doubt the above-chance results that have been obtained in now thousands of experiments carried out in most of the countries of the world, I have sometimes been tempted with an awful thought. It is one I hardly like to admit; yet I think it illustrates our quandary in regard to these card-guessing experiments. It is this. Is it possible that what all these experiments with cards are really demonstrating is a measurement of what we *in our ignorance* more usually call luck: that some people *are* in fact, at any rate at times, much luckier, whatever that may really mean, at card guessing than others? This indeed is a shocking thing for a scientist to say, but I say it because I want to make the point that this should in fact be *no more shocking* to the scientific position of today than the fact now statistically established by significance tests that there *are* a number of people who are able to guess correctly, more often than can be accounted for by the present theory of probability, which cards are which in a pack they haven't seen. The idea of luck and that of clairvoyance are *equally shocking* to our present scientific view of the universe. Is there something about probability which we do not understand, as suggested by Spencer Brown, or is there something about card guessing and perhaps the supposed "influencing" of dice (for most of the psychokinesis experiments have been done with dice) which is just as queer as what we call luck, but which scientific law has not yet got hold of?

These were the lines of thought that led me to design the experiments we are about to describe. I wanted to get away from the card-guessing procedures and to go back to an attempt to obtain evidence for the transference of whole patterns of thought, ideas, complex designs, and so on, rather than just guessing which of a few known symbols are being looked at; so I decided to work with drawings and photographs.

PLANNING THE EXPERIMENTS

Alister Hardy

Hitherto most of the experiments designed to test telepathy have been performed with just one or perhaps two or three people acting as agents in looking at a drawing or picture. I thought it possible that one might break new ground if one worked with, say, some two hundred people acting as agents—all considering the same idea—and say perhaps twenty people, isolated from everyone else, acting as percipients. There were several reasons for trying this plan.

Firstly, I thought that if we had some two hundred people all looking at the same picture, say of a balloon going up, there would be a greater influence (if telepathy was true) than if there were only one or two thinking of a balloon. Secondly, if we used such a number of agents and percipients, we might in each experiment have a better chance of coming across people who might be more gifted in such powers than others. And thirdly—this certainly a "long shot"—was the idea that since the laws of physics and chemistry, and so the repeatable experiments in these sciences, depend upon one dealing with very large numbers of atoms and molecules, the same might apply to psychic phenomena. If one confines oneself to experimenting with small numbers of atoms and molecules, the laws of physics and chemistry no longer hold; might it not be possible that if these paranormal phenomena depended upon some individual "psi" units we might never discover the laws regarding them if we only dealt with one or two minds at a time? It was just an idea perhaps worth trying.

The S.P.R. helped me both financially and in organization to set up just such experiments in the autumn of 1967. I am particularly grateful for all the work put in to make the arrangements a success by Sir George Joy, K.B.E., C.M.G., who was then Hon. Secretary to the Society, Mr. John H. Cutten, who later succeeded him in this capacity, and Mrs. Pauline Osborn, Secretary (later to become Lady Joy). One of the large lecture rooms of Caxton Hall, Westminster, was hired for seven consecutive Monday evenings from September 11th to October 23rd. All the members of the Society in London and the neighboring areas were invited to take part in the experiments, together with friends who would be interested, provided that they would agree to attend, as far as possible, at all seven sessions; in this way the cooperation of a group of some two hundred people was ensured for the whole series.

The arrangement of the hall for the experiments was as shown in Figures 2, 3 and 4. Towards the back twenty light-proof cubicles, made of double black-out material supported on metal frames, were arranged in four rows of five. In these would be seated the twenty people selected in each experiment to be the so-called percipients whilst around them, i.e., in front and on either side, the remainder of the two hundred people taking part would be seated to act as the so-called agents. Those who were in the cubicles could not see what all the others outside them could see in the way of drawings, symbols or photographs being displayed on the raised platform at the end of the hall. The people selected to be the "percipients" were chosen in alphabetical order and ten experiments were performed

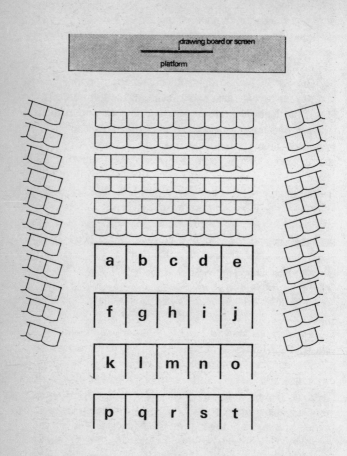

FIGURE 2 Plan of the usual arrangement for the Caxton Hall telepathy experiments. The cubicles in which the "percipients" sat (four rows of five) are shown in heavy line, lettered *a* to *t*, and intentionally drawn larger than they should be in relation to the size of the seating in the hall; actually there were "agents" seats at the ends of each row of cubicles as shown in the photographs opposite. The corresponding arrangement in the small experiments is shown in Figure 5.

FIGURE 3 Photograph of the cubicles as arranged in the typical large telepathy experiments in the Caxton Hall.

FIGURE 4 Another view of the arrangement at the Caxton Hall showing the platform and drawing board.

with each group of twenty; these would then be replaced by
the next twenty and so on. Two such sets of ten experiments
were performed on each of the seven evenings, making a
total of 140 experiments, so that all those taking part were
eventually tested. At the beginning of each session I explained the procedure being adopted and stressed the importance of everyone remaining absolutely silent whilst
any experiment was being conducted: to be careful, for
example, not to allow oneself to make even the slightest
involuntary sound such as a sigh, a gasp of surprise or a
little laugh which might indicate something of the nature
of the drawing or photograph being displayed. I will now
describe in detail how one such experiment was performed.

Let us suppose the twenty "percipients" are already
seated in their cubicles, screened at the sides and in front,
but open to a gangway behind which is patrolled by an
assistant who acts as a supervisor—one to each row of five
cubicles—to see that no attempt is made by the "percipients"
to communicate in any way with anyone in another cubicle
or outside the cubicles. Each "percipient" was provided
with a board, a sheet of paper and a felt pen. The essence
of each experiment was that the "percipients," on hearing
a buzzer telling them that either a drawing was being made
or a lantern slide being shown, should if possible make a
rough sketch or, if not, describe in a few words what impressions came into their minds: i.e., what they thought
was being shown by drawing or slide to the main body of
those in the hall and so possibly being transmitted from their
minds to them if telepathy was a reality.

Each sheet of paper was marked in the top right-hand
corner with the number of the experiment followed by a
small letter a, b, c or d, etc., which indicated its position in
the group of twenty cubicles: a, b, c, d and e forming the
first row; f, g, h, i, j, the second row, and k, l, m, n, o, and

p, q, r, s, t, being respectively those in the last two rows. By this means we could know the relative positions of all the results in each experiment, for example that *c* and *d* or *l* and *m* came from cubicles next-door to each other, whereas results *h* and *m* or *n* and *s* came from cubicles one behind the other or again that *l* and *h* or *n* and *t* were adjacent in a diagonal direction and so on. Then before any experiment began, each "percipient" was asked to write his name at the top left-hand corner, which would enable us to get in touch later, if we so wished, with anyone taking part, since we had all their addresses.

Now, let us suppose in the experiment I am describing that a drawing was being used as the target picture. The particular subject of the drawing was chosen in the following manner. The names of a hundred possible drawable objects were written on separate small cards and put in a box and shaken up; then as I went up to the screen to make the drawing, I invited some person in the front two or three rows, a different person each time, to put his hand into the box and draw out a card at random. This was the object I had to draw. I can draw very quickly—like a "lightning artist," some people say. The drawing was done in bold black chalk on a large white sheet of paper, large enough to be clearly seen by all those in the hall, except, of course, those in the cubicles. The first five drawings to be made, i.e., in the first five experiments, were for example a clown, a bat, a crown, a zebra and a dovecot. As soon as I started to draw, a buzzer sounded, letting those in the cubicles know that the experiment had started. At the end of a minute the buzzer went again, indicating that the experiment was over. In the first few experiments I varied the duration slightly, trying a minute and a half on one occasion, which was thought by those taking part to be too long, saying their thoughts wandered, and three-quarters of a minute, which was thought to be too short; so for the great majority of tests the drawing or slide was exposed for one minute. As soon as the "percipients" had finished making their drawing or written description, their papers were collected up by the supervisors and new sheets of paper appropriately numbered were issued for the next experiment. When all the papers from one experiment had been received, I then allowed the participants in the cubicles to stand up and look at the target drawing or slide to see if they had received any idea of it. This, perhaps, was a mistake, as I shall later explain; it was done, however, to keep up their morale, for it was felt that if they never knew whether they were getting near the target or not they would soon lose interest.

The procedure when showing a lantern slide was similar. The buzzer went as soon as the picture was thrown on the screen and again at the end of a minute when the picture was switched off. The lantern which was situated in front of the cubicles was worked by a professional operator who was given a black bag containing a hundred slides of different subjects into which he put his hand and drew out a slide at random. The subjects of the slides were all somewhat striking photographs having some emotional content, such for example as a ship sinking, children playing, a mountain peak, beautiful flowers, or a famous building. The first ten experiments made with the first twenty "percipients" consisted of five drawings and five with lantern slides and the same arrangement was followed in the second ten experiments. It was then suggested that better results might be obtained if, instead of using drawings of objects, a series of brightly colored simple designs or symbols were used; in subsequent experiments a number of tests were made with such symbols as for example an orange disk, a red cross, a green shamrock leaf, a black club, a blue fleur-de-lis, or a yellow star, in addition to drawings and slides in the following arrangements:

Experiments	21–30:	3	drawings,	3	symbols,	4	slides
	31–40:	3	"	3	"	4	"
"	41–50:	3	"	4	"	3	"
"	51–60:	3	"	4	"	3	"
"	61–70:	4	"	3	"	3	"
"	71–80:	4	"	3	"	3	"
"	81–90:	4	"	2	"	4	"
"	91–100:	4	"	2	"	4	"

It was then felt, on the preliminary examination of the results, that the use of symbols was giving no better results than with drawings or slides and also that they proved more difficult to judge; consequently in the remaining forty experiments, numbers 101 to 140, each series of ten consisted of seven drawings and three slides.

It should be stated that at the beginning of each experiment it was known to all, including the "percipients," whether the target was to be in the form of a drawing, a simple colored symbol or a photographic slide. In the case of the symbols the "percipients" were particularly asked to record any impression of color which came to them.

Before coming to the results, I should describe some other changes in procedure which were made in the course of the experiments. During the first four evening sessions, i.e., Experiments 1 to 80, the arrangement of the cubicles was as shown in Figure 2, i.e., twenty arranged in four rows of five. It was then thought that perhaps better results might be obtained if the "percipients" were not massed together in one block of cubicles, but had their cubicles more separated with seats for those acting as "agents" (those who could see the drawings or slides) between them, so that each "percipient" would be more surrounded by "agents" than in the former case. This arrangement was also prompted by the nature of some of the "apparent results" as will be presently explained when we come to them. Now the cubicles were constructed of metal frames, which could readily be assembled and taken down again, and for simplicity and economy were so made that three complete cubicles could be linked together to make a row of five just by adding a front panel between them. Since we now wished to separate them, we could only have four rows of three cubicles, i.e., twelve, with seats of "agents" between them, instead of the usual sets of twenty. Experiments 81 to 90 and 91 to 100 were thus made with only twelve "percipients" so separated, as shown in Figure 5. Experiments 101 to 130 were then made with the full complement again of twenty cubicles, and then in the last ten trials, 131 to 140, we went back to the separated conditions and so reduced the "percipients" to twelve.

From the foregoing we see that out of the total of 140 experiments, 110 were made with twenty "percipients" each (i.e., Experiments 1 to 80 and 101 to 130) which yielded a

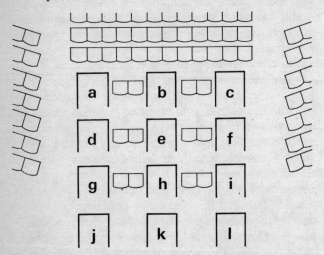

FIGURE 5 Plan of the arrangement of the cubicles in the small experiments.

total of 2,200 individual responses and 30 experiments were made with twelve "percipients" each (i.e., Experiments 81 to 100 and 131 to 140) yielding 360 individual responses. In the discussion of the results which follows, these two types of experiment are referred to as large and small experiments respectively. It is seen that altogether there were 2,560 responses. Of these, however, 448 were made to targets employing formal symbols which, as already explained, were found more difficult to compare with those made when drawings or photographs were used; for this reason they were excluded from the present study, leaving a total of 2,112 responses to be considered. To judge even this number, a great deal of work was involved.

My own examination made me realize how very difficult it was to make a proper assessment of the results and that the only way to demonstrate conclusively that they were other than could be accounted for by chance coincidences would be to devise some kind of "control experiment" in which numbers of different thoughts could be assembled at random to compare with the actual experimental responses. To make this further investigation and also later to carry out more experiments to test for telepathy, I required the assistance of a colleague who should be a psychology graduate with a training in statistical methods. With the help of a grant from the Parapsychology Foundation of New York and from the Society for Psychical Research I was enabled to appoint my colleague Mr. Robert Harvie, a graduate of London University with these qualifications. It was he who devised the nature of the "control experiments" we have used which are a great deal better and simpler than the ones I myself had envisaged. We will now together discuss the actual results of the original experiments as they were performed at the Caxton Hall, and then in a later section Robert Harvie will discuss the controls.

EXPERIMENTAL RESULTS

Alister Hardy & Robert Harvie

We shall deal first with what we shall call the direct hits, by which we mean drawings or written descriptions made by the "percipients" which we both judged to bear a close relation to the target drawing or slide being shown in the particular experiment concerned; these were the type of results which, if telepathy existed, the experiments had been designed to demonstrate. There were, indeed, what at first sight appeared to be some outstanding examples of such "direct hits"; their number, however, was small in relation to the number of percipients taking part. In addition, however, there were these other unexpected results which seemed to be even more striking: remarkably similar thoughts which occurred to two or more people within the cubicles in the same experiment but which had nothing to do with the "target" drawing or slide being shown. It is these "coincident thoughts," as we shall call them, which suggested that examples of spontaneous telepathy might be taking place in the experiments, and it is mainly with these that this part of the book will be concerned, so that we shall only deal very briefly with the so-called direct hits.

The ostensible direct hits

There were altogether 35 examples of what might be thought to be direct hits; these were out of the total of

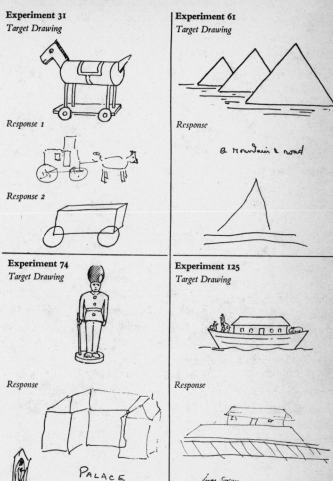

Experiment 31
Target Drawing

Response 1

Response 2

Experiment 61
Target Drawing

Response

a mountain & road

Experiment 74
Target Drawing

Response

PALACE

Experiment 125
Target Drawing

Response

Railway Station.

FIGURE 6 Four selected examples of ostensible "direct hits" in the telepathy experiments where drawings were used as targets. In each case the target drawing is shown immediately above the corresponding response. These results should be compared with those of the control "mock" experiments shown in Figure 37.

Experiment 9

Target slide

Response

Experiment 29

Target slide

Response

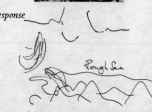

Experiment 58

Target slide

Response 1

Sea or watery scene

Response 2

Something to do with Sea
or Water

Experiment 68

Target slide

Response

FIGURE 7 Four selected examples of ostensible "direct hits" in the
telepathy experiments where photo-slides were used as targets. In
each case the target photograph is shown immediately above the corresponding response. These again should be compared with those of
the control "mock" experiments shown in Figure 38.

Experiment 88

Target slide

Response

This is something that gyrates — a
whirling feeling.

Experiment 97

Target slide

Response

Experiment 99

Target slide

Response

Experiment 100

Target slide

Response

Cat drinking

FIGURE 8 Four more selected examples of ostensible "direct hits" where photo-slides were used as targets, arranged as in Figure 7.

Experiment 109

Target slide

Response 1

Yacht with white sails on a river or estuary or bay with only rippling waves & a bank in the background of low ground

Response 2

boat on sea & arb behind

Experiment 119

Target slide

Response 1 Mountains. + snow.

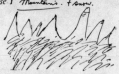

Response 2

Planes in sky

Mountains

Experiment 129

Target slide

Response Something to do with snow —

? children snowballing.

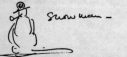

Snow man —

Experiment 139

Target slide

Response

A savage meal.

FIGURE 9 A further selection of possible "direct hits."

2,112 responses, making a percentage of only 1.6. Now, in spite of the small number and the results of the control tests to be discussed later, there were, as we have said, some very striking examples. Were they the results of telepathy or what we call coincidence? In Figure 6 we reproduce four examples from those where drawings were used as a target and in each of Figures 7, 8 and 9 four in which photograph slides were used. In each case facsimile reproductions of the response or responses are shown immediately below the target pictures. In Figure 6 it is surely tempting to suppose that the little guardsman drawn in the sentry-box outside the Palace in Experiment 74 has some relation to the drawing of the toy soldier; that the mountain and road drawn in Experiment 61 has a relation to the pyramids which were the target drawing; and that the railway station drawn in Experiment 125 is related to the target drawing of a Noah's ark, for it is almost identical *except* for the fact that the ends of the platform of the station slope down whereas those of the hull of the ark slope up. Or again, look at the photograph examples in Figure 7: the owl made in response to the owl photograph in Experiment 9 was the only owl *drawing* made in the whole series but with one other verbal response "owl" in Experiment 62; the drawing of the rough sea in response to the photograph in Experiment 29 is surely remarkable in that it represents the great wave thrown up in the background exactly like the photograph. The view of the snow mountains taken from an airplane used as the target in Experiment 119 (Figure 9) was accompanied by two snow mountain range responses, one of which had airplanes in the sky over them—just chance coincidence? Look also at the cannibal drawing labeled "a savage meal" made in response to the target of a native war dance in Experiment 139 (Figure 9), and is not the snowman, accompanied by the words "something to do with snow—? children snowballing," made in response to the penguin photograph in Experiment 129 (Figure 9) rather a nice association? We shall come back to these possible "direct hits" after we have come to the subsequent control tests (p. 107); before doing so, however, we must pass to these other seemingly extraordinary results which came out of the experiments, for it is with those coincident responses that we are mainly concerned and a consideration of them may influence our interpretation of these suggested direct hit responses.

Were there precognitive hits?

It may in passing be mentioned that we considered the possibility of there being some precognitive hits in our series, for at first sight it did appear as if this might be the case. When for instance a drawing of a butterfly formed the target for Experiment 15, it was found that a butterfly drawing had appeared as a response to Experiment 14, or when a wheelbarrow was drawn as the target for Experiment 42, a very similar drawing had appeared as a response in Experiment 41. A search was made for all such possible precognitive hits. In the whole series it was found that there were 16 such examples of similar drawings or ideas being expressed as responses in experiments immediately before those in which a corresponding target was used. Similar examinations were made for such examples as might occur when going back to two experiments before the targets, and again going back three, four and five times; these respectively yielded 14, 9, 12 and 17 responses which might be considered as possibly precognitive. These together with the score of 16 when going back to only the preceding experiments give an average of 13 out of the total of 2,112 responses, a mere 0.6 per cent. In view of the chance coincidences to be demonstrated later by the control tests for the possible direct hits, we can say at once that these cannot be regarded as significant.

The consideration of there being any post-cognitive hits was, of course, ruled out by the participants having been allowed, as explained above (p. 24), to see the target pictures after their papers had been collected at the end of each experiment.

Coincident thoughts

When one arranges the sets of twenty responses from each experiment in their relative positions as situated in the group of twenty cubicles, i.e., in four rows of five, one is often struck with the occurrence of remarkably similar drawings or written statements of ideas made by two or sometimes three, or very occasionally even four or five, of the "percipients" during the same experiment but which had no relationship to the drawing or photograph being used as a target. Very often these similar drawings or ideas came from cubicles in close proximity to one another, but it should be noted that, if they were adjacent, they were not always next-door to one another which to the skeptic might suggest some collusion between them, but just as often one behind the other, i.e., with a gangway in between under the scrutiny of the supervisor. It was as if there were small pockets of thought common to two or three localized participants. Sometimes the drawings were almost exact replicas of one another, as in those in Figure 10 (pp. 36–7), and it may be mentioned that in the whole series of 2,112 responses there were no other armchairs so much alike in form or perspective as those (which were next-door to each other) in Experiment 15, and the same is true for the lampposts of Experiment 111 which were one behind the other with an intervening row of cubicles in between. Also in

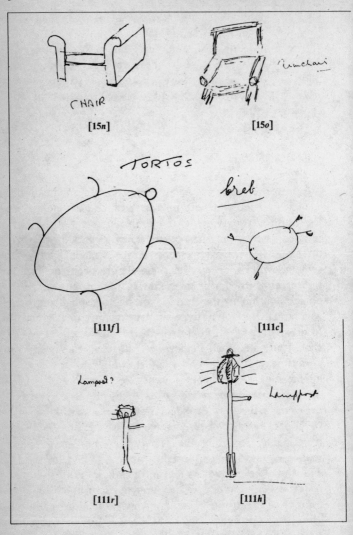

CHAIR

[15n]

armchair

[15o]

TORTOS

[111f]

breb

[111c]

Lampost?

[111r]

Lamppost

[111h]

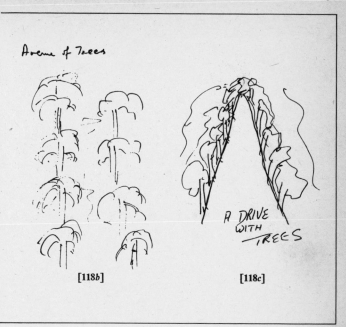

FIGURE 10 Examples of pairs of coincident thoughts occurring in the same experiments but bearing no relation to the target drawing or photograph; they appeared (at first sight) to suggest the occurrence of spontaneous telepathy.

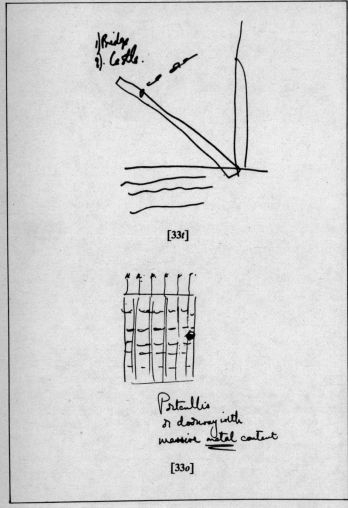

FIGURE 11 Two drawings made in cubicles which were one behind the other in the same experiment (33), which suggested a telepathic association of ideas.

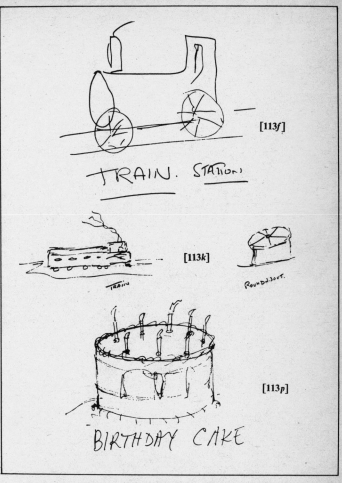

FIGURE 12 Three drawings made in cubicles one behind the other in Experiment 113. The person in the middle at *k* drew a train and what he called a roundabout; it almost suggests that he "picked up" the idea of the train from the person in front in cubicle *f* and that of the "roundabout" from the person behind in cubicle *p*, who drew a birthday cake which his so-called roundabout somewhat resembles.

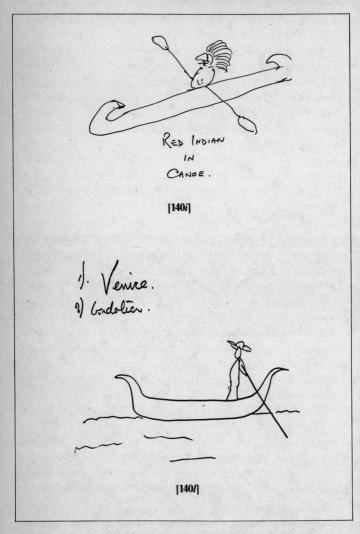

FIGURE 13 A further pair of coincident thoughts from Experiment
140 which suggest an association.

Figure 10 the two objects labeled "tortos" and "crab," while neither like a tortoise nor a crab, are remarkably similar in conception and there are no other drawings like them in any other experiment; the "crab" was third from the left in the front row of cubicles whilst the "tortos" was first on the left in the second row, i.e., two away from each other in a diagonal direction; and again the "avenue of trees" and the "drive with trees" (both in the first row of cubicles in Experiment 118 but with two cubicles in between) are also unique in the whole series.

Sometimes instead of there being similar drawings, there were closely associated ideas, as when in Experiment 33 one person in cubicle *o*, as shown in Figure 11, drew a portcullis while another directly behind in cubicle *t* drew a drawbridge; another example is that in Experiment 18 (Figure 15, pp. 46–7) where one person drew a throne with a crown at its head (labeling it "chair" or "throne") while the person in the next cubicle wrote "something commanding attention, such as presence of royalty. Awe-inspiring, something to be looked up to, austere, etc." Another example was in Experiment 128 where one person wrote "soldiers marching—formal parade in dress uniform," whilst the one next-door wrote "colour vivid—multi-coloured clothes—royalty, state function" and made a drawing (Figure 18, pp. 52–3).

Then we have an interesting example from Experiment 113 which might suggest that one person had received impressions from two other people; it is illustrated in Figure 12 (p. 39). The person in cubicle *f* drew a railway engine and labeled it "train" and the one in cubicle *p* behind and two rows away drew a birthday cake, whereas the person directly between the two in cubicle *k* drew both a train and an object which he called a roundabout but which in fact bore a distinct resemblance to the cake drawn by *p*. One more example of the more interesting drawings may be

picked out for special notice and is shown in Figure 13: it
came from Experiment 140 where in cubicle *i* is a drawing
of a Red Indian in a canoe and in *l* a gondola; the two
drawings are very similar in style but the ends of the two
craft curve in different directions (somewhat reminiscent
of the sloping ends, up in one and down in the other, of
the ark and station shown in Figure 6).

All the drawings agreed by the two of us to have sufficient
resemblance to, or association with, one another are reproduced in miniature, arranged in their pairs or triplets or,
in a few cases, quadruplets, in Figures 14 to 22 on pages
44 to 61; those from the "small" experiments follow those
from the "large." Where there is a verbal response that
appears similar to the idea expressed in a drawing by
another participant, it is shown against the drawing in
question. It should be pointed out that all the drawings
reproduced in Figures 6 to 13 are taken directly from the
originals and so are facsimiles, whereas all those in Figures
14 to 22 are *tracings* from the original drawings made in
rather thicker line to show up when reduced to a smaller
scale.

Not everyone will agree that all the pairs or triplets we
have chosen are sufficiently similar in their form or associated ideas to warrant inclusion in our selection of possible
significant matchings; no doubt also we have left out some
which others might feel should have been put in. If one or
the other of us was doubtful about any example it was
excluded. There is little need to comment individually on
those selected; some are indeed striking. It is sufficient to
turn the pages over to get the impression of the remarkable
frequency with which these coincident thoughts have occurred. In Figure 20 there is an example perhaps not un-
similar to that already illustrated in Figure 12; in cubicle
f of Experiment 101 was drawn a tree, adjacent at *g* was
a curious device and next-door again was another tree

together with a sun which might be thought to be influenced by the ideas in the other two cubicles.

In addition to the drawings there are a large number of coincident thoughts which are expressed entirely in words, and these are now given in the following lists where we show first of all those from the large experiments (i.e., those with twenty "percipients" taking part) arranged in their pairs, triplets or quadruplets; and these are followed by those from the much fewer small experiments (i.e., those with only twelve "percipients"). What a remarkable experiment was number 60: as shown on p. 66, it produced both a quadruplet and a quintuplet set of coincident thoughts as well as a possibly related pair (p. 63). It must be remembered that all such coincidental responses which we are considering in this section are quite unrelated to the targets that were shown in the particular experiments concerned.

The coincident thoughts in the experiments expressed verbally

(1) *Pairs of thoughts in the large experiments: in each case, in addition to the number of the experiment concerned, is shown the letter indicating in which cubicle the thought occurred*

1	k	sea, fish
	m	wave
3	b	flames and fire
	e	cat, warm interior, fire hearth
7	o	waterfall, landscape
	r	waterfall, garden

[*Continued on p. 62*]

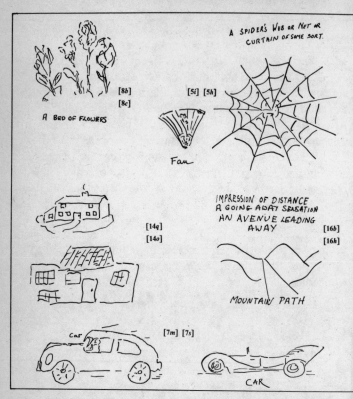

FIGURE 14 Here and in the four following figures (15 to 18) are shown miniature reproductions of tracings taken from all those drawings made in the Caxton Hall telepathy trials which show similar pairs of coincident thoughts turning up simultaneously in the various "large" experiments suggesting possibly spontaneous telepathy. In some cases a drawing may be matched with a written expression of a similar thought. The number of each experiment concerned is indicated against each drawing together with the letter indicating in which cubicle the thought occurred; by comparing these letters with those shown in the plan in Figure 2 it can be seen whether the "thoughts" occurred in adjacent cubicles or not. This series of paired coincidences should be compared with the similar series obtained in the control "mock" experiments shown in Figures 28 to 33.

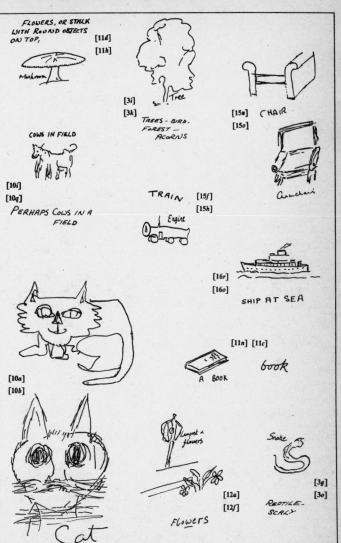

FLOWERS, OR STALK WITH ROUND OBJECTS ON TOP,

[11d]
[11h]

Mushroom

[3i]
[3k]

Tree

TREES - BIRD - FOREST — ACORNS

[15m]
[15o]

CHAIR

COWS IN FIELD

[10i]
[10g]

PERHAPS COWS IN A FIELD

Armchair

TRAIN

[15f]
[15h]

Engine

[16r]
[16o]

SHIP AT SEA

[11n] [11c]

book

A BOOK

[10a]
[10b]

Lamppost & flowers

Snake

[3g]
[3o]

REPTILE - SCALY

[12a]
[12f]

Flowers

Cat

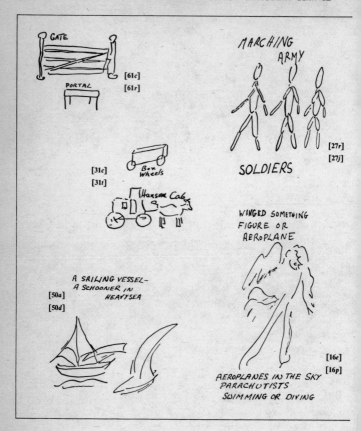

FIGURE 15 A continuation of the pairs of coincident drawings made in the "large" experiments arranged in the same way as in Figure 14.

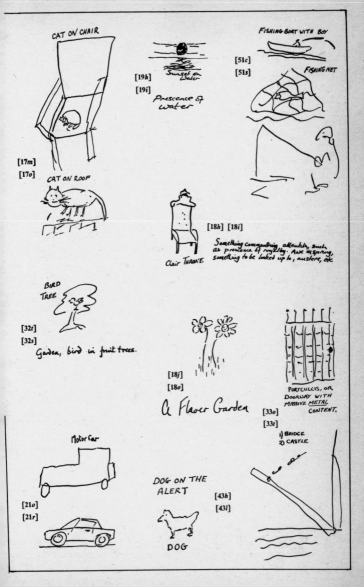

CAT ON CHAIR

[19h]
[19i]

Sunset on Water

Prescence of water

FISHING BOAT WITH BOY

[51c]
[51s]

FISHING NET

[17m]
[17o]

CAT ON ROOF

[18h] [18i]

Clair THRONE

Something commanding attention, such as presence of royalty. Awe inspiring, something to be looked up to, austere, etc.

BIRD TREE

[32r]
[32s]

Garden, bird in fruit trees.

[18j]
[18o]

A Flower Garden

PORTCULLIS, OR DOORWAY WITH MASSIVE METAL CONTENT.

[33o]
[33r]

1) BRIDGE
2) CASTLE

Motor Car

[21o]
[21r]

DOG ON THE ALERT

[43h]
[43l]

DOG

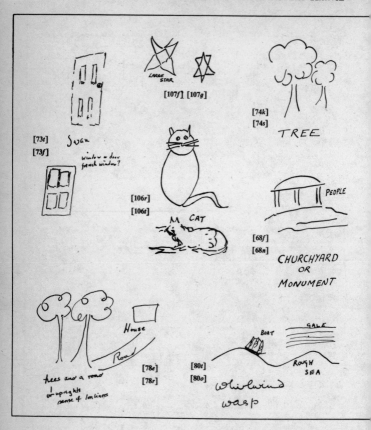

FIGURE 16 A continuation of the pairs of coincident drawings made in the "large" experiments arranged in the same way as in Figure 14.

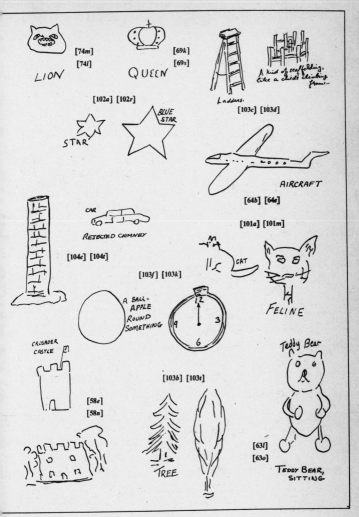

LION [74m] [74l]

QUEEN [69k] [69s]

[102a] [102r]

Ladders. [103c] [103d]

A kind of scaffolding, like a child climbing frame

STAR

BLUE STAR

AIRCRAFT [64b] [64e]

CAR

REJECTED CHIMNEY [104e] [104t]

[101a] [101m]

[103f] [103k]

CAT

FELINE

A BALL-APPLE ROUND SOMETHING

12
9 3
6

CRUSADER CASTLE

[58e] [58n]

[103b] [103t]

Teddy Bear

TREE

[63l] [63o]

TEDDY BEAR, SITTING

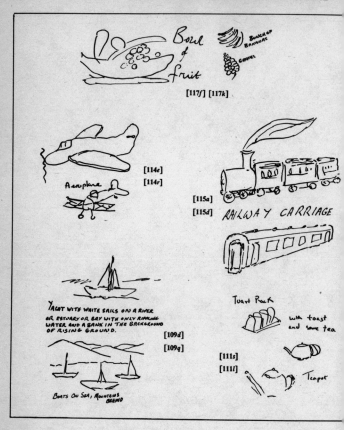

FIGURE 17 A continuation of the pairs of coincident drawings made in the "large" experiments arranged in the same way as in Figure 14.

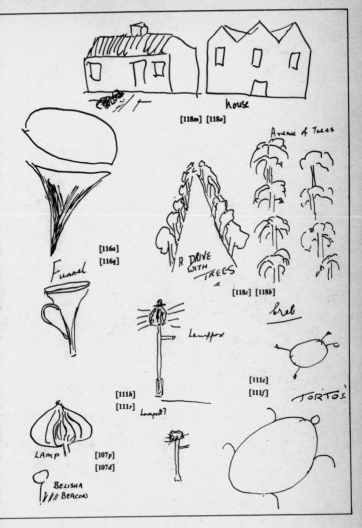

[118m] [118o]

house

Avenue of Trees

[116a]
[116g]

Funnel

R DRIVE WITH TREES

[118c] [118b]

treb

Lamppost

[111c]
[111f]

TORTOS

[111h]
[111r]   Lamppost?

LAMP   [107p]
        [107d]

BELISHA BEACON

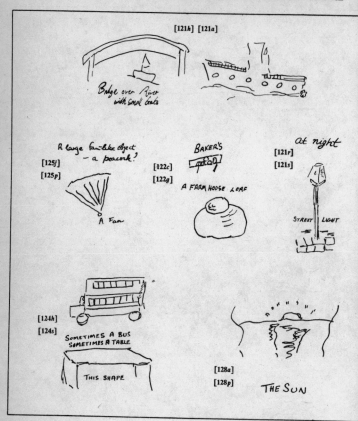

FIGURE 18 A continuation of the pairs of coincident drawings made in the "large" experiments arranged in the same way as in Figure 14.

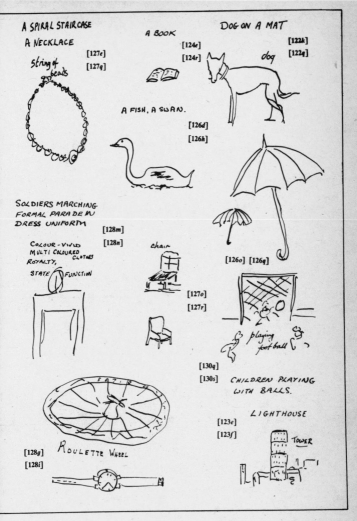

A SPIRAL STAIRCASE

A NECKLACE

[127e]

[127q]

String of beads

A BOOK

[124e]

[124r]

DOG ON A MAT

[122k]

[122q]

dog

A FISH, A SWAN.

[126d]

[126h]

SOLDIERS MARCHING
FORMAL PARADE IN
DRESS UNIFORM

[128m]

[128n]

COLOUR - VIVID
MULTI COLOURED
ROYALTY, CLOTHES

STATE FUNCTION

chair

[1260] [126q]

[1270]

[127r]

[130q]

[130s] CHILDREN PLAYING
WITH BALLS.

playing
football

ROULETTE WHEEL

[128g]

[128i]

LIGHTHOUSE

[123e]

[123f]

TOWER

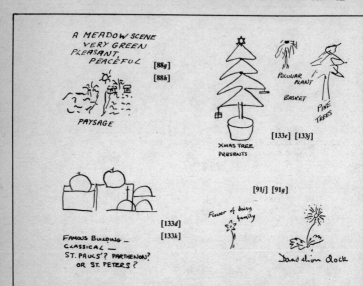

FIGURE 19 Pairs of coincident drawings made in the "small" experiments arranged as for the "large" experiments shown in the preceding figures.

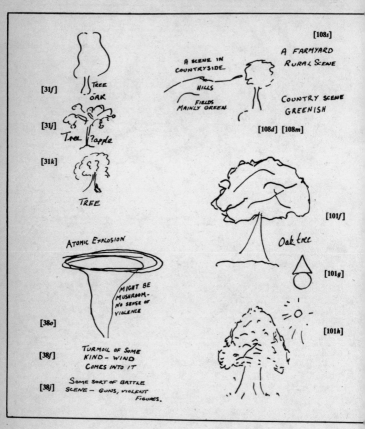

Figure 20 Triplets of coincident drawings or written expressions of similar thoughts arranged as were the pairs in preceding figures.

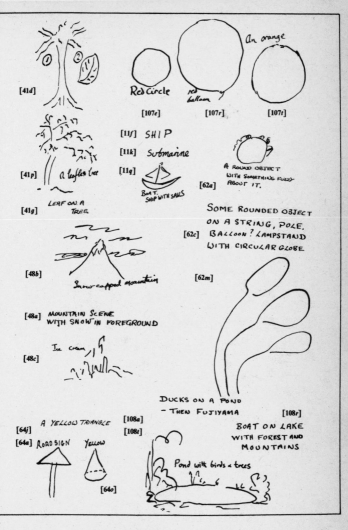

[41d]

Red Circle [107e]

red balloon [107r]

An orange [107t]

[41p] A leafless tree

[41g] LEAF ON A TREE

[11f] SHIP

[11k] Submarine

[11q] BOAT. SHIP WITH SAILS

[62a] A ROUND OBJECT WITH SOMETHING FUZZY ABOUT IT.

[62c] SOME ROUNDED OBJECT ON A STRING, POLE. BALLOON? LAMPSTAND WITH CIRCULAR GLOBE

[48b] Snow-capped mountain

[48a] MOUNTAIN SCENE WITH SNOW IN FOREGROUND

[48c] Ice cream

[62m]

[64j] A YELLOW TRIANGLE

[64a] ROAD SIGN

YELLOW [64o]

[108a]

[108t]

DUCKS ON A POND – THEN FUJIYAMA [108r]

BOAT ON LAKE WITH FOREST AND MOUNTAINS

Pond with birds & trees

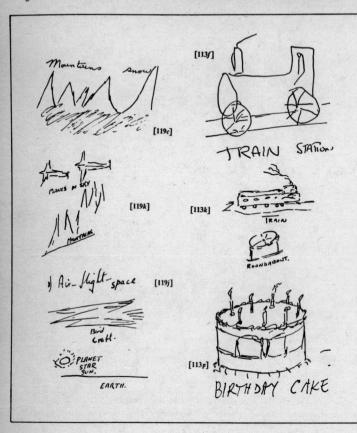

FIGURE 21 A further set of triplet coincident drawings or written expressions of similar thoughts.

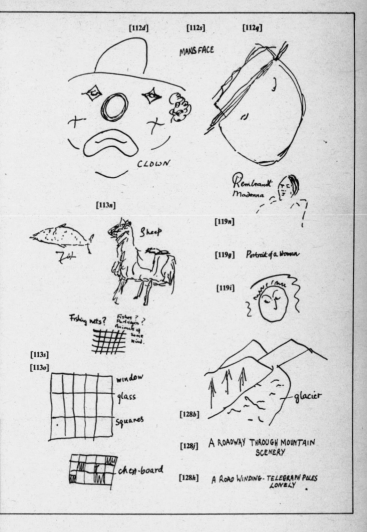

[112d] [112s] [112g]

MAN'S FACE

CLOWN

Rembrandt
Madonna

[113n]

Fish

Sheep

[119n]

[119g]   Portrait of a Woman

[119i]

Fishing nets?   Fishes?
Partridges?
Animals of
some
kind.

[113s]
[113o]

window
glass
squares

chess-board

glacier

[128b]

[128j]   A ROADWAY THROUGH MOUNTAIN
SCENERY

[128h]   A ROAD WINDING - TELEGRAPH POLES
LONELY .

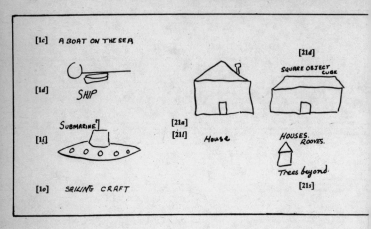

FIGURE 22 Multiple coincident drawings arranged as in earlier figures.

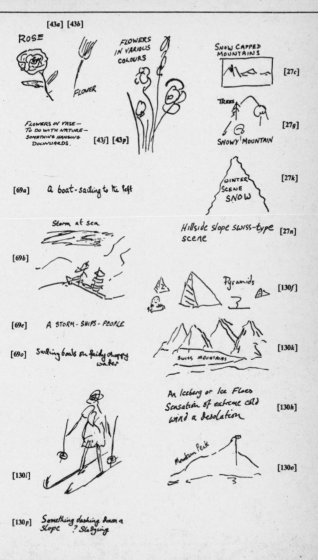

[43a] [43b]

ROSE

FLOWER

FLOWERS IN VARIOUS COLOURS

FLOWERS IN VASE—
TO DO WITH NATURE—
SOMETHING HANGING
DOWNWARDS. [43j] [43p]

SNOW CAPPED MOUNTAINS [27c]

TREES

SNOWY MOUNTAIN [27g]

WINTER SCENE SNOW [27k]

[69a] a boat - sailing to the left

Storm at sea

[69b]

Hillside slope swiss-type scene [27n]

Pyramids [130f]

[69c] A STORM - SHIPS - PEOPLE

[69o] Sailing boats on fairly choppy water

SWISS MOUNTAINS [130k]

An Iceberg or Ice Floes
Sensation of extreme cold
wind a desolation [130h]

Mountain Peak [130o]

[130i]

[130p] Something dashing down a slope ? Sledging

[*List continued from p. 43*]

| 9 | *j* | flowers |
| | *m* | flower or trees |

| 13 | *b* | an umbrella, clump of trees |
| | *i* | possibly an umbrella, something of a protecting nature, reassuring, comforting |

13	*g*	trees
	t	trees, animals in them
		(note possible triple with "clump of trees" at *b* in the same experiment, see above)

| 16 | *f* | head of old man |
| | *g* | W. G. Grace with beard |

| 27 | *e* | garden showing path up centre |
| | *l* | garden |

| 30 | *d* | animals with curly horns, outdoors |
| | *l* | pastureland, animals, cows |

| 30 | *n* | aeroplane, children |
| | *s* | aeroplane |

| 31 | *a* | happy picture with fish |
| | *n* | fish |

| 33 | *a* | a bookcase |
| | *g* | book |

| 37 | *d* | the sea and stretch of beach with birds |
| | *b* | again sea |

| 40 | *a* | round the fire |
| | *f* | fire, a feeling of fear |

| 40 | *j* | some wild animals, probably elephants |
| | *s* | zoo, animals |

| 48 | *e* | whale, high sea |
| | *m* | sea |

52	*i*	tree
	o	staircase, tree
58	*d*	sea or watery scene
	h	something to do with sea or water
58	*i*	volcano
	p	mountain
59	*c*	peaceful scene by river, trees, small boat, tall grass, bird like a heron
	e	pastoral scene, cows in meadow, trees, river
60	*g*	traffic
	j	traffic jam
70	*m*	veteran motor car
	q	large car
71	*b*	fruit
	f	fruit, apple
72	*g*	young boy, playing
	r	boy
74	*g*	kitten
	p	cat running after birds
78	*f*	church perhaps
	s	church
108	*e*	a garden with waterfall
	h	Niagara Falls
110	*e*	horses
	m	horses, soldiers
118	*r*	a gabled house in sunlight with blue sky above and white road in front
	s	hotel building, house by water, blue, stars

| 129 | *h* | an aircraft approaching or leaving airfield |
| | *n* | rocket, steam, clouds, airplane |

| 129 | *j* | catlike creature at left-hand side, crouching on a boulder |
| | *l* | train, engine, cat |

| 130 | *j* | I'll stay with feline, lion or tiger |
| | *l* | train, and I still want my cat creature (cf. responses of same two participants in Experiment 129) |

(2) *Pairs of thoughts in the small experiments*

| 84 | *h* | castle |
| | *j* | visor, helmet, armour, CASTLE, fashioned metal |

| 88 | *d* | children playing with a top |
| | *l* | children playing with beach ball near pool |

| 90 | *a* | crustacean (lobster) |
| | *f* | mushrooming blossoming effect, a creature too like an insect |

| 90 | *b* | children playing |
| | *g* | a child being run over |

| 90 | *c* | crowded street with people and bicycles |
| | *l* | man on cycle |

| 91 | *b* | rabbit |
| | *i* | a rabbit |

| 99 | *e* | lady in a gown |
| | *j* | woman in old-fashioned clothes by counter in shop |

| 137 | *a* | animal, small, not indigenous to Britain |
| | *f* | a small animal like hedgehog or mole with long snout |

139   *e*   an ancient building or church, interior of
              beautiful and rich design

         f   inside of building, beautiful lattice work like
              Alhambra, a square canopy overhead

(3) *Triplets of coincident thoughts (all in the large experiments) arranged as for the pairs above.*

6   *c*   park scattered with trees and a fountain

     g   green cool country scene, trees right, pool
          front

     n   a park of woods near a river

8   *e*   night scene, town, wet, lamps shining,
          pavements, a couple of people

     n   street scene

     o   village scene with lamp

18   *b*   a stream running into a broad quiet lake,
          country like Norway?

     d   river or stream, something in it—stones or
          islands, sense of flowing

     g   a subterranean tunnel with stream in it or
          coal seam

31   *l*   a flower

     m   roses

     p   dog, flowers

49   *n*   beach

     p   edge of yellow beach, blue green waves
          breaking on white surf

     s   sea scene, waves

52   *b*   horse, wooden, sun

     j   horse and chariot, cart, balloon

     p   horse

68   *e*   animals, possibly a zoo

     m   circus, sea lions

     q   train, elephants

79	d	the Queen
	l	a crowd outside Buckingham Palace
	p	admiring the Horse Guards

80	n	birds flying away
	p	seagulls
	s	bird, seagull

109	e	mountains
	r	snow scene with ski-lift and chalet
	c	range of mountain slopes, skiing

(4) *Quadruplet and quintuplet of coincident thoughts (both in the same large experiment 60, and note, as recorded (on page 63), there was also a pair of coincident thoughts in this experiment concerning traffic which might relate to the quintuplet)*

60	c	old-fashioned aircraft, biplane
	f	aeroplane
	h	connected with air, planes possibly
	p	something in flight

60	a	a street scene
	b	children in street
	e	street scene, shopping area
	l	houses in a street with people
	r	town, streets, houses

Now, the coming together of these similar thoughts at the same time must in many instances surely be due to "chance coincidence," i.e., to have happened simply by chance—and we shall consider what this means in a moment—rather than by some other factor such as possibly telepathy (if it exists). But can all the examples illustrated and recorded here be due simply to chance? That is the question. We can very quickly gain some indication of the part that may be played by "sheer coincidence" by making use of so-called random numbers. Those who work on various statistical studies often find it convenient to have available tables of such random numbers. In the example we are taking, we are using those given in Table 8 (p. 12) of the *Cambridge Elementary Statistical Tables*, compiled by D. V. Lindley and J. C. P. Miller (Cambridge University Press, 1966). Here are arranged two-digit numbers from 00 to 99 in random orders; they have been derived by each single digit of each two-digit number being taken independently at random from "a population" of digits in which those from 0 to 9 are equally represented, so that any one two-digit number has the same chance of appearing as any other. Each line of this table has, most suitably for our purpose, twenty such random two-digit numbers; for example the first row reads across as follows: 20, 17, 42, 28, 23, 17, 59, 66, 38, 61, 02, 10, 86, 10, 51, 55, 92, 52, 44, 25.

Already in the first twenty numbers of the table we see that the numbers 17 and 10 have occurred twice. Let us now write these twenty numbers from each line of the table in four rows of five numbers just as if they were "ideas" thought of by twenty people taking part in the cubicles of one of our experiments.

We have done this four times in Figure 23, i.e., taking the numbers from the first four lines of the table and making each line represent a separate imaginary experiment—as *a*, *b*, *c* and *d* in the figure—in which we will suppose that the participants have each been asked to record the first two-digit number that came into their minds. As just noted in "experiment *a*" we at once get two pairs of identical numbers: two 17s and two 10s; and in "experiment *b*" we get two pairs and a triplet: i.e., two 04s and two 94s and three 49s—and if this were a real experiment, should we not perhaps call attention to the 94s and 49s coming together at this same time as perhaps associated ideas? Pat-

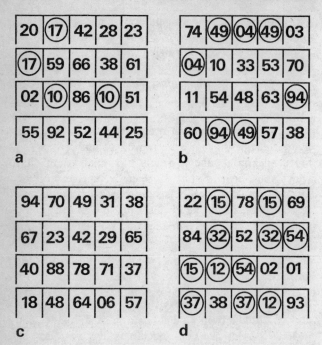

FIGURE 23 Random numbers arranged in groups of twenty as if they were separate "thoughts" in the telepathy experiments. The four examples *a,b,c* and *d* each represent the numbers given in a single row of figures taken from the table of random numbers in the *Cambridge Elementary Statistical Tables* (p. 12). Pairs or triplets of coincident numbers are ringed. For further examples see text.

terns of chance! In "experiment *c*" we get no coincidences at all, but in "experiment *d*" we get *four* pairs (12s, 32s, 37s and 54s) and a triplet of 15s!

This simple analogy surely has meaning for us. Supposing that each person taking part in our experiments was limited to just a hundred simple ideas, we would have more chance coincidences than actually occurred in our experiments. Now, if we asked a number of people to write down quickly a list of a hundred objects which came into their minds as possible target subjects in experiments such as we were making to test for possible telepathy, it might seem most likely that nearly all would have a number of familiar objects in common; it might well be thought that nearly all such lists would contain at least the following twenty "ideas": house, church, train, car, ship, tree, flower, mountain, river, sea, fish, airplane, bird, dog, cat, horse, teapot, cup, bottle, glass. If this were so for our participants, having in mind our groups of random numbers, it is obvious that by chance we should often get such simple objects occurring in pairs or even triplets in our own experiments. Actually, however, in our experiments the 193 people taking part by no means all thought of the objects we have just listed; whilst 76 thought of trees, 43 of houses, 39 of flowers and 36 of cats, only between 20 and 30 thought of horses, mountains, birds, airplanes, trains, motor cars, ships (or boats), dogs or churches (in that order of frequency) and only between 10 and 20 thought of fishes, sea or river, with teapots, cups, bottles and glasses all less than 10 (9, 6, 2 and 2 respectively). And what of the remarkable similarity of some of the drawings or associated ideas as illustrated for example in the ostensible "direct hits" in Figures 6 to 9, or that of the coincidental thoughts shown in Figures 11, 12 and 13? Are they not, perhaps, in rather a different category than that of just tree and tree, cat and cat, church and church coming together?

The variety of thoughts

It seemed worthwhile to make a catalogue or index of all the thoughts which were expressed either in drawings or in words during the course of the experiments to give some measure of their range and variety, and also the relative proportions of the more simple and the more complex ideas. We believe that it may be of some general interest, quite

apart from that of the experiments, to have such a catalogue
of the thoughts that occurred to 193 people, each having
expressed at least ten such ideas (i.e., having taken part
in at least ten experiments each and in some cases twenty
experiments), giving a total of 2,112 such expressions,
leaving out responses to symbols. The complete list of these
is given in Appendix III (p. 282), arranged in alphabetical
order, together with the numbers of the experiments, and
the cubicle in which each idea occurred, for example "accident, people taken to hospital" 100b; "ace of hearts" 15q,
to quote the first two items. If an idea occurred as an alternative to another one, each would be listed as a half,
e.g., "acorn 103$s\frac{1}{2}$," or if it was one of three ideas, it
would then be shown as for example "apple 116$s\frac{1}{3}$." Expressions such as "aeroplane, aeroplanes or aircraft," written
just as words, or as simple drawings, are classed together
and occur fourteen times; if, however, there is an additional
idea associated with the word "aeroplane" or "aircraft,"
such as for example "flying towards one," "in blue sky and
clouds," or "approaching airfield," this would be regarded
as a distinct thought and be shown as a sub-entry under
"aeroplane–aircraft." Altogether there are 1,573 such distinct ideas. What is the chance of two or three of these
distinct ideas of the same kind coming together by sheer
coincidence in the experiments we have made? Can we
make a measure of it? That is the problem.

It is possible to construct groups of twenty numbers like
those shown in Figure 23 but made up of three- and four-
digit numbers derived from random-number tables—and
this was tried by Alister Hardy in the beginning; such,
however, gives little help. In the ones that were made there
were many fewer coincident numbers coming together than
there were coincident thoughts in our experiments, and no
triplets; it is, however, really impossible to compare such
numbers with various ideas. Should we only match, say,

353 with another 353, or should we also match it with 352 and 354 as being closely similar? One cannot judge. The only way in which one can test whether our results are due to telepathy or to chance is to devise "control experiments" using expressions of thought randomly arranged in groups of twenty or of twelve, as in our tests, and see if there is any significant difference between the number of coincidences in the controls and that in the experiments.

THE CONTROL
OR MOCK "EXPERIMENTS"

Robert Harvie

In scientific parlance the word "control" is used to signify a "standard of comparison for checking inferences deduced from experiments."[9] One method of obtaining controls to test for telepathy in the Caxton Hall experiments would be to ask two thousand or so people to record a single guess as to what was being shown on a screen, hidden from their view, during a minute-long interval (the screen could be quite blank). If each person recorded his guess at a different time, we would eventually possess a pool of responses from which twenty at a time could be randomly drawn to form control groups made up of quite independently produced responses. An obvious drawback to this procedure is analogous to that of the famous recipe which begins "First catch your hare . . . ," which in our case becomes "First catch your two thousand people. . . ." Whilst considering this rather daunting pursuit, we realized that the hare had, in effect, already been caught in the sessions at Caxton Hall. We decided to form mock experiments by selecting groups of twenty (or twelve) responses from amongst those which had come out of the Caxton Hall series in such a way that all the responses of a mock "experiment" should have been produced at different times by different individuals. The procedure we chose was designed to test the suggestion that the *simultaneous* coincident thoughts found in the original experiments were attributable to telepathy. In this way we hoped to determine the number of coincident thoughts that could be expected to occur between the subjects taking part in the Caxton Hall experiments when the possibility of telepathy is excluded but who are otherwise responding under the very same conditions as were present in the sessions at the Caxton Hall. If it should turn out that in our mock experiments, or controls, there are the same number of coincident thoughts as in our original experiments, then it is unlikely that the result of the latter could be attributed to telepathy.

From the ninety large group experiments, comprising 1,800 responses, we obtained ninety control "experiments," each made up of twenty responses, as before. Each control group contained responses randomly selected from the set of ninety original experiments. There were, however, three constraints placed upon the make-up of the control groups.

Firstly, each response from the original experiments occurred only once in the whole set of ninety control groups.

Secondly, each response within a control group was derived from a different original experiment; thus each response had been drawn or written on a different occasion.

Thirdly, all the responses within a control group had been produced by different individuals.

The full details of the rather elaborate randomizing procedure by which the control groups were obtained are given in Appendix 1(a) (p. 276). The responses of each control group were arranged in four rows of five, replicating the original formation of the cubicles (see Figure 2). Those responses within each control group which were appreciably similar to one another were recorded and their positions relative to one another within the four-by-five array were also noted. These positions were denoted by the letters *a* to *t* as in the original experiments. Thus response *a* is at the top left corner of the array and response *t* at the lower

right-hand corner. The control groups were numbered 1 to
90 by simply following the order in which they were inspected.

The twenty-six small group experiments yielded 312 responses. The controls for these experiments were obtained
simply by hand shuffling, with some thoroughness, all these
responses and laying them out in groups of twelve. Again
by arranging the responses in four rows of three we could
replicate the original arrangement of the cubicles and so
record the relative positions of the similar responses within
a control group.

Results

All those responses in the control groups which were
judged to be, either in form or in association of ideas, as
similar to one another as were those classed as coincident
thoughts in the original experiments, are reproduced in the
following pages in just the same way. It would indeed seem
that the coincidences in these control tests are just as
striking as those in the earlier series. We will first of all
select a few of the more interesting examples as we did
before and then present the full set of them.

We feel that the coincidences found in the control groups
are of just such a nature as those of the original experiments.
In Figure 24 (pp. 76–7) the two vases, and the rocket and
pencil both inclined at an angle of 45°, parallel in their near
identity of form the armchairs and lamp-posts of Figure
10. Again in Figure 24 the goldfish in their bowls are the
only two in the entire control series and in the particularity
of the idea expressed may be compared to the "tortos" and
"crab" shown in Figure 10.

Again we find closely associated ideas as in the example
of "impression of distance, etc." and the drawing of the

road in striking perspective illustrated in Figure 25. As in Experiment 113, shown in Figure 12, the responses "tunnel" and "train, steam, tracks" almost seem to have contributed to the third response in Figure 26 which includes both the funnel and train motifs. The similarity in style of the drawings labeled "balustrade" and "railway station" in Figure 27 call to mind the gondola and Indian canoe of Experiment 140 illustrated in Figure 13.

The complete set of coincident thoughts from the control groups presented as drawings are shown in Figures 28 to 36 on pages 88–104, whilst those which are entirely verbal in expression are given in the following list arranged in the same way as those from the original experiments. The two series of results, experimental and controls, should be carefully compared.

Verbal coincidences in the control groups

(1) *Pairs of thoughts in the large control groups: in each case, in addition to the number of the group which represents a "mock" experiment, is shown the letter indicating in which position in the layout the thought occurred*

| 4 | *m* | mother and child hand in hand |
| | *r* | child or children, perhaps happy |

| 5 | *i* | hillside and trees |
| | *r* | pastoral scene, cows in meadow, stream, trees, etc. |

| 6 | *f* | river |
| | *g* | river or reeds with boat |

| 9 | *p* | a lighthouse |
| | *c* | a feeling of height, tall, pole, pylon or tower |

[*Continued on p. 81*]

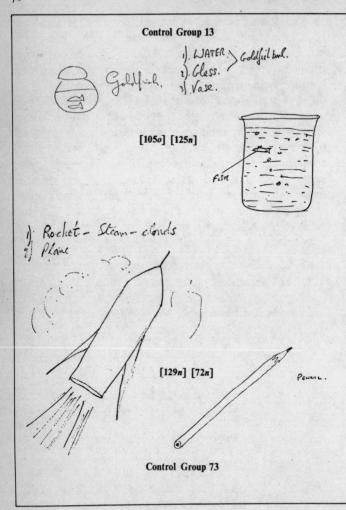

FIGURE 24 Examples of pairs of coincident drawings which occurred in the control "mock" experiments; these should be compared with those from the real experiments shown in Figure 10.

[43d] [53d]

Control Group 75

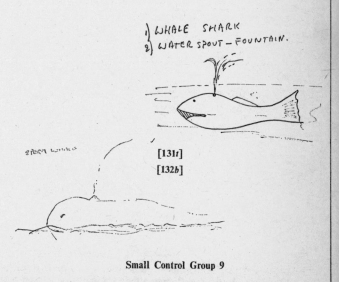

1) WHALE SHARK
2) WATER SPOUT — FOUNTAIN.

SPERM WHALE

[131t]
[132b]

Small Control Group 9

[120m]

[16b]

an impression of distance
with flowers + trees — a "going away"
sensation — a long view — somebody
walking away.... an avenue
perhaps — leading away.

Control Group 33

FIGURE 25 A pair of associated ideas from the control "mock" experiments which may be compared with similar ones in the real experiments as for example in Figure 11.

[128s]

Looking through a tunnel to the light at the end

[53s]

FUNNEL

TONNEL

[28s]

TRAIN, STEAM, Tracks.

Control Group 81

FIGURE 26 A triplet of associated ideas from the control "mock" experiments.

[118d]

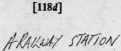

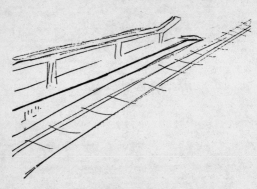

[50b] [59b]

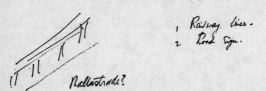

Control Group 2

FIGURE 27 Somewhat similar drawings of "station" and "balustrade" which might have suggested spontaneous telepathy but are taken from the control "mock" experiments, together with a third "thought" of "railway lines," all taken from the same control group.

[*List continued from p. 75*]

10	*k*	a group of people
	p	faces, people, girls
10	*l*	car and traffic, policemen
	q	policemen
15	*k*	children playing happily
	n	child on swing
17	*d*	at night
	n	moon shining on trees
17	*j*	children playing with balls
	m	boy and girls playing ball
17	*l*	leaves
	r	grass, leaves, country scene
21	*d*	aeroplane
	k	biplane, possible first World War—old fashioned aircraft
26	*n*	cross or swastika, aeroplane
	k	connected with the air, planes possibly, clouds
30	*d*	foliage, air, discipline, order
	j	tree
31	*a*	tree
	g	tree
31	*o*	apple
	s	apple
36	*i*	Buckingham Palace
	q	Houses of Parliament, bridge block
38	*h*	cars
	m	traffic, motor cars

42	*b*	something moving over water from left to right, water skier
	r	to do with sea, could be boat sailing, wind
44	*a*	monkey
	q	monkey
46	*e*	flowers
	s	bowl of flowers
53	*a*	bird, seagull
	k	penguin
59	*m*	lion, jungle, hunters, danger
	r	something lit and beautiful, vague feeling of menace
60	*m*	Westminster Abbey
	p	London, Westminster
64	*g*	animals feeding
	h	animals, possibly a zoo
68	*j*	panda
	t	bear
69	*g*	coastline, sea
	o	something to do with sea or water
70	*a*	ducks, water, birds
	g	boat on river or swan
74	*a*	landscape
	z	a lake with mountains in background
77	*k*	mountains or perhaps iceberg or some large mass
	d	hills, mountains

78	*l*	motor racing track with cars going round
	m	car smash, injured lying on road, saloon cars not a race track

81	*h*	sheep, harvest time
	j	farmyard, rural scene

84	*e*	large animal's head with horns
	p	cow? tail waving

87	*e*	sea or water scene
	q	waterfall

88	*p*	ship like a schooner, sailing on ocean, sun shining on it, birds flying around
	r	sailing boat

89	*b*	toadstool, rejected sailing boat
	e	sailing boat

(2) *Pairs of coincident thoughts in the small control groups*

2	*e*	bananas
	g	fruit

5	*e*	lighthouse
	g	this is something that gyrates, a whirling feeling

5	*h*	castle overlooking a valley
	i	Edinburgh Castle

7	*i*	insect on leafy branch
	l	small bird on leafy branch

7	*f*	horse and cart, roadway
	h	donkey with panniers going up a hill, Italy?

| 11 | g | crabs |
| | h | crustacean (lobster?) |

| 12 | a | an inn, country pub |
| | i | a country cottage |

| 14 | b | a line of geese, children playing with a top |
| | l | children in snow, sledge, rabbit |

| 19 | c | animal, small not indigenous to Britain |
| | f | a mouselike creature, long tail, dragonfly |

(3) *Triplets of coincident thoughts in the controls (all in the large groups) arranged as for the pairs above*

25	c	some kind of fruit, apple
	f	fruit, apple
	m	apple

70	d	game
	c	children playing by a school
	s	young boy playing

76	d	houseboat
	j	boat on lake with forest and mountains
	q	house by a harbour

(4) *Quadruplet of similar thoughts, in the large experiments controls*

4	r	peaceful scene by river, trees, small boat, tall grass, bird like heron
	n	trees, fields
	l	park scattered with trees and a fountain
	k	river or stream, something in it, stones or islands, sense of flowing

While the quality of the coincidences in the controls compares well with that of the actual experiments, we are just as interested in making a quantitative comparison of the two series.

When the coincident thoughts in the original experiments are counted (including both drawings and verbal responses), we find that there are, in the large groups,

107 pairs
 27 triplets
  7 quadruplets } of similar responses
  1 quintuplet

while in the small groups there are just 20 pairs of similar responses.

Thus in the large groups there are altogether 328 responses which are found to resemble at least one other response in their respective experiments.

Now, in the controls we find that there are, in the large groups,

131 pairs
 17 triplets } of similar responses
  2 quadruplets

and in the small groups we find that there are 23 pairs of coinciding thoughts.

In the large control groups there is a total of 321 responses which resemble at least one other response in their respective groups.

Clearly the number of coincidences found in both the original large and small experiments is insignificantly different from that observed in their controls.

It looks as though we must say that there is, after all, no evidence that the simultaneous coincident thoughts in the original experiments could be attributed to telepathy.

There are nevertheless some interesting differences between the original experiments and their controls. We could mention the greater incidence of multiplicities of thought—triplets and quadruplets—in the experimental groups as perhaps suggestive of a tendency towards "clustering" which is neglected in the simple comparison of the absolute numbers of coincident responses.

There is, in addition, an important aspect of the results which we have not yet dealt with. We have said (p. 35) that in the original experiments similar responses very often occurred in close proximity to one another. Now from our records we can count up the number of coincident thoughts which fell adjacently to one another. (By adjacent I mean either directly to the side, front, or back—the cardinal points of the compass—but not diagonally. Thus the cubicles *c*, *g*, *i* and *m* are adjacent to *h*, whereas *l*, *n*, *d* and *b* at the diagonals are not adjacent.)

When we count up the number of adjacent coincidences in the large control groups, we find that just 69 out of the total of 321 coincidences are adjacent. This is in fact a slightly greater proportion than probability theory would lead one to expect (see Appendix 1 [b]). On the average one would expect that out of 321 coincidences about 51 would occur in adjacent positions, which is not significantly different from the 69 found. Where the control groups are concerned, everything is as it should be if the results are attributable to chance.

However, when we return to the original experiments, a rather different picture emerges. From our records we find that of the 325 coincident thoughts in the large groups as many as 98 similar responses occur in adjacent positions. This is almost double the number that, on the average, we would expect to find by chance. Furthermore when we compare the proportion of adjacent coincidences in the originals with the proportion found in the controls, we find that the difference is statistically significant. To be precise, we should expect such a difference to arise just by chance in only about one in every hundred repetitions of the whole experiment (see also Appendix 1 [b]).

If there is a tendency for the coincidences to occur in close proximity to each other to an extent that is not attributable to chance alone, what can we say about it? Paradoxically, it appears that this spatial grouping of similar responses, while probably not attributable to chance, is not attributable to telepathy either. If as a result of proximity there had been some telepathic contact (or collusion!) between subjects, then there would surely have been an appreciable difference between the absolute numbers of coincidences found in the originals and the controls. But we have seen that the numbers are practically equal, and for that reason we have rejected the telepathy hypothesis. Puzzling, is it not?

In relation to the coincidences in the controls we feel we should mention an idea that has been put to us on more than one occasion but which we have thought to be so unlikely that we have not hitherto referred to it. Nevertheless perhaps it should be aired. It has been suggested that the results of our control experiments and their numerical similarity to those of the real experiments are actually to be explained by a form of telepathy: a supposed telepathic pool of ideas being shared among all those taking part over the seven weeks of the tests. We think this most unlikely because even if there were such a telepathic pool effect, then surely the results from the real experiments, which were concerned with thoughts occurring at the same moments of time, should be greater than those drawn at random from the whole stock of odd thoughts recorded over the seven weeks.

The "ostensible direct hits" and their controls

We have said that in the original experiments there was a small proportion of responses which might well be thought

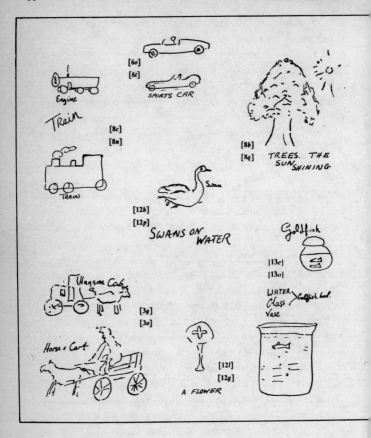

FIGURE 28 Here and in the five following figures (29–33) are shown miniature reproductions of tracings taken from all the drawings showing pairs of coincidences appearing in the "large" control "mock" experiments, arranged as in Figure 14 for the real experiments.

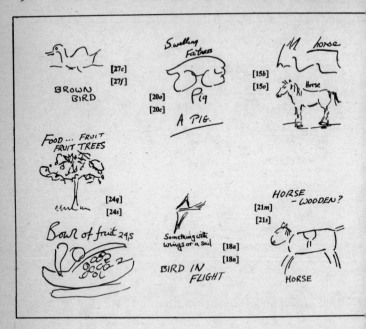

FIGURE 29 A continuation of the pairs of coincident drawings found in the "large" control "mock" experiments as in Figure 28.

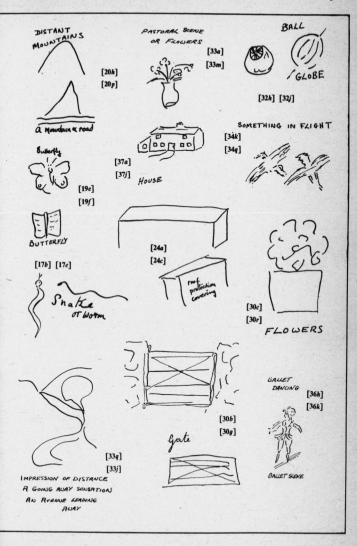

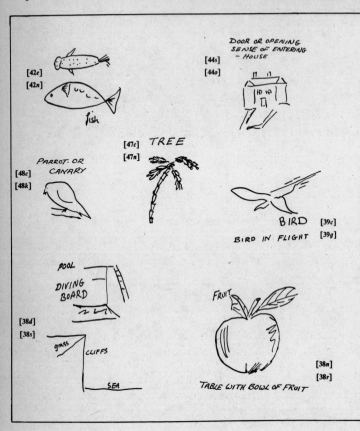

FIGURE 30 A continuation of the pairs of coincident drawings found in the "large" control "mock" experiments as in Figure 28.

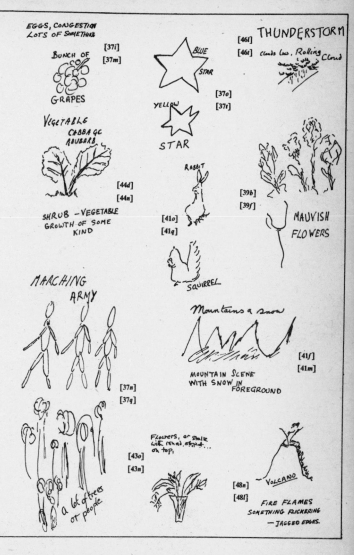

EGGS, CONGESTION
LOTS OF SOMETHING

[37i]
[37m]

BUNCH OF
GRAPES

VEGETABLE
CABBAGE
RHUBARB

[44d]
[44n]

SHRUB — VEGETABLE
GROWTH OF SOME
KIND

BLUE
STAR

[37o]
[37t]

YELLOW
STAR

RABBIT

[41o]
[41g]

SQUIRREL

THUNDERSTORM

[46f]
[46k] Clouds low, Rolling
Cloud

[39b]
[39f]

MAUVISH
FLOWERS

MARCHING
ARMY

[37n]
[37g]

a lot of trees
or people

Mountains & snow

[41f]
[41m]

MOUNTAIN SCENE
WITH SNOW IN
FOREGROUND

Flowers, or stalk
with round object...
on top;

[43o]
[43n]

[48n]
[48f]

VOLCANO

FIRE FLAMES
SOMETHING FLICKERING
— JAGGED EDGES.

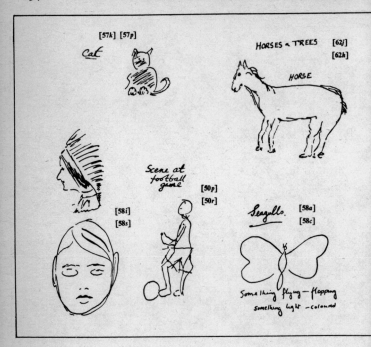

FIGURE 31 A continuation of the pairs of coincident drawings found
in the "large" control "mock" experiments as in Figure 28.

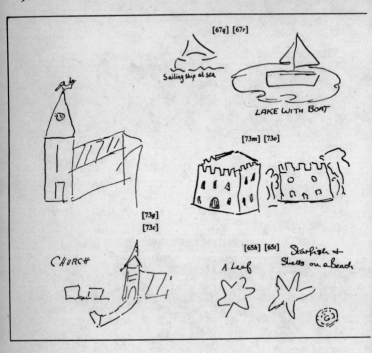

FIGURE 32 A continuation of the pairs of coincident drawings found in the "large" control "mock" experiments as in Figure 28.

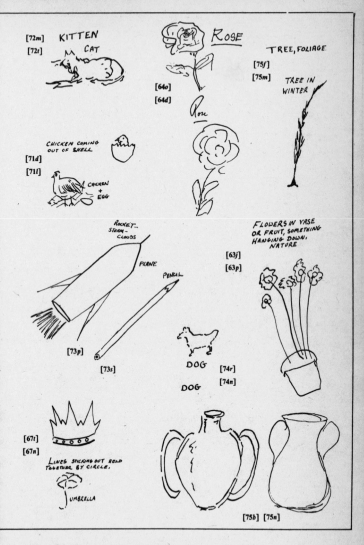

FIGURE 33 A continuation of the pairs of coincident drawings found in the "large" control "mock" experiments as in Figure 28.

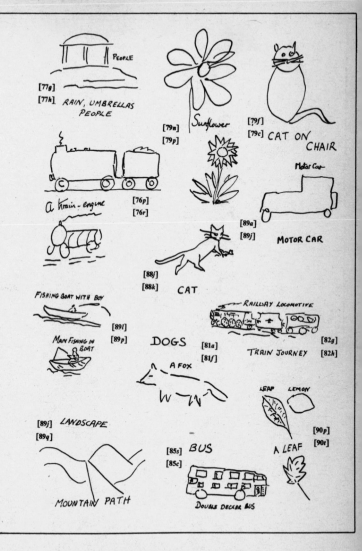

[77g]
[77h] *RAIN, UMBRELLAS PEOPLE*

PEOPLE

Sunflower
[79n]
[79p]

[79f]
[79c] CAT ON CHAIR

a train - engine
[76p]
[76r]

Motor Car

[89a]
[89j]

MOTOR CAR

[88j]
[88k] CAT

FISHING BOAT WITH BOY
[89l]
[89p]
MAN FISHING IN BOAT

DOGS [81a]
[81f]

A FOX

RAILWAY LOCOMOTIVE
[82g]
[82h]
TRAIN JOURNEY

[89j] LANDSCAPE
[89q]

BUS [85s]
[85c]

LEAP LEMON

A LEAF
[90p]
[90r]

MOUNTAIN PATH

DOUBLE DECKER BUS

FIGURE 34 Pairs of coincident drawings found in the "small" control "mock" experiments.

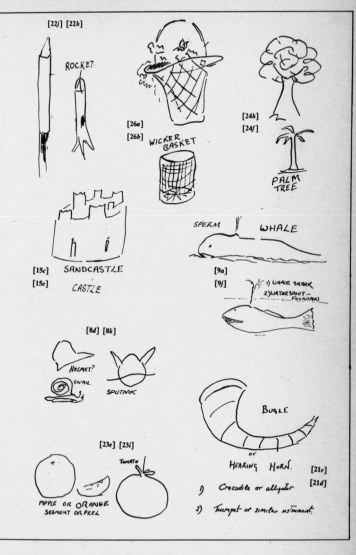

[22j] [22h]

ROCKET

[26a]
[26b]

WICKER
BASKET

[24h]
[24f]

PALM
TREE

[15c]
[15e]

SANDCASTLE

CASTLE

SPERM   WHALE

[9a]

[9j]

1) WHALE SHARK
2) WATERSPOUT—
   FOUNTAIN

[8d] [8k]

HELMET?

SNAIL

SPUTNIK

BUGLE

or

HEARING HORN.   [21c]

[21d]

[23e] [23i]

TOMATO

APPLE OR ORANGE
SEGMENT OR PEEL

1) Crocodile or alligator

2) Trumpet or similar instrument

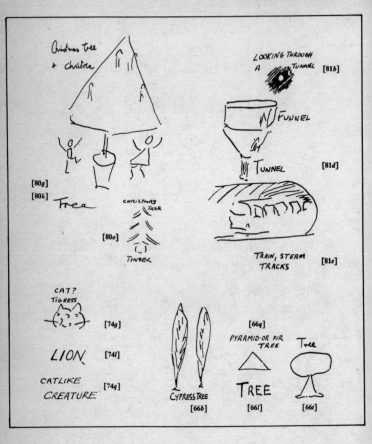

Figure 35 Triplets of coincident drawings found in the control "mock" experiments.

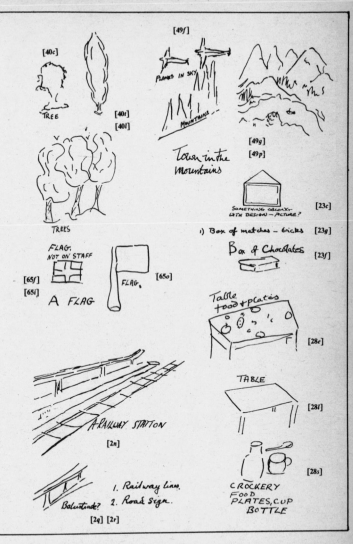

[40c]

TREE

[40r]

[40l]

TREES

[49f]

PLANES IN SKY

MOUNTAINS

Town in the Mountains

[49g]

[49p]

SOMETHING OBLONG-WITH DESIGN — PICTURE?

[23c]

1) Box of matches — 6ricks [23g]

Box of Chocolates [23f]

FLAG.
NOT ON STAFF

[65f]

[65i]

A FLAG

FLAG.

[65o]

Table food + plates

[28e]

TABLE

[28l]

A RAILWAY STATION

[2n]

Balustrade?

1. Railway lines.
2. Road sign.

[2g] [2r]

CROCKERY
FOOD
PLATES, CUP
BOTTLE

[28s]

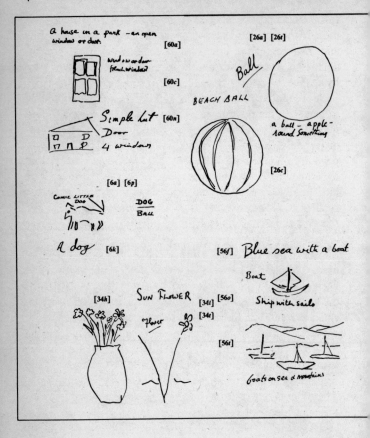

FIGURE 36 Further triplets and one quadruplet found in the control "mock" experiments.

to be "direct hits" on the target slides or drawings. Although the resemblance between the apparent direct hits and their respective targets is in some cases truly remarkable, is it again possible that such similarities could arise by chance?

Suppose that these apparent direct hits were attributable to chance; then if we took the targets at random and matched each in turn against randomly selected groups of responses, we would expect to find about the same proportion of "ostensible direct hits" to arise as in our original experiments. If on the other hand the "ostensible direct hits" really were telepathic hits, then we would expect a smaller proportion of apparent direct hits to occur in the random matchings. This we proceeded to test.

When we came to making up the controls, we realized that only half the targets and half the responses could be used. This was because after each of the experiments had been completed the subjects were encouraged (as explained on p. 24) to stand up and look at the target drawing or slide. We must therefore admit the possibility that the responses could in some cases have been influenced by the nature of the preceding targets. To have matched randomly selected responses against targets which had preceded these responses could have weakened the validity of the controls. Therefore in our controls we only matched responses against targets which had succeeded these responses.

The controls were obtained by the following procedure. There were altogether 116 target slides and drawings. The second 58 of these targets provided the target pool for the controls. The responses, however, were selected from the first 58 experiments for the reasons just stated.

If the "ostensible direct hits" in the 116 original experiments are chance coincidences, then we would expect to find, using only 58 targets in the controls, about half the number of apparent direct hits.

Each control group was selected by reference to random-number tables. The 58 experimental groups from the *first half* of the series were numbered 1 to 58. A control set of twenty responses would be set up by selecting each response from a different original experiment by reading off the numbers met with in the table between 1 and 58 and then selecting each particular response from each such experimental set by a further reference to the random table. It was an elaborate method but it was felt to ensure the greatest possible randomization for our controls. The same procedure was followed to give us each of the control groups.

The 58 targets from the *second half* of the experimental series were now numbered 1 to 58 and each of the 58 control groups of responses (made up as just explained) was allotted a target drawing or photograph from this series by reference to another page of the random numbers. When each group had been allotted a target in this way, they were examined to see how many, if any, of these control responses came sufficiently near to their target to be classed as a possible "direct hit." When this was done, we found 17 such apparent "hits," i.e., those judged by the two of us to be so classed. Four examples of these in which the allotted targets were drawings are shown in Figure 37 and four in which the targets were photographs in Figure 38. These should be compared with the experimental ostensible direct hits in Figures 6 to 9. Are they not just as striking? If the sunrise over the sea or the church correspondences shown in Figure 37 had been obtained in a real experiment, one would surely have been inclined to suppose that telepathy might be a possible explanation; or, again, are not the examples in Figure 38 just as remarkable? Since there are 17 of these correspondences for the control groups, their number compares very well with the 35 obtained in double the number of original experiments.

At this point it seemed that the controls had ruled out

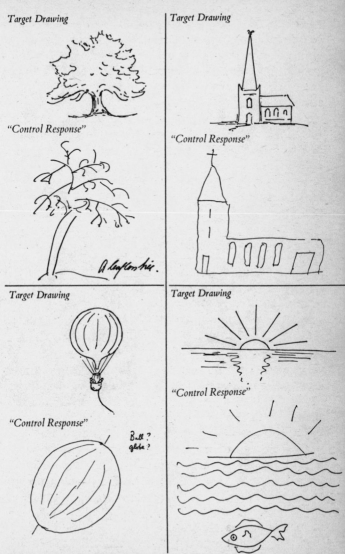

Target Drawing

"Control Response"

Target Drawing

"Control Response"

Target Drawing

"Control Response"

Target Drawing

"Control Response"

FIGURE 37 Four selected examples of apparent (although false) "direct hit results" taken from the control "mock" experiments where drawings were the targets.

Target Slide

Target Slide

"Control Response"

1) kite on cloud

"Control Response" 1

Animal(s) feeding

"Control Response" 2

Dog

Target Slide

"Control Response" 1

A range of mountains

"Control Response" 2

Snow-capped mountain

Target Slide

"Control Response"

A ship like a schooner sailing on
the ocean, the sun shining on it, + birds
flying around it

FIGURE 38 Four selected examples of apparent (although false)
"direct hit results" taken from the control "mock" experiments
where photo-slides were the targets.

the telepathy explanation entirely, and a consideration of the results from the control tests for the coincident thoughts strengthened such a view. Subsequently, however, after we had made the tests for possible precognitive hits referred to on p. 34, it was realized that there was an equally valid and less elaborate method of making a similar control, and four such further tests were made which perhaps make our judgment less certain. Fifty-eight targets from the second half of the series were selected at random and each one was matched against one of the sets of twenty responses, again selected at random, but from those which had been made in the first half of the series. The first control test of this kind with 58 targets randomly matched with 58 sets of responses yielded a score of 15 apparent direct hits which was close enough to that of the 17 found in the former control; but three further tests made in the same manner, only with different random matchings of targets and responses, yielded only 8, 8 and 11 apparent hits respectively. We now have the results from five control experiments giving an average of 12 apparent hits for a set of 58 targets. If we double this to correspond with the full set of 116 experiments in the original series, we see that the score of 24 apparent direct hits from the control tests is only about two-thirds of the 35 such ostensible direct hits in the original experiments. Perhaps just a small fraction was really due to telepathy? But let us proceed to a more general discussion.

GENERAL DISCUSSION

Alister Hardy & Robert Harvie

It would certainly seem that at any rate the majority of the results in the original experiments, which at first sight might have suggested telepathy, can now just as well be explained by the coincidental coming together in time of similar ideas, as has been so well demonstrated in the control experiments. We say "at any rate the majority" of examples because perhaps it may be that there is a suggestion that there might be something of *both* effects taking part in the so-called direct hit results; in comparing those from the experiments and the controls it may be felt that some of the results from the former appear to be a little more remarkable than those from the latter—perhaps more psychologically associative than the controls: for example the Palace guardsman, the savage meal, and the snowman? Clearly more work must be done.

Now, in regard to the "control experiments" we should point out a difference between the controls for the "direct hits" and those for the coincident thoughts. In the actual experiments the thoughts expressed by the participants were drawn from an almost infinite range of different ideas that might be possible, whereas in the controls the range of ideas was limited to the fixed number already expressed in the experiments. This again would seem to suggest that the experimental results for the "direct hits" are really somewhat

better than the controls suggest. In regard to the controls
for the coincident thoughts this difference does not really
arise, for the test must be applied to the actual number and
range of ideas already expressed by the participants: there
were in the course of the experiments 1,573 different ideas
recorded; for the control test of the coincident thoughts
it is *this range* that must be considered (as we have done)
and *not* an infinity of ideas. It was, of course, the object of
the controls to see how often these 1,573 ideas came together by chance and whether such chance coincidences
equaled those of the experiments.

But what of these other curious effects, relating to the
adjacent coincidences, mentioned above—what are we to
think of them? What are we to think of coincidences in
general? Are they just to be dismissed as "sheer coincidence"? If these experiments have done nothing else, they
have provided the material for a closer study of the extent
to which such remarkable "comings together in time" may
occur in an apparently random fashion. Is there something
more to it than meets the eye? Is it related to some of the
effects in the card-guessing experiments we discussed
earlier? Robert Harvie makes a study of random numbers
in the next part of the book which suggests something very
queer in this unusual field. Is it related to the coincidences
which again and again occur in everyday life?

We are lucky to be joined in this book by one who has
made a special study of the problem of coincidence in general. Arthur Koestler's book *The Roots of Coincidence* appeared just after we had made these control experiments;
we therefore invited him to come and inspect the results we
had obtained in our systematic "laboratory study" of
coincidence. He did so with the satisfying result that he
agreed to collaborate in the present volume. In the third
part of the book he presents what might perhaps be termed
a natural history of coincidence: a review of many examples

of coincidence in everyday life taken in part from his own collection and in part from the files of our Religious Experience Research Unit at Manchester College, Oxford, where we receive a great many records of personal experiences, many of which exhibit examples of coincidence. In relation to religion it is interesting to recall the saying attributed to Archbishop William Temple: "When I pray," he said, "coincidences happen; when I don't, they don't"[10] There are many religious people who would support his view. Coincidence is certainly a subject worthy of study, whether it is "sheer chance" or not. And what do we mean by sheer chance? This is the question to which Arthur Koestler devotes the final part of the book.

It would be well in concluding this first part for us to assert that, in spite of the negative results of our experiments in regard to the demonstration of telepathy, we believe that there is now in existence a considerable body of other experimental evidence to support its existence quite apart from the card-guessing work which was discussed in the introductory section.

We will briefly summarize some of the more striking examples. In the 1930s, but only published much later in 1962, and translated into English the following year,[11] the late L. L. Vasiliev, Professor of Physiology in the University of Leningrad, carried out a number of experiments which confirmed still earlier ones made in France in the 1880s by Professor P. Janet and Dr. M. Gillat in Le Havre and again repeated in Paris by the famous physiologist Professor Charles Richet. In these French experiments "a healthy peasant woman of 50 years of age" was induced to go into a hypnotic sleep by telepathic suggestion at distances ranging from a quarter to half a mile in the Le Havre trials and later over somewhat longer distances in those made with the same subject by Professor Richet in Paris. At the second all-Russian Congress of Psychoneurology at Petrograd in

1924, Professor K. I. Platonov referred to the earlier French work and in a lecture demonstrated similar experiments, but over a much shorter distance. Professor Vasiliev, who attended the Congress, resolved to investigate this phenomenon himself and later, together with Dr. I. F. Tomashevsky, who joined him in the study, experimented with two hysteria patients who proved to be particularly good at being made not only to go to sleep, but also to awaken in response to telepathic mental suggestion. Their experiments completely confirmed, but with greater refinement, the earlier results of the French investigations. Vasiliev then took a new step forward.

When he began his work, it was generally supposed in Russia that telepathy, if it existed, must be produced by some radio-like electromagnetic wave system. Vasiliev therefore repeated the experiments with the hypnotist enclosed within a metal screening chamber to cut out any such radiations and subsequently made a further series of tests with the subject also screened, but by a different system: the so-called Faraday Chamber. In either case the screening made no difference at all to the results. If these results are confirmed by other workers, it must surely prove to be the most important advance yet made in the study of telepathy.

Another series of experiments which appears to give a strong indication of telepathy is that made by Drs. Stanley Krippner and Montague Ullman and their colleagues at the famous Dream Laboratory at the Maimonides Medical Center at Brooklyn. It is now well known that in a sleeping person his or her "rapid-eye movements" as recorded on an electroencephalograph indicate a state of dreaming and that if such subjects are woken up immediately after such eye-movements cease, they are then able to give a very good account of their dreams if they are asked at once to do so. In these particular experiments, while the subject was sleeping the person acting as agent concentrated on some picture in an adjacent room and attempted to influence the dream pattern of the sleeper. The picture was chosen at random, while the subject was asleep, from a pool of such pictures, all contained in sealed envelopes. An experimenter recorded the subject's rapid-eye movements and as soon as they were over woke him up, saying, "Please tell me your dream," and then recorded his reply on tape; this would be done several times during the night, and in the morning the experimenter had a further post-sleep interview with the subject. The transcripts of the recordings, together with a complete set of all the pictures in the pool, including that chosen, were sent to outside judges who then had to evaluate the results by deciding which, if any, of the pictures could be matched with the subject's dream impressions; they judged them by an elaborate system of scoring hits and misses. There were altogether 74 such telepathic sessions with many different persons acting as agents and subjects; of these, 52 were judged to be telepathic hits and 22, misses. Standard statistical tests showed that the probability of such a score occurring by chance is less than one in a thousand.[12]

One more example of the more modern work is that of Dr. Thelma Moss, Assistant Professor of Medical Psychology, and Dr. J. A. Gengerelli, Professor of Psychology, both of the University of California, Los Angeles.[13] They had been impressed, as have others, that such a large number of examples of supposed spontaneous telepathy in the anecdotal history of the subject have been associated with some highly emotional incident such as an accident, serious illness or the death of a close relative or friend; consequently they resolved to experiment by generating emotional, affective states. It had also long been suggested that those who believed in ESP got better results in experiments than those who were skeptical. Combined with the production of emotional states, they set out to test whether those who believed in ESP would in fact produce statistically more significant results in rigidly controlled telepathy experiments than those who were convinced that ESP could not take place.

They worked with 144 volunteers, both male and female, ranging in age from fourteen to sixty-five, from various walks of life. The subjects worked in teams of two, i.e., 72 pairs, which were divided into three groups of 24 pairs each: the *ESP Group,* being those who believed in ESP and thought they had had such experiences in the past; the *ESP? Group*, those who believed in ESP to some extent, but did not believe they had the faculty; and the *Non-ESP Group*, who were convinced that ESP did not exist. The essence of each experiment was this. One member of each pair, whom we may call the transmitter, was placed in a soundproof chamber in one room and shown a series of emotional pictures—colored slides projected on a screen all bearing on a similar theme—whilst at the same time hearing through headphones music, voices, animal sounds, etc., appropriate to the situation presented; the other member of the pair, the receiver, sat in a comfortable reclining chair in another room which was separated from the transmitter's room by a distance of twenty feet. There was an experimenter present in each room and in the receiver's room there were two screens upon which *two* lantern-slide pictures could be simultaneously projected from two lanterns electrically controlled. The receiver was asked to relax and "receive" impressions of what his partner was experiencing in the other room and then speak his impressions into the microphone of a recorder. He was then shown a pair of slides, one of which was the same as that shown to his partner and the other quite different, and he was asked to choose the one that corresponded better than the other with his impressions. If he had no impressions, he was asked to guess which of the two slides was the one his partner had seen. Each experiment consisted of three such trials. In these first experiments the teams of the *ESP Group* scored with a probability against the result being due to chance of 1 in 3,000, whereas the other two groups scored no more than chance expectation. Further experiments were done contrasting those who were artists or had professionally some kind of creative ability (i.e., writers, musicians, actors, painters, etc.) and those whose profession gave no hint of such qualities (i.e., those in business, trade, etc.); here again the artistic group had a highly significant positive result, whereas the others failed to score above chance.

More recently, Dr. Moss and her colleagues[14] have done perhaps the most remarkable telepathy experiment of all: they have attempted and got significant results in tests for what appears to be telepathic communication across the world from Los Angeles to Sussex in England. Incredible it seems, yet their experiments have beautifully designed controls; it is these which make them so noteworthy.

Instead of there being many teams of just two subjects, one transmitter and one receiver in each test, there was a group of 22 subjects acting together as transmitters, whilst all looking at the same picture and hearing the same sounds in a room in Los Angeles, and three other groups acting as receivers in different parts of the world: 28 in another room in Los Angeles, 15 in a room in New York and another 14 in a room at Sussex University in England. Now, in addition to three pairs of alternative emotional episodes or themes as in the former experiments, there were introduced, as a control, three non-emotional "episodes": one consisted of nine slides on each of which was a single letter of the alphabet (m, l, e, c, t, p, r, f, z), another consisted of nine slides on each of which was a single short black line, each drawn at a different angle, and the third consisted of a series of nine slides on each of which was a number (3, 8, 1, 5, 4, 7, 9, 4, 5)—all of these were shown for ten seconds each. The order in which the experimental (i.e., the emotional) themes and the control (non-emotional) themes was presented was randomly determined. Scoring for success or otherwise was by a system similar to that employed in the previous experiments. The times at which the trials took place were exactly synchronized: those in Los Angeles beginning at 12 noon, those in New York at 3 P.M. and those in Sussex at 8 P.M. The results show that for the experimental (emotional) episodes the receivers in all three places scored better than chance expectation, but, surprisingly, those in Sussex did very much better than those in New York.* Taken altogether, the receivers scored significantly beyond chance for the experimental (emotional) episodes, with a calculated probability of 3,000 to 1 against it being just chance, whereas for the control (non-emotional) "episodes" they only scored at chance level.

Not only did the statistical tests significantly support the hypothesis of telepathic transmission, but there was interesting supporting qualitative evidence. As in the earlier experiments, the receivers, before they were asked to choose which was the correct slide being shown, were asked to write down their impressions of what the transmitters were thinking of. In regard to a "Space" episode, four of the receivers in New York wrote respectively the following sentences: "Dark edges, a centred pinpoint of light . . . a swinging weightlessness"; "A black void"; "Shafts of light from the sky. Perhaps lightning, but more vague, more like rays of light amidst dark amorphous cloudiness"; "Moon or sun . . . someone falling through . . . something bursting brightly." And at the University of Sussex for the same episode three of the receivers wrote thus: *"War of the Worlds,* by H. G. Wells? Or the next war, involving death by the use of satellites and flying platforms"; "I can see the

---

* A speculative thought occurs to one—could it be that there was more mental "noise" in the greater city which interfered with clearer reception?

world as if I were in a space ship—I'm in a cabin which is
very clear and . . . everything is floating"; and the third
said "Outer space with a space ship heading for the moon
. . . hundreds of stars"; and there were similar statements
at Los Angeles. The authors go on to say that it might be
argued that, as space travel is so much in the minds of people today, one might well expect such phrases to occur by
sheer coincidence; however, they add that "in *no other
episode* did descriptions even remotely resembling space
travel appear." And there is something else of qualitative
interest to be noted. The transmitters were also asked to
write down their reactions to the episodes which they experienced and here, in addition to some similar words being
used by both transmitters and receivers such as, for example,
in the space episode, "weightless" and "weightlessness" respectively, there appeared some interesting possible dis-
tortions: whilst three transmitters wrote the word "weightlessness," one receiver wrote *"white lightness,"* and again
during the control episode showing nonsense letters, one
transmitter wrote the words "nonsense script" whilst a
receiver wrote "nondescript." It is also perhaps worth
mentioning that when the control slides of short black lines
were being shown to the transmitters, two of the receivers
(in different areas) wrote "short black lines" or "slanting
lines."

There is indeed increasing scientific evidence for what
may be called "real" telepathy, i.e., the influence of one
mind upon another at a distance. Likewise the evidence is
mounting for the existence of what has been called a "psi"
factor, whatever that may be, which appears to be present
in all the card-guessing, dice-throwing experiments of
modern parapsychology. A recent questionnaire inviting the
opinions of readers of the journal *New Scientist* revealed a
striking change in the attitude of scientists (including
engineers) to the findings of parapsychology.[15] Over 1,500

readers completed the questionnaire form: of these, 63 per cent held university degrees of some kind; included in these were 29 per cent of the total who had higher degrees; a further 13 per cent were university students; and only 5 per cent admitted to no further education after leaving school. The results of the operation showed that 25 per cent regarded ESP as an established fact, with a further 42 per cent declaring it to be a likely possibility. In contrast only 3 per cent thought ESP an impossibility, while of the remainder, 19 percent regarded it as a "remote possibility" and 12 per cent called ESP "merely an unknown." There is certainly a wind of change blowing in the scientific world of today.

Finally we should say that all the data of our experiments and their controls, with the original drawings and written responses made by the participants, are filed in the Religious Experience Research Unit, Manchester College, Oxford, and may be further worked upon by bona fide investigators who apply to the Director with their credentials and are prepared to come to Oxford to study them. Apart from the fact that we may be doing further work on them ourselves, we do not wish to run the risk of loss or damage by dispatching the bulky records to other centers of work.

References to Part One

1. *The Living Stream* (London 1965) and *The Divine Flame* (London 1966).

2. *The Advancement of Science*, vol. 6, pp. 213–23 (London 1949).

3. *The Hibbert Journal*, vol. 47, p. 105 (1949).

4. *Enquiry*, vol. 1, p. 1 (1948).

5. *Proceedings of the Society for Psychical Research*: vol. I, pp. 263–83 (1883); II, pp. 24–42 (1884); and III, pp. 424–52 (1885).

6. Ibid., vol. II, pp. 189–200 (1884).

7. Spencer Brown, G., *Probability and Scientific Inference* (Longmans, London 1957).

8. Thouless, R. H., *From Anecdote to Experiment in Psychical Research*, p. 35 (London 1972).

9. *The Concise Oxford Dictionary.*

10. Quoted by Douglas Steere in *Dimensions of Prayer*, p. 85 (London 1965).

11. Vasiliev, L. L., *Experiments in Mental Suggestion*, translated and published by the Institute for the Study of Mental Images, Church Crooham, Hampshire (1963).

12. Krippner, S., "Electrophysiological Studies of ESP in Dreams . . . ," *Journal of the American Society for Psychical Research*, vol. 64, pp. 277–85 (1970).

13. Moss, T., and Gengerelli, J. A., "ESP Effects Generated by Affective States," *The Journal of Parapsychology*, vol. 32, pp. 90–100 (1968).

14. Moss, T., Chang, A. F., and Levitt, M., "Long-Distance ESP: A Controlled Study," *Journal of Abnormal Psychology*, vol. 76, pp. 288–94 (1970).

15. *New Scientist* (25 January 1973, p. 209).

PART TWO

Probability and serendipity

ROBERT HARVIE

The real constitution of things is accustomed to hide itself.
HERACLITUS, *The Cosmic Fragments*

In the ancient world the commonest randomizing device was the astragalus, the ankle bone of the sheep or any other cloven-footed animal. The bone has four nearly flat sides and rounded ends; when thrown, it tends to fall on one or the other of the pair of narrower faces. The cubical die with which we are familiar is an early development of the astragalus. Egyptian dice of the second millennium B.C., beautifully fashioned from bone or ivory, are found to throw absolutely true. The bones and dice enabled both gaming and the art of divination to flourish.

Gambling was so popular in the Roman empire that it came to be forbidden by law except during the month of December, the Saturnalia. However this prohibition was widely ignored and several of the emperors were apparently in the grip of gambling fever. Of Augustus Caesar, for example, Suetonius writes:

Augustus did not mind being called a gambler; he diced openly, in his old age, too, simply because he enjoyed the game—not only in December, when the licence of the Saturnalia justified it, but on other holidays, too, and actually on working days. That this is quite true a letter in his own handwriting proves:

"My dear Tiberius,

. . . we had the same company for dinner, except that Vinicius and the elder Silius were also invited; and we gambled like old men all through the meal and until yesterday turned into today. Anyone who threw the Dog—two aces—or a six, put a silver piece in the pool for each of the dice; and anyone who threw the Venus—when each of the dice shows a different number—scooped the lot."[1]

Dice and astragali were used widely for divinatory purposes, both in the public temple ceremonial and in private soothsaying. In the temple ritual the supplicant stated his wish and the bones were cast by an attendant votary. The answer was given by referring the outcome to the oracular tablets on which the throws and their meanings were described. The Venus cast, for example, was a favorable outcome; the Dog, disastrous. Both in the religious context of fortune-telling and in the secular context of gambling, the fall of the dice was assumed to be governed by the wish of the gods.

In his essay *De Divinatione*, Cicero scorns the idea of divine intervention with some astringent remarks:

For we do not apply the words "chance," "luck," "accident," or "casualty" except to an event which has so occurred or happened that it either might not have occurred at all, or might have occurred in any other way. How then is it possible to foresee or to predict an event that happens at random, as the result of blind accident, or of unstable chance?[2]

Cicero is here describing the concept of the random event by applying the criterion of the principle of insufficient reason. A random event is one for which we have no good, or sufficient, reason to suppose that it should have happened in any other way than that it in fact did.

---

[1] Superior figures refer to end-of-part notes.

In another passage Cicero invokes what we generally call the "law of averages"—that the unusual may be expected in the long run:

Nothing is so uncertain as a cast of dice and yet there is no one who plays often who does not sometimes make a Venus throw and occasionally twice or thrice in succession. Then are we, like fools, to prefer to say that it happened by the direction of Venus rather than by chance?[3]

The lucidity of Cicero's approach to matters of chance remained in isolation until the Renaissance when men rejected the idea that, in Walter Raleigh's words, "God hath shut up all the light of learning within the Lanthorn of Aristotle's brains," and felt free to speculate, to conjecture and to invent.

Girolamo Cardano, physician, mathematician and notable eccentric, was born at Pavia in 1501 and died insane at the age of seventy-five. Amongst the huge number of manuscripts which he left behind him were his famous autobiography, *De Vita Propria Liber*, and the book which concerns us at present, *Liber de Ludo Aleae* (The Book of Games of Chance). In this work Cardano compiles a scrapbook of the moral, historical, practical and arithmetical aspects of gambling. He warns his readers that if they are to gamble at all they should gamble for small stakes and choose opponents of "suitable station in life." He also advises on such matters as cheats who use soapy cards and mirrors in their rings to reflect the playing surfaces. Amongst these trivia we find, like a jewel in the midden, the first expression of the mathematical concept of probability. Talking of the "cast of one die," Cardano writes:

One half the total number of faces always represent equality; thus the chances are equal that a given point will turn up in three throws, for the total circuit is completed in six, or again that one of three given points will turn up in one throw. For example I can as easily throw one, three or five as two, four or six. The wagers therefore are laid in accordance with this equality if the die is honest.[4]

In this seminal passage Cardano states the fundamental axiom of probability theory. The probability of an event is the ratio of the number of cases favorable to that event, to the total number of possible cases, where all are of equal weight or likelihood. The probability of an event may therefore be expressed as a proper fraction lying between naught and one. An event with zero probability never happens; with a probability of one, an event happens invariably. Where there are two equally likely possible cases, as with an idealized and unbiased coin, the probability of the single favorable case is given by the ratio 1:2. The importance of Cardano's generalization from empirical observation is immense. From this insight of great simplicity and power stem the elegant intricacies of probability theory and the statistical edifices of modern science. Cardano's use for his innovation was more mundane. He goes on to show how the gambler can avoid taking on unfavorable wagers by calculating the probabilities associated with the various combinations for the throw of two dice and three dice.

Although Cardano had written *Liber de Ludo Aleae* in about 1563, it remained unpublished until nearly a century later. Whilst gambling was certainly widespread and intense, there is no record of any other discussion of probability in the sixteenth century. Nevertheless the knowledge of how to calculate a probability had somehow percolated amongst mathematicians, so that we find Galileo, in a fragment written between the years 1613 and 1623, treating the matter as something self-evident.[5]

Galileo was asked, probably by his patron Cosmo II, Duke of Tuscany, to solve a dicing problem: Three dice are thrown. Although there are six numerical partitions of nine, and likewise six partitions of ten,* "long observation has made dice players consider ten to be more advantageous than nine." Why? Galileo tackles the problem by first stating the total number of throws with three dice, i.e., 216. He then tabulates, like Cardano, the possible combinations resulting from the throws of three dice which give the outcomes 10, 9, 8, 7, 6, 5, 4 and 3, and points out that the combinations for the outcomes 11–18 are symmetrical with these. From his table the number of possible throws or combinations which give the outcome 10 is seen to be 27, and the number of combinations giving 9 is seen to be 25. If we assume that all of the 216 distinguishable combinations or throws are equally likely, then the difference between the ratios 25/216 and 27/216, that is, 2/216 or 1/108, expresses the empirically observed advantage to wagering on the ten as against the nine.

Galileo's short excursion into probability is again an isolated instance of inquiry into the subject. Interest in questions of probability began to spread and show evidence of real vitality as a consequence of the famous debate between Pascal and the great mathematician Pierre de Fermat in 1654.[6,7] Pascal had been asked by the Chevalier de Méré, a courtier with a poor opinion of mathematicians, to solve two gaming problems. The first, the Problem of Points, had first been discussed in a treatise by Fra Luca Paciolo in 1494. While well known in Pascal's time, figuring in a number of standard textbooks, it had apparently never been correctly solved. On each play of a game, one of two players scores a point, and the two players have equal chances of winning the point. Three points are required to win. If for some reason the players are forced to break off at some stage, how should the stakes be divided? If it is assumed that the players are of equal opportunity, an

* i.e., for 9, (6,2,1) (5,3,1) (5,2,2) (4,4,1) (4,3,2) (3,3,3)
  and for 10, (6,3,1) (6,2,2) (5,4,1) (5,3,2) (4,3,3) (4,4,2)

equitable distribution of the stakes should be made in proportion to the respective probabilities of the players of winning the game, and these probabilities depend upon the number of points still lacking.

Pascal gives an original and ingenious method for solving problems of this type, where just two players are involved, which depends upon the use of binomial coefficients. In this he was aided by his studies of the Arithmetical Triangle, later to become known as Pascal's Triangle. Fermat's method was based upon the enumeration of possible combinations, an approach fundamentally the same as that of Galileo and Cardano. Fermat's method proved undoubtedly superior where more than two players are involved; a fact that Pascal first of all denied, then grudgingly acknowledged. This defeat caused Pascal to withdraw from the debate; shortly afterwards he gave up mathematical speculation altogether and only returned to this interest for a brief period, as a distraction from the discomfort of toothache, towards the end of his life.

The Chevalier was additionally vexed by a dicing conundrum which he called a "*grande scandale*" and which led him to say that "Arithmetic is demented." While there is an advantage in wagering small favorable odds on throwing at least one six in four throws of a single die, there is a disadvantage in placing similar odds on throwing at least one double six in twenty-four throws of two dice. But, said de Méré, the ratio 24/36 (the number of pairings of the faces of two dice) is equal to the ratio 4/6 (the number of faces of one die); therefore the expectations should be equal for the two cases. Fermat's resolution of the Chevalier's difficulty is missing from the correspondence. Pascal either found the question beyond his capacity, or, more likely, was nonplused by de Méré's reasoning; at any rate he passed it on to Fermat without comment.

Rumors of this debate spread rapidly in scientific circles. Christiaan Huygens, visiting Paris in 1655, became sufficiently intrigued by the Problem of Points to set about work on a treatise on probability on his return to Holland. *On Reasoning on Games of Chance,* which appeared in 1657, is the first systematic treatment of probability theory. Huygens sets out all the principles and propositions of the theory which were then known, together with a number of problems and exercises. Although Huygens made few innovations, his treatise, which marks the entry of probability into the field of interest of mathematicians generally, remained a standard work for nearly half a century.

Cicero pointed out that the exceptional, lucky event can be expected to occur at some point in a sufficiently long chance series. This insight was given precise expression by James Bernoulli in what he called his Golden Theorem—the fruit of twenty years of meditation on the subject. He described it as "a problem of which the novelty, as well as the high utility, together with its grave difficulty, exceed in weight and value all the remaining chapters of my doctrine."[8] (Bernoulli is referring to his book *Ars Conjectandi,* published in 1713—eight years after his death.)

Bernoulli's theorem, the law of large numbers, is first of all a mathematical exercise. Like any other algebraic theorem its proof is arrived at deductively from propositions which are taken to be true by definition. In its verbal form the Golden Theorem asserts the following: The probability tends towards certainty that the proportion of successes observed in a binomial experiment (to be explained in a moment) approaches without limit the true probability of success on a single trial as the number of trials approaches infinity.

A binomial trial is one for which there are two possible outcomes, success or failure (non-success). For example, in drawing cards from a pack, any red card might be a success, any black card a failure. In studying genetic inheritance the property "blue-eyed" may be counted a success, and any other eye-color a failure. A binomial experiment must furthermore have the following features: the number of trials is fixed in advance, the trials are independent, and all trials have identical probabilities of success. Trials are independent provided that the outcome of any trial cannot be affected by any other trial in the experiment. In the idealized experiment for which these conditions are fulfilled, Bernoulli's theorem suggests that the relative frequency of successes continually approaches nearer to some stable value as the length of the experiment increases, and this stable value is equal to what we had at first presumed the probability of a success on a single trial to be. The a priori, or presumed, probability of success being the ratio of favorable cases to possible cases, assuming that these are equally likely, the presumed probability is thus the "true probability." So, for example, in an experiment in which an idealized penny (for which the a priori probability is, say, $1:2$) is tossed repeatedly, we expect the number of heads to be as close as we like to 50 per cent and we can be virtually certain of this as the number of tosses approaches infinity.

Bernoulli went on to reverse the argument, thereby giving the theorem a practical and controversial application. Suppose we have a pack of cards in which the relative proportions of red and black cards are unknown. We draw a card, replace it into the pack, shuffle thoroughly, draw another card and so on, repeating the process a large number of times. If we find that a red card is drawn R times and a black card S times, then, claims Bernoulli, we can infer that the proportion of red cards is $R/R+S$. And by implication this is the probability of drawing a red on a single trial.

We could of course keep on drawing the cards, replacing, and shuffling ad infinitum in order to approach certainty, but it would be simpler to turn the pack over and count the numbers of red and black cards. This, however, we cannot do in other examples such as in tossing a coin, casting a die, spinning a roulette wheel; in these cases there is no way of arriving at the true probability of a success with certainty other than by an infinite number of trials. We are not just forbidden to look at the cards, we cannot; infinity is ever receding. The Golden Theorem suggests that infinity can be truly represented by a large, but finite, number of trials. Since we can never hope to reach infinity, this suggestion is neither verifiable nor falsifiable but may be called a fundamental presupposition.

Why should this presupposition be true? Bernoulli answers by shyly invoking Fate, in former times a goddess of destiny.

If thus all events through all eternity could be repeated, by which we could go from probability to certainty, one would find that everything in the world happens from definite causes and according to definite rules, and that we would be forced to assume amongst the most apparently fortuitous things a certain necessity, or, so to say, F A T E.[9]

With Bernoulli the study of probability had matured from being a guide to wagering to a true theory of probability. Bernoulli's calculus, greatly refined by de Moivre and others, accurately describes the orderliness of individual single events when taken en masse. So widely applicable did it prove to be that a hundred years later Laplace could say:

The theory of probabilities is at bottom only common sense reduced to calculus; it makes us appreciate with exactitude that which exact minds feel by a sort of instinct without being able oftimes to give a reason for it. It leaves no arbitrariness in the choice of opinions and sides to be taken; and by its use can always be determined the most advantageous choice. Thereby it supplements most happily the ignorance and the weakness of the human mind.[10]

Common sense or divine destiny? However we like to look at it there is little doubt that probability theory does work.

In his essay *What is Life?*, Erwin Schrödinger has called the statistical orderliness, which arises from individually unpredictable random events, "the 'order from disorder' principle." While many of the phenomena with which physics deals are statistical in nature, the "order from disorder" principle appears most irreducibly at the subatomic level. It is a basic postulate of quantum theory, the fundamental theory of matter, that individual events at the subatomic level are neither reproducible at will, by experiment, nor predictable in theory. For example, the disintegration of the nucleus of a radioactive isotope is a process of spontaneous decay which cannot in any way, in theory or by experiment, be predicted in advance.

Radioactivity is a nuclear phenomenon which proceeds quite independently of the chemical combination of the atom with other atoms; neither is it affected by ordinary physical influences like temperature and pressure. Radioactivity consists of the spontaneous emission by the substance of certain kinds of rays or particles. Whatever kind of ray or particle is emitted, it is found that the radiation from a given sample decreases gradually with time according to a definite law which states that the intensity of radiation decreases by half every T seconds. The number, T, called the half-life, is constant for each radioactive isotope, but it varies widely from substance to substance.

Thus although in a collection of, say, one million nuclei of the same kind, it is impossible to say exactly when any one of them will disintegrate, we know that after a time equivalent to the half-life only half a million will survive unchanged. The concept of probability represents the connection between the irreproducible, unpredictable, single event and the predictability and uniformity of multiple events. The situation is vividly put by Schrödinger:

The disintegration of a single radioactive atom is observable (it emits a projectile which causes a visible scintillation on a fluorescent screen). But if you are given a single atom, its probable lifetime is much less certain than that of a healthy sparrow. Indeed, nothing more can be said about it than this: as long as it lives (and that may be for thousands of years) the chance of its blowing up within the next second, whether large or small, remains the same. This patent lack of individual determination nevertheless results in the exact exponential law of decay of a large number of radioactive atoms of the same kind.[11]

At the subatomic level the principle of sufficient reason breaks down for isolated events while, at the same time, being retained for the same events in an ensemble. Orthodox quantum theory attempts to resolve this paradox by asserting the probabilistic nature of matter at the microscopic level. But a further paradox remains—that of probability itself. The laws of probability describe *how* a collection of single random events can add up to a large-scale certainty, but not *why*. Why do not the million nuclei explode at once? Why should we expect that a symmetrically balanced penny will not fall "heads" on every toss from now to eternity? The question is evidently unanswerable save by the postulation of an unknown Fate, or by appealing, as did Laplace, to the "instinct" of "exact minds," or by other similar ploys.

The "order from disorder" principle seems to be irreducible, inexplicably "just there." To ask why is akin to asking "Why is the universe?" or "Why has space three dimensions?" (if indeed it has).

From Bernoulli's theorem we would expect that the exceptional, irregular event will be swamped by a long-run regularity. An actual coin-tossing experiment illustrates this. The coin was tossed ten times and fell heads nine times. The coin looks suspiciously biased, but would we be justified in rejecting it as "unfair"? The coin was tossed ninety

times more. The table below shows the number of heads
in each set of ten tosses and the cumulative number of heads
as the experiment proceeds.

Number of tosses	Number of heads per ten tosses	Cumulative
10	9	9
20	5	14
30	5	19
40	6	25
50	6	31
60	5	36
70	5	41
80	5	46
90	6	52
100	4	56

The proportion of heads at the end of 100 tosses is 56
per cent. The initial run of 90 per cent heads has shrunk to a
more modest proportion. It seems fairly clear that the first
ten tosses were exceptional and gave a heavily biased estimate of a coin which is probably reasonably "fair." It is
interesting to note that the initial run of nine heads was not
compensated by a later run of nine tails but was swamped
by an averaging-out process over the relatively long term.

This swamping tendency of chance events over the long
term is poignantly illustrated by the failure of a well-known
gambling system which purports to be based on the law of
large numbers: the Biarritz system. A roulette wheel has
thirty-seven numbers, each of which are equally likely to
come up. According to the Biarritz system, the player before
placing any stakes notes the results of at least one hundred
and eleven spins of the wheel. Having noted the numbers
which have come up with less than a certain frequency, the

player stakes on those, on the supposition that their former rarity will be offset by an immediate glut. There is nothing in the law of large numbers to suggest that this will happen, and if such a system were to be regularly successful, we could no longer assume that the separate outcomes were causally independent.

The assumption, following Bernoulli's lead, that the probability calculus can accurately describe the real world is at the basis of statistical reasoning. The calculus enables one to estimate the probable limits within which a chance set-up approximates a priori expectation for any length of experiment. We have seen that the degree of approximation diminishes, with a corresponding approach to certainty, as the number of trials grows larger. Conversely, any consistent deviation from chance expectation becomes increasingly improbable as the number of trials increases. If in an experiment we find that such a consistent deviation from chance expectation occurs, we are likely to believe that this expectation was wrong and that the observed proportion of successes gives a truer estimate of the probability of success on a single trial.

The practice of statistical reasoning may be illustrated by the late Sir Ronald Fisher's famous teacup experiment, which he describes in *The Design of Experiments*.[12] A lady claims that she can tell by sipping a cup of tea whether her hostess added the milk before or after pouring out the tea itself. To show off her confidence, she agrees to submit to a test in which she has to identify eight cups, four of which received milk first, the other four tea first, but which are otherwise the same. She receives no other information than that four cups are of one sort and four of the other. We give them to her in a random order. There are two possible outcomes. The lady may do no better than she would by guessing; alternatively, she may do better than we would expect by chance. We should stipulate, before the start of the experiment, the odds we will accept as being "better than chance." In this example we could place the odds at 50 to 1.

Now we find that she identifies all the cups correctly. There are seventy possible arrangements of eight things of two different kinds, and in this particular case only one of these is the correct arrangement. The probability of picking out this one correct arrangement by chance is therefore 1/70. If there were no grounds for the lady's claim and the experiment had been repeated a large number of times, we would expect her to identify all the cups correctly only about once in every seventy times. Accordingly, we say that the odds are 69 to 1 against selecting the correct order at one trial, if there were no grounds for the claim. These odds are better than the odds of 50 to 1 which we had set in advance. We would therefore be inclined to accept the alternative hypothesis of better-than-chance and interpret this as supporting the lady's claim to a special connoisseurship.

A statistical experiment is a sort of dialogue between hypotheses. To begin with, we assume that our experimental set-up is a chance set-up; this is the hypothesis of chance, or "null hypothesis." Against this we propose the "alternative hypothesis." If the results are such that it is likely, on the basis of our calculations, that there is a very small probability that they occurred by chance, then the alternative hypothesis is accepted and the null hypothesis rejected. The "level of significance" of a result expresses the probability of the result having occurred by chance. The significance level tells us how unlikely it is that the result is a "fluke." The alternative hypothesis is a hypothesis of non-chance. To accept the alternative hypothesis is to say with a certain degree of confidence that the results are not attributable to chance.

The logic of the standard type of ESP or PK (psychokinesis) experiment is identical to that of Fisher's parable of the teacups. In those ESP experiments in which a guessing, or choice, technique is used, the percipient attempts to

guess the order of a random sequence of targets. The target
for each call, or guess, is one of a limited number of alterna-
tives. The targets most commonly used are the traditional
Zener cards (p. 14). These have five symbols—star, cross,
wavy lines, square and circle. If all normal sensory clues are
excluded and the percipient is merely guessing blindly at
the order of the cards, we would expect about one-fifth of
the guesses to be correct in the long run. This is the chance
hypothesis. If the number of correct guesses proves to be
significantly greater than, or smaller than, one-fifth of the
total number of guesses, then the null hypothesis is unlikely
to be correct. The relation between guesses and targets appears to be something other than chance. In a PK experiment in which the subject attempts to influence the fall of
dice, the object may be to have a predetermined die-face
fall uppermost. If the chosen face should fall uppermost
more frequently than would be expected by chance, then
again we consider that the relation between the subject's
wishes and the behavior of the dice is other than chance.

The greater the level of significance, the more reason we
have to suppose that the results are not attributable to
chance. Broadly speaking, the experimental evidence for
the reality of psi phenomena (to use the more neutral, and
more general term for ESP and PK) relies heavily on obtaining very significantly beyond chance results. The magnitude of the odds against the chance hypothesis obtained in
some card-guessing experiments is colossal. In an early test
at Duke University, the famous Pratt-Pearce experiment,
the number of calls made by the percipient, Hubert Pearce,
was 1,850. The most probable number of "hits" or correct
guesses, on the chance hypothesis, is 370. The actual number exceeded this by 188. The odds against obtaining such
a deviation by chance alone are quoted[13] as being well over
8 million million million to 1 (actually 8×10^{26} to 1). A
series of experiments carried out by Dr. Soal in 1941 with
Basil Shackleton as percipient had results of even greater

statistical significance.[14] An earlier pilot experiment had
shown that Shackleton seemed to be guessing not at the card
at which the agent was looking but the card ahead of that.
In the confirmatory series of experiments in which nearly
four thousand guesses were made, Shackleton continued to
guess successfully at the card ahead, getting about 300 hits
above the mean chance expectation of 800. The odds against
the chance hypothesis are indeed astronomical (10^{36} to 1).
More recently, a series of experiments by Dr. Helmut
Schmidt have brought in similarly striking results. In one
precognition experiment the subjects were faced with four
colored lamps which were lit in a random sequence governed by a radioactive source. The subjects were required
to guess which of the four lamps would light up next and to
press the button corresponding to this lamp. In a series of
nearly 74,000 guesses three subjects succeeded in making
about 900 more correct guesses than would be expected by
chance. In the task of attempting to predict which of the
lamps would *not* light up, two subjects were able to score
strikingly below chance expectation. The below-chance, or
negative, deviation in 9,000 trials was over 200. The probability of obtaining these scores by chance is less than one
in ten thousand million.[15] It is evident that such improbable
coincidences cannot be dismissed as mere flukes. It has
been estimated that in order for the deviation observed in
the Soal–Shackleton experiment to turn up by chance, more
experiments would be required than the whole history of
the world would allow for.

These experiments, which do not stand alone, illustrate
the levels of significance which may be attained in experiments with highly successful subjects. The relation between
guesses and targets appears to be something other than
chance, judging by the statistical evidence. Writers on ESP
generally interpret this non-chance relationship as indicating a causal relationship. Dr. R. H. Thouless, for example,
writes:

The problem with which tests of significance are concerned is that of how likely a given numerical result would have been if there had been no special cause (such as ESP) operating to produce it. . . . If the likelihood of the result occurring in the absence of any special cause producing it (i.e., by chance) is large, there is obviously no reason to look for a cause; if however this likelihood is very small, it is reasonable to suppose that there was some special cause producing the result, and the lower is the chance likelihood, the more likely is it that some cause was at work.[16]

Parapsychologists are only too aware that a statistically significant result in an ESP test does not, as is the case in the physical and biological sciences generally, mean that the phenomena are reproducible at will. But a statistically significant result usually *does* imply that a phenomenon is predictable under some specified conditions. "In relation to the test of significance," writes Fisher, "we may say that a phenomenon is experimentally demonstable when we know how to conduct an experiment which will rarely fail to give us a statistically significant result."[17]

But successful ESP experiments are elusive and, in the sense that they are not repeatable at will, evade being fully experimentally demonstrable. Is this because the phenomena of telepathy, clairvoyance and precognition which are said to be involved are by their very nature elusive? Or will more sophisticated methods of measurement and control bring forth the fully repeatable experiment from the "hidden channels of the mind"? Until the repeatable experiment has been recognizably attained, the critic can with some justice query the scientific credentials of ESP experiments.

One such critic taking a skeptical standpoint, suggested that many card-guessing and dice-influencing experiments were not demonstrating telepathy, and so forth, but something quite different though just as interesting. George Spencer Brown claimed, somewhat controversially, that the apparent successes of ESP experiments are really the failures of probability theory to apply to reality: "They [the results of psychical research] comprise, in fact, the most prominent empirical reason for beginning to doubt the universal applicability of classical frequency probability." The failure of probability theory to work as well as we should like it to, Spencer Brown attributed to a "vagueness in the very concept of randomness itself." He went on to assert:

. . . any attempt to randomise, of which tables of random numbers and psychical research experiments are both typical examples, will lead all too frequently to the curious results which have been thought in the past by psychical researchers to be evidence of telepathy and whatnot. My suggestion in *Nature* in 1953 was simply that if many of the psychical research scores were, as I suspected, merely examples of the "failures" likely to occur in our attempts to randomise, then similar examples should be found in such sources of randomisation as published random numbers themselves.[18]

It is only fair to say that the technical arguments Spencer Brown put forward to support his claim excited largely adverse criticism.[19] However, the empirical challenge was quickly taken up by Mr. A. T. Oram,[20] who published his results in an interesting paper entitled "An Experiment with Random Numbers." In this experiment Oram matched pairs of digits from the whole of a well-known series of random numbers, that of M. G. Kendall and B. Babington Smith. The first digit of a pair was taken to represent the "guess" and the second digit the "target" of a card-guessing experiment. The number of hits (when both digits of a pair were the same) was in accordance with probability theory. However, the pattern of scores which emerged from the experiment coincided in a remarkable way with that found in certain psycho-kinetic experiments with dice. This appeared to be a largely fortuitous coincidence in that it mainly arose out of the way in which Oram had chosen to arrange the data.[21,22] The outcome of the whole experiment was thus clouded by ambiguity and seemed neither to convincingly refute nor to confirm Spencer Brown's suggestion. Perhaps some apparently successful ESP experiments are indeed pointing to an unknown property of that insubstantial territory which we call randomness? In what follows we hope to re-open the question by taking the exploration of this territory a little farther.

The procedure adopted was designed to simulate an experiment of the card-guessing or dice-influencing type while excluding the influence of paranormal causes.

An ESP experiment of the guessing variety requires a series of guesses to be matched against a randomly selected set of targets. In our simulation the targets were digits taken from published tables of random numbers. The guesses, or rather mock guesses were intended to be digits generated automatically by computer. Modern, high-speed computers can be programmed in a great variety of ways to generate and print out what are rather confusingly known as "pseudo-random" digits.*

The main purpose of this experiment was to see whether, in matching the guess sequences against the target digits, a notable deviation from the most probable number of coincidences or "hits" to be expected by chance would occur.

---

* The prefix "pseudo" arises from the method by which the sequence of digits is produced and not from possible deviations from some ideal standard of randomness in the constitution of the sequence. Given the program, or algorithm, and the necessary skills required to interpret it, the sequence would become predictable. The successive decimal digits of π, for example, might appear to be random to someone who did not know how they had been produced. Once in the secret (given the algorithm "divide $22/7$"), the sequence would become predictable.

As a subsidiary interest, I also wanted to examine the data for evidence of so-called position effects.

In the literature of parapsychology it has very frequently been noted that percipients may at the beginning of an ESP (or PK) test score beyond chance, only to score at the chance level as the test continues. The scoring rate may decline over a long period of testing, or there may be a decline in scoring within an experimental occasion which is followed by a pick-up in the scoring rate at the start of the next occasion. The first kind of decline has been called "long-term" decline; it tends to be permanent. The second may be called "episodic" decline.

Both of these patterns of scoring have been found so repeatedly that declines appear to be the best attested and most consistently observed phenomena of parapsychology. Episodic declines are thought to be part of the more general phenomena of "position effects" in which a percipient may tend to score successfully in some parts of every experimental occasion while scoring at the chance level in other parts of the session. It may also happen that the subject scores above chance at the start of a run or session and below chance expectation towards the end, so that the average of his scores is at the chance level.

Position effects are perhaps the most nearly lawful phenomena of parapsychology. Dr. J. B. Rhine says of them:

. . . position effects have been a familiar phenomenon in experimental parapsychology almost from its beginning and have almost reached the status of being a criterion of evidence of psi activity. . . .[23] Obviously, if nothing takes place but chance guessing in a chance series, there will be no position effects. Therefore, when any lawful position effect pattern is produced in a proper psi test, it must be because the psi process has intruded its influence into the varying patterns of the chance responses.[24]

In order to look for episodic declines in the simulated ESP experiment, there had to be some method of identifying an "episode." Fortunately the means were to hand.

Some months before, I had carried out, quite informally, a guessing experiment on a small scale. In this the subjects had been asked to write down the digits 0 to 9 in the most varied order they could manage. They were asked to write down 400 digits altogether—200 on one day, 200 on the following day. They were also asked to record each set of 200 digits in two separate blocks of 100 digits each, and to leave an interval of some minutes between writing down these two blocks. In this way four blocks of 100 digits apiece were obtained from each subject. For the purposes of the experiment let us call each set of 200 digits an episode. Would there be decline effects within episodes? That is, would there be some marked difference in the rate of scoring between the two blocks of 100 digits produced on the same day?

Each person's guesses were then matched against four hundred consecutive digits of a table of random numbers; these constituted the targets. A random point of entry was made into the tables for each person's set of targets. A hit is scored when the same digit occurs at the same point in the guess sequence and the target sequence. The ten digits 0 to 9 have an equal probability of occurrence in the random tables, so the probability of a "hit" or coincidence is $1/10$. The mean chance expectation, the most probable number of hits if chance alone is operating, for a block of 100 guesses is therefore ten, i.e., $100 \times 1/10$.

The results of this experiment are only of interest because this pilot experiment provided a model on which the simulation experiment which was to follow could be based. I shall mention them in order to illustrate the scheme of the inquiry.

Only five subjects were tested, giving a total of 2,000 guesses, i.e., 5×400. In Table 1 the matching scores for each block of 100 digits are shown. The columns A and B denote respectively the first and second block of guesses on each day.

The totals for each column are only trivially different from the mean chance expectation of 50 (each column represents the scores of 500 guesses).

The total overall score is 202, almost exactly the mean chance expectation of 200. However, there is the mildest suggestion of a decline between the A and B blocks on each day, the column totals of the A blocks being slightly greater than the B block totals. The differences are not significant,

TABLE I

Subject	First-day scores		Second-day scores	
	A block	B block	A block	B block
I.M.	14	6	9	14
V.W.	8	8	14	9
P.L.	13	14	10	6
B.T.	6	6	10	11
B.H.	13	11	12	8
TOTALS	54	45	55	48

but the effect might have been enhanced by further testing of the subjects whose scores contributed notably to the decline (e.g., subjects B.H. and V.W.). As it is, we can leave these results to illustrate the sort of shape that position effects may be expected to take.

The simulated inquiry followed the general schema of the pilot experiment. In advance I had set the required number of "guesses" at about 25,000 (more exactly, 24,800—following the pilot experiment, an exact multiple of 400 was desirable).

I asked friends and acquaintances who had access to computers to donate pseudo-random digits. The real purpose of the request was not divulged, and they were obtained under the pretext that I was interested in the degree of randomness of pseudo-random sequences. I gave no hint that the sequences were to be matched against random number tables. The number of digits per sequence was left to the free decision of the donor.

Eventually three sequences of pseudo-random digits were obtained from separate sources. Each being generated by different programs, the guess sequences were, hopefully, fairly varied. At this point only 17,600 digits had been obtained. The immediate prospects of obtaining further material from such sources appeared to be very slight, so that the remaining 7,200 digits were taken from a standard set of random-number tables, that of Fisher and Yates.[25]

The number of digits or "guesses" in each of the four sequences is shown in Table 2.

The pseudo-random sequences were, on request, printed

TABLE 2

Sequence	Number of digits
1	8,000
2	4,800
3	4,800
4	7,200

out in blocks of one hundred—ten rows of ten digits each. The blocks were labeled alternately A and B, in imitation of the pilot experiment. Four successive blocks may be called a series, each having 400 digits, equal to the number of guesses made by each subject in the pilot experiment.

At the first stage of the inquiry the target digits were

taken from the tables of M. G. Kendall and B. Babington Smith.[26] Each series of guesses was matched against a different section of these tables, which are printed in one hundred blocks of a thousand digits apiece. Each block contains twenty-five rows of forty digits. A few of the blocks, which are known to be biased in certain ways, have been asterisked by the authors and these blocks are avoided. The blocks which were to provide the target series were selected by reference to another set of random digits. Successive pairs of digits, reading from the first row of these new tables, were used to select the target block in the Kendall and Smith numbers. The target series in the selected block started either at the first or the twelfth of the twenty-five rows in the block; this row was selected by tossing a coin.

The selection of target digits for each series of guesses was not purely at random, as no target series could be used more than once—technically, sampling was without replacement. The method described simply maximized the variety of target series while reducing to a minimum the experimenter's deliberate choice. All the target series for each guess sequence were selected before I had looked at any of the sequences.

The guess and target series were then matched digit by digit and any hits or coincidences were ringed. The number of coincidences in each block was counted and recorded. An example of this procedure for a single series is given in Table 3.

The most striking feature of the scores after all the digits had been matched was that the number of coincidences fell considerably below mean chance expectation. The explanation which immediately springs to mind is that this deficiency is attributable to errors in matching. The task is certainly monotonous and tedious and under these conditions errors are very likely to be made. It is likely that coincidences which are really there are missed. An independ-

TABLE 3
Example of "Guess" and "Target" Series of 400 Digits
The coincidences are shown in heavy type

Block	"Guesses"	"Targets"	Matching Score
	1 7 6 3 1 1 0 7 6 0	2 8 7 1 0 2 2 3 4 3	
	6 3 3 5 8 4 7 4 0 1	0 6 9 7 1 5 6 4 3 8	
	6 3 2 1 3 1 6 3 4 **3**	**6** 7 7 7 4 6 7 1 2 **3**	
	9 1 4 2 0 4 3 5 7 4	6 0 3 3 8 2 2 6 8 6	
A	0 1 5 8 8 4 6 3 2 3	8 7 6 7 6 8 2 7 9 2	8
	1 2 9 1 3 8 4 2 5 8	7 6 8 4 2 7 7 8 0 5	
	0 5 1 1 0 5 5 0 2 7	1 1 4 5 0 3 5 3 5 8	
	5 6 5 2 6 8 2 0 8 4	6 1 1 8 3 4 6 2 8 3	
	1 5 9 0 8 5 4 9 6 4	4 6 9 1 7 2 1 5 0 1	
	0 9 2 7 1 9 8 9 9 9	6 6 7 7 0 4 9 1 1 5	
	6 7 7 0 9 4 6 1 7 4	1 5 9 0 7 1 3 0 7 1	
	8 1 7 2 6 1 8 8 8 1	1 3 3 6 4 6 5 5 7 9	
	0 0 0 7 6 5 1 3 2 6	5 1 5 8 0 1 4 7 3 8	
	7 9 6 4 9 1 1 9 4 1	9 9 0 4 1 3 0 6 6 3	
B	6 3 4 7 9 1 2 9 3 4	3 8 9 6 2 1 0 0 3 5	13
	0 7 1 1 0 3 8 4 2 2	1 6 7 1 6 9 0 9 3 4	
	6 2 0 9 6 9 9 8 8 0	8 2 5 7 9 7 5 5 3 5	
	3 2 8 7 5 9 9 9 7 0	0 8 4 0 7 2 1 4 7 0	
	4 7 6 7 7 7 4 2 5 6	1 4 3 2 0 3 6 2 2 6	
	0 3 5 2 7 7 0 1 9 2	8 8 5 0 3 6 6 3 1 7	
	8 4 3 5 0 8 5 3 6 0	3 8 8 1 5 9 3 4 2 6	
	0 6 2 5 1 9 5 7 0 7	8 2 5 3 2 6 9 3 1 9	
	9 3 2 4 7 0 4 3 9 9	3 1 5 0 8 4 1 9 8 4	
	4 7 8 7 1 1 8 0 9 3	2 5 1 1 9 3 5 1 3 2	
A	7 6 2 2 8 7 5 7 3 9	3 1 6 3 5 4 7 3 8 9	7
	2 2 4 0 5 3 9 2 6 2	3 5 2 1 8 6 6 8 6 6	
	6 2 4 9 6 9 3 5 9 2	4 2 1 6 3 8 0 1 9 2	
	6 1 9 3 7 4 4 1 7 9	5 8 5 7 9 0 0 4 7 7	
	0 4 9 4 9 0 3 1 3 8	7 4 0 7 2 1 9 2 7 1	
	7 5 2 0 8 1 3 9 7 4	3 9 6 4 3 0 6 4 5 9	
	1 6 9 2 2 9 1 5 1 0	9 6 6 1 4 9 3 1 2 0	
	7 4 0 5 9 4 8 1 0 2	1 3 9 6 5 5 4 2 2 6	
	9 7 3 6 7 4 8 4 7 7	6 9 8 8 9 2 2 7 0 7	
	7 0 8 6 6 3 6 6 2 3	9 7 5 6 1 8 0 7 6 9	
B	8 0 3 4 1 0 4 0 1 9	3 3 3 4 5 4 8 7 1 0	15
	8 2 6 7 2 2 9 0 7 0	0 7 7 7 2 0 2 3 6 0	
	7 3 9 2 6 4 9 7 4 8	8 8 5 8 5 4 7 8 5 3	
	1 3 9 9 2 7 1 3 0 5	8 7 1 8 1 0 0 1 9 2	
	8 9 1 0 3 7 5 3 5 0	2 8 9 7 8 7 4 2 9 1	
	7 3 5 3 5 9 4 4 4 0	2 2 5 3 3 4 6 9 2 4	

ent comparison of four thousand guesses and targets by a colleague gave results substantially in accordance with mine but with some minor discrepancies which suggested that I had indeed erred towards missing out possible coincidences. I therefore checked all the sequences twice, over a period of about four months. The first check showed, as expected, that a number of coincidences had been missed on the first comparison. The second check gave the same results as the first check, there were no discrepancies between the matching scores, so I am fairly confident that the final matching scores are accurate.

The overall score points to a deficiency of hits: there are fewer coincidences than are to be expected on the chance hypothesis. Table 4 gives the scores for each sequence and the deviations from mean chance expectation (MCE).

TABLE 4

Sequence	Number of guesses	MCE	Matching score	Deviation
1	8,000	800	763	−37
2	4,800	480	429	−31
3	4,800	480	492	+12
4	7,200	720	660	−60
TOTALS	24,800	2,480	2,364	−116

(C.R. $= 2.41$; $p = .016$)

Three out of the four sequences produced a negative deviation in the matching scores.

In order to estimate the probability of a deviation of −116 having occurred by chance alone, we can apply a standard statistical test—the normal approximation to the binomial distribution (Appendix II, p. 280). This gives a level of significance $p = .016$. Thus we would expect the observed deviation from mean chance expectation of 116 to occur by chance about sixteen times in every thousand experiments. The odds against the chance hypothesis are 62 to 1. These odds bear no comparison to the odds of millions or billions to one against the chance hypothesis derived from the performance of a few high-scoring ESP subjects. Nevertheless the level of significance is greater than that commonly accepted as evidence of, rather than as convincing near-proof of the reality of, the presence of ESP in guessing experiments. According to the *Journal of Parapsychology* the criterion level of significance commonly used today is a probability value of .02, i.e., odds of 50 to 1 against the chance hypothesis.

What can be said about these results? On the one hand the case for paranormal causation in conventional ESP and PK experiments can hardly be prejudiced by an isolated result with a fairly low level of significance. The evidence for ESP and PK rests not only on the successes of the few high-scoring subjects but also on the accumulation of experiments in which deviations from chance are less extreme. Although some of these results may be attributable to chance, it would hardly be plausible to argue on the basis of a single instance that all of them are. On the other hand the results are curious, and intuitively surprising. It is certainly odd that a negative deviation should be maintained over the large number of trials involved without being, in the long run, swamped. The results would at least suggest caution in inferring a cause on the basis of statistical arguments alone.

The scores on the A and B blocks were summed separately in order to examine the data for position effects. Table 5 shows that there was a tendency for the A blocks to deviate more strongly from chance expectation than the B blocks.

Three of the four sequences show a similar pattern of

scores—a larger negative deviation in the A block progressing to a smaller (negative or positive) deviation in the B
block. For the series as a whole the A block negative deviation is nearly three times as great as the B block deviation.
When the subject is scoring below chance expectation ("psi-
missing") in a proper ESP test, this kind of fall-off in score
is sometimes called an "incline effect," using an obvious
spatial metaphor. However, as the effect is one of a reduc-
tion in scoring between occasions, one may as well stick to
calling it a decline effect.

TABLE 5

Sequence	Number of guesses in A blocks (= number of guesses in B blocks)	MCE	Deviation A	B
I	4,000	400	—46	+9
2	2,400	240	—22	—9
3	2,400	240	+24	—12
4	3,600	360	—41	—19
TOTALS	12,400	1,240	—85	—31

The difference between the A and B block scores is not
statistically significant; such a difference would be expected
by chance with a probability of about 0.3 (odds of 10 to 3
against). Nevertheless, in a conventional ESP test the observed position effects might well have been taken to cor-
roborate the evidence for the presence of psi suggested by
the overall significant negative deviation.

Since the possibility of psi phenomena appears to have
been excluded in this experiment, one can only presume
that the results are attributable to chance or to some un-

suspected non-randomness of the target series. In either case one would suppose that if the whole operation were repeated with the same set of "guesses" matched against a new series of random digits, then the anomalies of the first experiment would vanish or fade into insignificance.

In the second stage of the inquiry the same four sequences were matched against digits from random-number tables published by the Rand Corporation.[27] The target series were selected from pages 2–12 of these tables—these pages happened to be to hand—in the same manner as in the previous experiment.

In the second experiment the null hypothesis was that the scores would be insignificantly different from chance expectation. On the basis of the previous experiment we can couch the alternative hypothesis as a specific prediction, namely that the overall matching scores will fall significantly below chance expectation. We might also predict that the same pattern of decline effects will be displayed.

As before, I checked the initial matchings twice. Eight thousand "guesses" and targets were matched independently by two colleagues and the accuracy of the scores was confirmed.

The results were again unfavorable to the null hypothesis. Table 6 shows that in line with the prediction made, the overall scores again fell below chance expectation.

Again three sequences gave a negative deviation. The overall deviation is less than before; the probability of a deviation of −95 having occurred by chance is in this instance .02. The odds against the chance hypothesis are therefore 50 to 1.

The outcome of the second experiment, if considered by itself, is perhaps not unduly disturbing. But it is surely very odd that the matching scores should fall below chance expectation yet again. If we take the two parts of the experi-

TABLE 6

Sequence	Number of guesses	MCE	Score	Deviation
1	8,000	800	761	−39
2	4,800	480	432	−48
3	4,800	480	455	−25
4	7,200	720	737	+17
				−95

(C.R. $=2.0$; $p=.02$, one tailed)

ments in conjunction, the probability of both the observed negative deviations having occurred together by chance is smaller than either having happened individually in unconnected experiments. From Table 7 we see that the accumulated negative deviation is 211.

TABLE 7

	No. of guesses	MCE	Score
Experiment 1	24,800	2,480	−116
Experiment 2	24,800	2,480	−95
	49,600	4,960	−211

(C.R. $=3.15$; p less than .0008)

The probability of finding a negative deviation of 211 in a sequence as long as 49,600 is about .0008. So the odds against the outcome of the two experiments taken together having arisen by chance alone are 10,000 to 8, or 1,250 to 1.

This is certainly a respectably high level of significance, great enough to persuade one to believe with fair confidence that a paranormal cause is acting in the context of a proper

ESP or PK test. For example, a recent experiment by Dr. Helmut Schmidt in which subjects apparently influenced the behavior of a randomizer governed by a radioactive source gave odds of about 1,000 to 1 against the chance hypothesis. This experiment attracted unusual attention outside of the journals of parapsychology.[28]

The data were examined for position effects as before. Table 8 shows the A and B block scores for each sequence.

TABLE 8

Sequence	Number of guesses in A blocks (= number of guesses in B blocks)	MCE	Deviation A	B
1	4,000	400	−11	−28
2	2,400	240	−16	−32
3	2,400	240	−25	0
4	3,600	360	−15	+32
TOTALS	12,400	1,240	−67	−28

The cumulative scores over the A and B blocks of all four sequences display the same kind of decline effect as before but to a lesser degree. But the A block deviation is larger in only one case, that of sequence three, so that the evidence for the predicted decline effect is not without ambiguity.

In the two experiments described, each target series of 400 digits had been haphazardly selected from the random-number tables concerned. There is an extremely remote possibility that some of these target series had been biased in some unsuspected fashion that corresponded to a similar bias in the guess sequences. Suppose, for example, that there was a deficiency of the digit 8 in many of the target series selected and that there was an excess of eights in the guess sequences. The negative deviations observed would perhaps then be attributable to deviations from the theoretical frequencies of the digits 0 to 9.

As a countercheck to this contingency, a third series of matchings was made. The target digits were once more from pages 2–12 of the Rand tables. But on this occasion the guess sequences were matched against target digits taken in their original book order.

Again two checks were made on the initial set of matchings.

The outcome of this third experiment is set out in Tables 9 and 10, in the accustomed manner. Table 9 shows the deviations from chance expectation of each sequence, while Table 10 displays the extent of the differential scoring between the A and B blocks of each sequence.

TABLE 9

Sequence	Number of guesses	MCE	Score	Deviation
1	8,000	800	766	—34
2	4,800	480	459	—21
3	4,800	480	517	+37
4	7,200	720	647	—73
TOTALS	24,800	2,480	2,389	—91

(C.R. = 1.98; for which p = .024, one tailed)

On this occasion the decline effect between the A and B blocks when all four sequences are considered together is in the reverse direction from that of the preceding experi-

TABLE 10

Sequence	Number of guesses in A blocks (= number of guesses in B blocks)	MCE	Deviation A	B
I	4,000	400	−3	−31
2	2,400	240	−17	−4
3	2,400	240	+10	+27
4	3,600	360	−29	−44
			−39	−52

ments. Moreover, the differential scoring between the A and B blocks is comparatively minute.

The principal effect of modifying the target order in the third experiment has been the disappearance of a particular position effect. Like an old familiar tune the overall negative deviation returns. The negative deviation of 91 may reasonably be taken to exclude the possibility of bias having been introduced by the particular method of target selection in the first two experiments.

These results are certainly extremely odd. If all other explanations are excluded then they can only be attributable to something akin to chance. So far as I am aware, the alternative explanations which are possible are

(1) Errors in scoring
(2) Non-randomness of the target digits
(3) Paranormal causation.

I shall discuss these in turn.

(1) Errors in scoring

While I am confident that inaccuracies have been reduced to a bare minimum by the three checks made on all the sequences by myself, and the independent comparisons by others, certainty can only be attained by a number of further independent checks of the material. However, the energy involved in this could be fruitfully expended in repeating the experiment with fresh material. Presumably the whole matching operation could be carried out rapidly and efficiently with the use of a suitably programmed automatic computer.

(2) Non-randomness of the target digits

This may take two forms: (a) aberrations from the required theoretical frequency of the digits; (b) the presence of subtle and unsuspected patterns in the order in which the digits occur.

(a) The tables are thoroughly inspected before publication in order to ensure conformity to the required theoretical frequencies, provided that large enough samples are taken. A sample size of over twenty thousand digits, as in the present experiment, would certainly be more than adequate. The possibility of bias having been fortuitously introduced by the selection of relatively short target series has been effectively ruled out as the explanation of the results by the negative deviation obtained in the third experiment where the target digits were taken without disruption to the book order.

(b) This demands that the target series possess repetitive patterns which are in turn counter similar to a recurring pattern or recurring patterns in the four guess sequences used. Again, this contingency seems highly improbable. However, the improbable is clearly not impossible.

In favor of the pattern hypothesis one could point to the position effects obtained between the A and B blocks, when these are summed over all four sequences, in the first two experiments. However, this seems to be partly artifactual. When the individual sequences are considered, it can be seen that the A block deviation is greater in exactly six cases out of twelve. Ignoring the sign of the deviation, it is greater in the A block for Sequence 3 in the second experiment, Sequence 2 in the third experiment, and all four sequences in the first experiment.

A stronger argument against the hidden pattern hypothesis can be constructed by considering the case of Sequence 4. This sequence was derived from the random-number tables of Fisher and Yates. These tables have been elaborately and minutely tested by Mr. Fraser Nicol for any signs of systematic ordering. His tests gave no indication of the presence of such patterns.[29] However, the deviation from chance expectation in the matching scores of Sequence 4 was quite considerable in two of the present experiments. In the light of the tests made by Fraser Nicol we can conclude that absence of pattern does not preclude scoring significantly beyond chance expectation. One can fairly dispose of the pattern hypothesis as *the* explanation of the results.

(3) Paranormal causation

This is the heart of the matter. It would be possible to construct all sorts of ad hoc explanations of these results involving paranormal causation (precognition of the target series, etc.). But this would be an entirely circular argument based on the assumption that any deviation from chance observed in a purely statistical experiment where all other causes are absent is due to paranormal cause or causes.

There is at least one experiment in the annals of parapsychology which is comparable with the present one. This is an experiment carried out by Dr. Lucien Warner and published in the first volume of the *Journal of Parapsychology*.[30] Dr. Warner matched packs of ESP (Zener) cards against each other. One pack represented the targets, the other pack the mock calls or guesses. Both packs were thoroughly shuffled and were therefore putatively random. A large number of packs were matched by this method and altogether over one hundred thousand "guesses" were made. The results were in accordance with chance expectation. This experiment is commonly accepted as being adequately controlled for ESP, i.e., any paranormal influence was safely excluded. If this is the case where Dr. Warner's experiment is concerned, then it must surely be so in the present experiment.

It looks as though the results obtained in the present experiment can only be attributable to "chance." If so, however, is it then possible to discriminate between the presence and absence of paranormal causation in purely statistical experiments which yield a relatively low level of significance to support an ESP (or PK) hypothesis? It may well be that the ostensibly non-chance results obtained in some ESP and PK experiments are after all attributable to "chance"—which in these cases perhaps could better be described as mischance. Further experiments along the same lines are needed to test this conjecture.

If, however, similar control experiments were to show that highly significant deviations from chance expectation could be obtained in the absence of any possible normal or paranormal cause, then our commonsensical notions of chance are in for a rude shock.

There is an anecdote about G. K. Chesterton as a small boy. Walking with his mother, the young Chesterton spotted another small boy. After gazing at this child for a few moments Chesterton turned to his mother to ask "What's he *for*, Mother?" What are the chance aberrations of psi for? If the statistical aberrations of parapsychology are chance coincidences, are they *merely* chance, *mere* coincidences?

While card-guessing experiments are a fruitful source of evidence for some real, if inexplicable, phenomena, they tend at best to be little more than rather trivial exercises in communication. The foibles of random digits seem to have even less import. A recent crop of somewhat unusual experiments suggests however that the caprices of randomness may have a biological value. Walter J. Levy and Eve André, working at the Institute for Parapsychology, placed newly hatched chicks under a heat lamp coupled to a randomizing device governed by a radioactive source.[31] At set intervals the lamp was switched on or off, according to the dictates of the randomizer. The number of "offs" and "ons" was recorded automatically. With the lamp on, the chicks were "relaxed and showed every sign of enjoyment"; with the lamp off, they were "huddled and peeping miserably." The chicks were left with this automated "hen" for a number of nights; on each occasion the number of "ons" was significantly greater than the number of "offs." However, when the apparatus was left to run by itself with no chicks under the lamp, the number of "offs" and "ons" were equal—in accordance with chance expectation.

An even more remarkable experiment was carried out by Levy.[32] Using the same apparatus, not chicks, but fertile chicken eggs were placed under the heat lamp. The lamp came on or stayed off every twenty-four seconds, according to the selection of the randomizer. When no eggs (or only hard-boiled eggs!) were present, the number of "offs" equaled the number of "ons." When fertile eggs were placed in the incubator, the lamp came on more often than not. In the first experimental series of 4,500 trials the light came on 2,358 times, as opposed to the 2,250 times expected by chance. In the second series of 6,506 trials the lamp came on 3,416 times, whereas the chance expectation is 3,253. The adaptive value of these chance deviations, if confirmed by further work, is clear in a way that is not obvious in the general run of guessing experiments.

Perhaps what we call chance embraces a pair of supplementary principles, firstly the "order from disorder" principle, and secondly what we might tentatively call a "coincidence factor," of which parapsychology provides a wealth of examples. The scope of such a principle may well extend beyond the conundrums and riddles of psi. Dr. Stewart Kauffman, working at the Massachusetts Institute of Technology, has proposed that living organisms are, in a fundamental respect, randomly constructed.[33]

Kauffman studied the behavior of randomly constructed systems—or "nets"—of binary elements. These nets, which were simulated by computer, were comprised of elements, analogous to switches, each of which could be either "on" or "off."

The interconnections between the elements of a net were made at random. Each element scanned the input ("on" or "off") from two other elements, and had an output ("on" or "off") to one other element. The response, or output, from each element was prescribed by a randomizing device.

Nets containing between fifteen and two thousand elements were studied and found to behave in a surprisingly orderly manner. For any such net there is a finite but very large number of possible states, or configurations of its elements. (A net containing N elements has 2^N possible states.) Starting from an arbitrarily chosen inital state, in which the elements are placed on or off at random, one would perhaps expect a randomly constructed system to pass through a sequence or all possible states, returning eventually to the initial state, and then to traverse the whole cycle again, and so on indefinitely. Far from this being the case, Kauffman found the system tended to cycle through a very small number of states. Furthermore, the number of different configurations displayed by the system when started from different initial states was also unexpectedly small. When perturbed by arbitrarily reversing one element (from on to off or vice versa) as the system cycled through successive states, the systems exhibited a marked stability. In 90 per cent of the cases the system returned to the cycle of states from which it had been disturbed. Like a missile homing in on its target, the system returned to its original path when subjected to minor, random interference. These networks of disorderly construction gave every appearance of orderly patterning and stability in behavior.

Kauffman suggests that the metabolic activity and development of contemporary organisms may be governed by large randomly connected nets of genes which interact in a similar fashion to randomly constructed networks of binary elements. The behavior of such nets displays the stability characteristic of, and necessary for, life. This hypothesis is supported by the accuracy of predictions with regard to, for example, the rate of cellular differentiation and cell replication observed in organisms of varying complexity, which Kauffman based on the observation of his binary nets. In concluding this argument Kauffman writes:

A living thing is a richly connected net of chemical reactions. One can little doubt that the earliest proto-organisms aggregated their reaction nets at random in the primaeval seas; or that mutation continues to modify living metabolic nets in random ways. Evolution, therefore, probably had as its initial substrata the behaviour of randomly aggregated reaction nets.

It is a fundamental question whether two billion years of survival pressure have succeeded in selecting from a myriad of unorderly reaction nets those few improbable, that is nonrandom and ordered, metabolic nets which alone behave with the stability requisite for life; or whether living things are akin to randomly constructed automata whose characteristic behavior reflects their unorderly construction no matter how evolution selected the surviving forms. . . . Large, randomly assembled nets of binary elements behave with simplicity, stability and order. It seems unlikely that Nature has made no use of such probable and reliable systems, both to initiate evolution and protect its progeny.[34]

Thus Kauffman's random nets seem to point to a formative tendency present in apparent disorderliness. Principally through the processes of natural selection, Nature shapes out of chaos the intricate and highly organized forms of living organisms. In contrast to inanimate matter, the living world is one of increasing orderliness. While the physical universe, like a runaway horse, tends towards increasing entropy, or disorder, the living world flows against this current by constantly creating order, or negative entropy. Is not the orderliness emerging from the free-for-all antics of Kauffman's automata reminiscent of the harmonies that may resonate from the otherwise surd digits of random-number tables?

If the "order from disorder" principle ensures the uniformity and continuity of chance events, perhaps the "co-incidence factor" is marked by the creative accident. Jung maintained that the occurrence of meaningful coincidences required the postulation of an explanatory principle to be added to the concepts of space, time and causality.[35] This principle, the synchronicity principle, is based on a universal order of meaning which is complementary to causality. He suggests that meaningful coincidences, or synchronistic events, indicate a "self-subsistent meaning" based upon "an order of the microcosm and macrocosm which is independent of our will." For Jung the meaning of coincidences is, as it were, pointed to by the activation of postulated archetypal processes: archetypes mediate the functions of the collective unconscious and consciousness—they are the messengers of the psyche. Consciousness is for Jung discriminative and structured, acquiring knowledge within the limitations of time and space; the unconscious, on the other hand, is formless and is in its acquisition of knowledge unconditioned by the constraints of space and time. The processes of the unconscious reflect processes which are external to the psyche; the microcosm and macrocosm are in harmony. Jung suggests that it is the revelation of this universal order which is responsible for a sense of the numinous which often accompanies the experience of certain coincidences, or acausal concurrences. By his postulation of "archetypal processes" Jung provides a psychological context for what I have called the "coincidence factor."

In the next part we leave behind us these puzzling statistical quirks which are encountered in psychical research; here Arthur Koestler considers those equally enigmatic "synchronistic" events which are encountered in everyday life, the coincidences which range from the trivial to the numinous-laden, from the commonplace to the unique.

References to Part Two

1. Suetonius, *The Twelve Caesars*, p. 90, trans. Robert Graves (Penguin, London 1972).
2. Cicero, *De Divinatione*, II.vi, p. 387, Loeb (London 1938).
3. Cicero, ibid., p. 507.
4. Cardano, G., quoted by Oystein Ore, *Cardano: The Gambling Scholar* (Princeton 1953).
5. Galileo, G., "Sopra Le Scoperte Dei Dadi," *Opere*, 8, pp. 591–4 (Firenze 1898).
6. Fermat, P., *Oeuvres de Fermat*, vol. II, Ed. Tannery, P., and Henry, C. (Paris 1894).
7. Ore, Oystein, "Pascal and the Invention of Probability Theory," *American Mathematical Monthly*, vol. 67, 5, pp. 409–19 (1960).
8. Bernoulli, J., quoted by David, F. N., *Games, Gods and Gambling*, p. 136 (London 1962).

9. Bernoulli, J., ibid., p. 137.

10. Laplace, P. S., *A Philosophical Essay on Probabilities*, p. 196 (New York 1951).

11. Schrödinger, Erwin, *What is Life?*, p. 83 (Cambridge 1969).

12. Fisher, R. A., *The Design of Experiments* (London 1947).

13. Rhine, J. B., and Pratt, J. G., "A Review of the Pearce-Pratt Distance Series of ESP Tests," *Journal of Parapsychology*, XVIII, pp. 156–77 (1954).

14. Soal, S. G., and Bateman, F., *Modern Experiments in Telepathy* (London 1954).

15. Schmidt, H., "Precognition of a Quantum Process," *Journal of Parapsychology*, XXXIII, pp. 99–108 (1969).

16. Thouless, R. H., *From Anecdote to Experiment in Psychical Research*, p. 69 (London 1972).

17. Fisher, R. A., op. cit., p. 13.

18. Spencer Brown, G., *Probability and Scientific Inference*, p. 116 (Longmans, London 1957).

19. Scott, C., "G. Spencer Brown and Probability," *Journal of Society for Psychical Research*, vol. 39, pp. 217–34 (1958).

20. Oram, A. T., "An Experiment with Random Numbers," *Journal of Society for Psychical Research*, Vol. 37, pp. 369–77 (1954).

21. Spencer Brown, G., Letter in *Journal of Society for Psychical Research*, vol. 38, pp. 38–40 (1955).

22. Oram, A. T., op. cit., pp. 40–3.

23. Rhine, J. B., *Journal of Parapsychology*, XXXIII, p. 137 (1969).

24. Rhine, J. B., ibid., p. 146.

25. Fisher, R. A., & Yates, F., *Statistical Tables for Biological, Agricultural and Medical Research* (Edinburgh 1938).

26. Kendall, M. G., and Babington Smith, B., *Tables of Random Sampling Numbers* (Cambridge 1971).

27. Rand Corporation, *Million Random Digits* (Glencoe, Ill., 1955).

28. Schmidt, H., "Mental Influence on Random Events," *New Scientist* (June 24, 1971).

29. Fraser Nicol, J., "Randomness: The Background and Some New Investigations," *Journal of Society for Psychical Research*, vol. 38, pp. 71–86 (1955).

30. Warner, L., "The Role of Luck in ESP Data," *Journal of Parapsychology* I, pp. 84–92 (1937).

31. Levy, W. J., and André, E., Abstract in *Journal of Parapsychology*, **XXXIV** (September 1970).

32. Levy, W. J., Abstract in *Journal of Parapsychology*, **XXXV** (December 1971).

33. Kauffman, S., "Metabolic Stability and Epigenesis in Randomly Constructed Genetic Nets," *Journal of Theoretical Biology*, no. 22, pp. 437–67 (1969).

34. Kauffman, S., ibid., p. 465.

35. Jung, C. G., *Structure and Dynamics of the Psyche*, Collected Works, vol. VIII, trans. R. F. C. Hull (London 1960).

PART THREE

Anecdotal cases

ARTHUR KOESTLER

The study of parapsychology is concerned with two types of events: (a) the results of laboratory experiments, (b) phenomena which occur spontaneously in everyday life. The latter are usually referred to, somewhat contemptuously, as "anecdotal material," because the value of such reports depends in most cases on subjective assessments of the reliability of the reporter; they do not qualify as scientific evidence in the strict sense. Well-authenticated cases are rare, and even when, initially, the evidence seems to be strong and unequivocal, it tends, with the passing of time, to become elusive, ambiguous and finally to vanish into thin air amidst a flutter of mislaid documents, lost diaries, of eyewitnesses having second thoughts, or moving to an unknown address, or dying an untimely death. It looks as if the phenomena in question had a tendency to leave a smoke screen in their trail to confuse their pursuers. This frustrating experience is so common that it deserves a name: we might call it the ink-fish effect.

Another variety of the ink-fish operates in the minds of the skeptically inclined. As one correspondent[1]—a biochemist—wrote in response to a letter of mine in the *New Scientist* asking for reports of "coincidental" experiences:

[1] Superior figures refer to end-of-part notes.

So *many* such experiences occur in one's life—having varying degrees of impact, ranging from the trivial and humorous to incredulity and wonder—but for lack of any rational or conventional framework of explanation into which they may fit and be ordered, they are rapidly expelled from our "normal" consciousness and quickly disintegrate and fade away in our memories. As you know, the common dustbin is labelled "coincidences," "accidents," "fate," "chance," etc.

But while most such events of the "trivial or humorous" type land in the dustbins of memory, there are others with a dramatic impact which may have a lasting effect and lead to profound changes in a person's mental outlook—changes ranging from religious conversion in extreme cases, to a mere agnostic willingness to admit the existence of levels of reality beyond the vocabulary of rational thought. It seems that the majority of serious people engaged in parapsychological research—even of the dreariest card-guessing kind—derive their motivation from such spontaneous, quasi-traumatic experiences, which are subjectively more convincing to them than the best-designed laboratory experiment. Thus the ultimate roots of parapsychology—in terms of subjective experience—are in the "anecdotal material," though it would not stand up as evidence in court; whereas the statistical evidence, however impressive, may satisfy the rational strata of the mind but leaves the deeper levels unsatisfied and hungry for meaning. Statistics is the daily bread of science, but even science does not live by bread alone—quite apart from the disturbing problems concerning the nature of statistical probability, chance and design, discussed in other sections of this book. Thus it seemed justified to include this part comprising anecdotal material on apparently meaningful coincidental events. It does not aim at convincing the determined skeptic; it merely aims at providing some food for thought to those with an open mind, driven by perhaps no more than a playful curiosity, which prompts them to search for patterns in the mosaic of random events—for the face hidden in the tree.

The collection of "anecdotal cases" in this part is based on readers' letters to the authors, personal communications from friends, answers to a questionnaire sent out by the Religious Experience Research Unit (RERU) at Manchester College, Oxford, and on the letter to *New Scientist* mentioned above—with a sprinkling of first-hand experiences. The guiding principle of selection was emphasis on the "coincidental" nature of the experience—i.e., a preference for cases which appear to resist explanation not only in terms of physical causality, but also in terms of telepathy and other categories of "classical" ESP. Accordingly, some of the most dramatic cases, such as telepathic dreams or premonitions of death or accident, had to be reluctantly excluded.

However, it is obviously impossible to draw a rigid categorical distinction, because "coincidental" and "ESP-type" phenomena overlap—see Part One—and we do not have even the beginning of a methodology which would enable us to decide whether some event with astronomical odds against chance should be interpreted as a manifestation of ESP—or in terms of "synchronicity" or the "clustering effect" to be discussed later on.

The library angel

To start with, a trivial experience which is typical of a frequently recurring pattern.

In the spring of 1972, the *Sunday Times* invited me to write about the chess world championship match between Boris Spassky and Robert Fischer, which was to take place later that year in Reykjavik, Iceland. Chess has been a hobby since my student days, but I felt the need to catch up on recent developments, and also to learn something about Iceland, where I had only spent some hours in transit on a transatlantic flight during the war. So one day in May I went to the London Library, St. James's Square, to take home some books on these two unrelated subjects. I hesitated for a moment whether to go to the "C" for "chess" section first, or to the "I" for "Iceland" section, but chose the former because it was nearer. There were about twenty to thirty books on chess on the shelves, and the first that caught my eye was a bulky volume with the title:

CHESS IN ICELAND AND IN ICELANDIC LITERATURE
by Williard Fiske

It was published in 1905, by—of all things—"The Florentine Typographical Society, Florence, Italy."

This type of coincidence, involving libraries, books, quotations, references or single words in special contexts, is so frequent that one almost regards them as one's due. Here are a few more examples.

Excerpts from a letter by Dame Rebecca West, D.B.E., undated, received on October 6, 1972:

On a lawn at a sale in the Thames Valley I found four lithographs by the great Delpeche (of horses drawn by Charles Vernet). I bought the four for a pound and hung them in Henry's [her husband's] room as he was horse-mad.

One day I found myself in the London Library, standing at the counter while an assistant fetched me the memoirs of Gounod. An American came up and asked me if I was me, and said he was writing an article on Delpeche, and he had heard I had four of Delpeche's lithographs, and I said I had. As we stood talking the assistant interrupted and said she had only the English translation of Gounod's memoirs, would it do. I said I would look, and opened it at a page where Gounod describes how kind Delpeche was to his mother when she was left penniless with a family. . . .

A second "library case" reported by Dame Rebecca provides an added twist. She went to Chatham House (the Royal Institute of International Affairs) to check up on a certain episode related by Fritsche—one of the accused in the so-called minor Nuremberg (war crime) trials:

I looked up the trials in the library and was horrified to find they are published in a form almost useless to the researcher. They are abstracts, and are catalogued under arbitrary headings. After hours of search I went along the line of shelves to an assistant librarian and said: "I can't find it, there's no clue, it may be in any of these volumes." (There are shelves of them.) I put my hand on one volume and took it out and carelessly looked at it, and it was not only the right volume, but I had opened it at the right page.

The added twist here is that while her *systematic* search had remained fruitless, her apparently *random guess* was instantly rewarded, as if it had been guided by intuition.

Another typical "library case," quoted from the replies to the RERU questionnaire (case no. 1320):*

At the time of my father's very sudden death he was engaged on a book based on his American lectures. It was in uncorrected typescript and he said it had engrossed him more than any other book he had written. He had left a note asking that I should see it through the press if he died before it was published and asked that two scholars who were his friends should, before publication, read it. . . .

There were many footnotes which were incomplete and without the references. It took me six months to check and verify

---

* As the questionnaire assured all respondents that their identity would be treated as confidential, I can only refer to the case numbers in the files.

the references etc. Finally I got them all, except one, quoted from the "Sacred Books of the East" in (36 volumes). C., a professor who was an authority on Indian religions, could not help me.

Finally I borrowed from the University library 3 volumes which he had once had out. With them I sat down late one night in his study chair. I gave a "sort of prayer"—"Can't he be allowed to help me?" Then I took up one of the three volumes at random and it opened at the place! My task was complete.

Such happenings may seem dull to the outsider, but they are fraught with emotion for the person who experiences them. De Maistre has a nice phrase: "*L'ange distributeur des pensées*." After reading through a score of "library cases" one is tempted to think of library angels in charge of providing cross references. In a letter dated October, 1972, Mrs. Rosalind Heywood (author of *The Sixth Sense*, etc.), quotes the following among several other examples:

A week or two ago I was thinking of the line "*Venus toute entière a sa proie attachée*," but I couldn't remember the second and third words. Within two days I found the line quoted in a mystery story where one would not expect to find Racine. . . .

The next report (RERU case no. 785) will probably ring a bell in many long-married couples' ears:

Yesterday my husband was deeply immersed in a book whilst I, browsing somewhat idly through the *Penguin Dictionary of Quotations*, found myself on page 392 reading Terence. At this juncture my husband interrupted me and read aloud from page 21 of his book—Jung's *Psychological Types* . . .

"*Certum est quia impossibile est* . . . this is certain because it is impossible" (Tertullian).

I discussed this for some time with him and then returned to the page still open in my book. The first words to catch my eye were the following: "*Credo quia impossibile*—I believe because it is impossible."

Can this be dismissed as pure coincidence? Two such totally divorced works being linked by a single quotation at a specific point in time and/or ESP between us—surely the substance of Tertullian's words, mocking as they do accepted modes of logical thought, may lead us to expect otherwise?

In the next case the library angel seems to operate over a distance of several hundred miles. Excerpt from a letter from Mr. Ivone Kirkpatrick, O.B.E., T.D., of Wimborne, Dorset, dated May 15, 1972:

One of the most remarkable coincidences I have experienced was one day before the last war. I happened to be reading a passage from Goethe's *Gespräche mit Eckermann* and I switched on my radio which happened to be tuned into a German station. To my astonishment the man was reading from the same passage as I was.

Another "quotation case" with a strangely lyrical quality, from the RERU files (no. 1575).

In 1968 my daughter was jilted for the second time and I could not comfort her or stay her weeping. I went into the kitchen to get a drink and prayed desperately to be able to give her words of comfort as I am usually inarticulate in such situations, although I feel keenly. As I waited for the kettle to boil I distinctly heard the words "As the sun sets, it also rises." At the time I accepted this without astonishment, and only afterwards did the full impact of that voice come to me. However, I went back to the lounge to my distraught daughter. Giving her a drink I said, "As the sun sets, it also rises." She seemed quieter and I went to bed.

A year afterwards my daughter was getting married. I booked the reception at a country Jacobean mansion recommended to me, and having photos taken it was decided that the lack of sun at the main entrance would not make for a good picture, so we went to the garden entrance where steps lead down on to a terrace. Cut there in the old stone of the door lintel under which the happy pair were standing was "As the sun sets, it also rises."

In the next case the librarian angel seems to assume the role of literary agent. It concerns an earlier book of mine, *The Case of the Midwife Toad*[2]—a biography of the Austrian biologist Paul Kammerer, who throughout his life was fascinated by serial coincidences and wrote a book on the subject. The following excerpt is from a letter by Mr. Bent Henius, Science Editor of the leading Danish newspaper, *Berlingske Tidende*:[3]

Dear Mr. Koestler,

I have just finished translating your . . . book about the midwife toad for Gyldendal [the publishers] here in Denmark.

I have been specially interested in the law of seriality (a difficult word to translate into Danish) and thought you might be interested in a couple of examples. I often have such experiences.

If a colleague at my newspaper finds something of interest for me in a foreign paper, he cuts it out and sends it to me. Two months ago I received a cutting from a British paper. I receive such cuts every day, and often it will take some weeks before I get time to read them, especially if they are about literature and not "hot news." However, that day I had to go to the doctor, and I took the cutting along to read it if I had to wait in the waiting room. I had to, and for the first time I read about your toad-book. When I came back to my office later in the afternoon, Gyldendal called and asked if I would like to translate the book.

I shall conclude this section with another personal experience, witnessed by four people.

In June, 1961, my wife and I moved into a house we had

built as a summer residence in the mountain village of
Alpbach, in the Austrian Tyrol. Alpbach is a place with a
strong Catholic tradition, and though we are not Catholics,
we agreed to have the house blessed by the parish priest,
Herr Pfarrer Danninger, to comply with local custom. On
the morning of Sunday, June 25, the day appointed for the
ceremony, while waiting for Pfarrer Danninger, I was reading André Maurois' biography of Alexander Fleming.[4] It
contains a passage where Maurois discusses the hypothesis
that the biblical hyssop, which the ancient Hebrews used in
their purification rites during the harvest feast, was a plant
which carried the mold *penicillium*; and he quotes verse 7
from Psalm 51: "Purge me with hyssop and I shall be
clean." When I got to this passage my wife called, "The
Herr Pfarrer is here"; so I put a bookmark in that page and
went downstairs. Our neighbors, the farmer Othmar Rad-
inger and his wife, joined in; and after the traditional glasses
of *Schnaps*, Pfarrer Danninger performed the ceremony—
which culminated in his sprinkling the walls with holy water
and reading out, in German, Psalm 51, verse 7: "Purge
me with hyssop and I shall be clean."

When it was over, I showed the guests the Maurois
volume with the bookmark in it. They were not unduly
impressed, as they simply took it for granted that "such
things happen."

Something curiously similar seems to have happened to
a Mr. X (age fifty-eight, case no. 1468 in the RERU file):

For a long time I lived in an old cottage on the Berkshire
Downs. The plaster was peeling in my bedroom through long
neglect and I gradually came to see that the area of about a
square yard over my head made a picture of the crucifixion,
with two Roman soldiers in the foreground, dicing for the robes.
I saw this for weeks, perhaps months, on end, both by daylight
on waking, and by lamplight (there was no electricity) on going

to bed. Eventually I made careful drawings of the picture, then scraped it off and repainted.

Gradually over the years I came to see it as a sort of warning: I was wasting my time not doing nearly enough work, and in fact dicing against the background of the crucifixion.

Then during my Christmas holidays in Greece in 1968 I was working on a palindromic poem. I have invented a new kind, where it is the words and not the letters that go backwards in the second half. I was so engrossed with the technical difficulties that I was content with rather vague meaning, until I suddenly saw that the words were so to speak guiding themselves in the direction of my picture. I started to make a conscious effort to describe, at least at a symbolic level, what I had seen so long ago.

I had finished working on the poem on January 6 and was typing the final version. Just as I finished the last line of the third stanza "Cross that I built"—the doorbell rang and there was an Orthodox priest. He offered me the Cross to kiss (the only time in my life that I have kissed the Cross) and then went around asperging the flat. I had not realised it was Epiphany Day, still less that it is the custom of the Orthodox Church to carry out the ceremony on this day.

"Deus ex machina"

After the ghosts in the library, the ghost in the machine. The previous section dealt with coincidental events of a verbal nature. In the following section I shall cite a few bizarre cases involving mechanics and engineering.

Among the letters I received after publication of a recent book, *The Roots of Coincidence*,[5] there was a particularly amusing one from Mr. Jeffrey Simmons, Managing Director of W. H. Allen & Co, the publishers. I was so intrigued by it that I wrote back several times, asking for more details, which Mr. Simmons was kind enough to provide. In the interest of a continuous narrative, I have inserted passages from his later letters where they fill gaps in the first.

Letter dated March 20, 1972

Dear Mr. Koestler,
The problem of coincidence has fascinated me for years, and I read your latest book with obvious interest. I was debating with myself whether to write to you—I cannot recall ever writing a fan letter, or writing to an author at all for that matter except in my professional capacity—when Robin Maugham* told me that he had just left you. . . . Whether or not this constituted a coincidence, it made up my mind for me.

My purpose in writing is to put on record for you something that happened to me which is, in many ways, more puzzling than anything similar I have read about. . . . I have been a publisher for 25 years. During this time I have had occasion only once to pulp a book. . . .

To "pulp" a book means to destroy the whole stock by putting it through a mill and turning it into pulp. In a subsequent letter (dated May 8) Mr. Simmons explained why he felt obliged to resort to this drastic procedure:

For a time after the war, a subsidiary company of ours published some of Edgar Rice Burroughs' Tarzan books in paperback editions. . . . As near as I can recollect, the year was perhaps 1950. A letter reached me from a naïve, but also very irate, lady who wrote that she had always regarded the Tarzan books as suitable for children, but that she was disgusted to discover that they were filled with descriptions of sex and flagellation, and how dared we publish such filth? The explanation for this extraordinary outburst was that the books were printed by a small printer—a refugee from Hitler—who happened also to

---

* Viscount Maugham, the author—nephew of Somerset Maugham.

print the books by Hank Janson which by the standards of the time were considered pornographic by those who make that sort of judgment. He had mistakenly bound the Tarzan books in the Janson covers, and vice-versa!—so it was cheaper for them to reprint de novo than to replace the covers. It was he who suggested that we pulp the books and return to him the proceeds. . . .

But how does a respectable publishing firm set about pulping a book? We now revert to the narrative in Mr. Simmons's first letter:

. . . I went upstairs to our Production Manager and asked him whether he knew a firm that could do the job. He said "No," adding that he had never needed to pulp a book during his 40 years in publishing. By an unusual chance, a young boy from our warehouse was delivering a message to the Production Manager at that very time, and he told me that he lived in Battersea and that there was a firm called Phillips Mills (of whom I had not then heard). Using the Production Manager's telephone, I asked our switchboard operator to look up their number and telephone them for me. "Their representative is here," was her reply. I thought at first she was joking, but in fact he had walked in literally seconds before I spoke to the operator. He was an old man, and told me that my office was on his beat and that, apart from a short time during the war when he was ill, he had passed the office almost every weekday for years, but had never before called in. I asked him what had made him call in now, and he said he did not know; something just told him to do so. (Incidentally, he never called again, as far as I am aware.)

It seems worthwhile to recapitulate briefly the sequence of coincidental events in this crazy story. First, Mr. Simmons hesitates whether to write to an author whom he has never met, when a third person arrives at his office coming straight from that author's house. Next, faced with the momentous problem how one is to set about pulping Tarzans, he happens to run into an office boy who happens to know of a pulping mill. And, to crown it all, the *deus ex machina* from Battersea happens to pay just at that moment his first and last visit to W. H. Allen & Co.

Mr. Simmons's comments, at the end of his first letter, reflect the way many people react when faced with experiences of this kind:

The amazing implications of this story will not be lost on you. Telepathy can explain why the man called in, but in order for it to have operated he had to be passing at the very instant I wanted him, and by chance even heard of his firm—on the one and only occasion I needed him. Was this pre-ordained? At the very least there was some extraordinary chain of circumstances working in my favour. Why should it do so for something so seemingly unimportant—for, after all, it would have made no material difference if I had had to telephone Phillips Mills and their representative had visited me the following week? If there are helpful forces operating in unimportant matters, may they not also be operating, unknown to me, in important cases? And if helpful forces are around, may there not be unhelpful ones, alas? How much control do we have over our own destiny?

The next case leads from pulping to pumping. It was reported by a friend, as a rejoinder to the former, and subsequently confirmed in writing:

On May 20, 1972, a group of people were standing round a swimming pool in the garden of the Hon. Mark Bonham-Carter's house near the small village of Ripe in Sussex. . . . The pool had been emptied to be relined, but at the bottom there remained a quantity of water too low to go down the draining hole, which made it impossible to start work.

Various ideas of how to proceed were discussed and rejected, till one of the guests, the local architect, said: "What we need is a builder's pump, but the problem is how to get hold of one."

At that moment a loud noise was heard from the road (about 40 yards away), and a lorry rattled slowly by, carrying a builder's pump. The architect leapt into his car, caught up with the lorry, and the pool was promptly drained.

Another case (RERU no. 1268), by an Army officer, sounds like a variation on the same theme:

One day I was engaged in directing people to a car park. During the period of waiting I picked up a dirty looking pebble, but after rubbing off the mud found it was a marble.

When my host came down to see me he denied it belonged to his children. So, though I have not needed a marble since childhood 60 years ago, I put it into my pocket rather than throw it away.

That afternoon I filled up with petrol at a garage where the attendant was not a regular and a bit "ham fisted." When I asked him to fill the battery with water he knocked off one of the stoppers and though we uncoupled the battery and lifted it and examined the roadway, we could not find it. Then I remembered my marble and put it where it fitted exactly. Was it a coincidence?

What if instead of an unseen hand, an unknown man had handed me the marble and passed on!

These were cases of some trivial but unusual need being satisfied by some very improbable, whimsical event—one might call them *miraculets*. The next case, however, though also of the *deus ex machina* type, belongs to an altogether different category. To spare the feelings of those involved, I have to camouflage their identities, but the facts are correct in every detail.*

On a certain day in November, 1971, a gifted young

---

* Photostats of the correspondence relating to this and all other cases (except those contained in the RERU files) have been deposited in the archives of the S.P.R.

architect (unknown to me) who had suffered a nervous breakdown, threw himself in front of an incoming train in a London Underground station, and was taken to hospital. His injuries were severe: a fractured pelvis, punctured abdomen with extrusion of intestine, lacerated back and severe bruising. However, he pulled through.

I learned about this incident from a relative of the victim (also unknown to me), who, after reading *The Roots of Coincidence*, wrote to me about the strange circumstances surrounding it:

Some days after the event I was talking to one of the doctors at the Hospital who asked me if I had heard the full story. He said the case was engrossing the interest of London Transport. Apparently Harold's life was saved not at all because the train driver saw him and applied the brakes in time. Quite independently, and with no knowledge of Harold or of what he intended to do, some passenger on the train had pulled down the "Emergency" handle. And again independently of Harold's case, London Transport had interviewed this passenger with a view to a prosecution on the ground that he had no reasonable cause for pulling the handle.

This passenger's pulling the handle must have saved Harold's life. They had to jack up the train to get him out, therefore he must have been well under it. On the other hand a wheel cannot have passed over him or he would have been killed. Pulling the "Emergency" handle applies the brakes automatically. The difference between life and death must have been measured in nanoseconds.

If one had precise figures for the incidence of suicides by this method at this station, the incidence of "false alarm" calls by passengers etc., etc., a calculation of statistical probability could be made, but one supposes the chances are infinitesimally small.

A friend of mine, Mr. Tom Tickell, on the editorial staff of *The Guardian*, volunteered to investigate the case. He contacted London Transport, but ran into the traditional barrier of red tape. The identity of the passenger who had pulled the emergency handle was allegedly unknown. The name of the driver of the train was eventually disclosed, and his address given c/o the Divisional Manager of his branch. A letter to the driver sent to that address remained unanswered. Thus the case petered out, leaving but a muddy trail—the ink-fish effect once more.

The only hard evidence proving that there *was a* passenger who pulled the emergency handle is a letter in my possession to a relative of the victim from London Transport, Travel Inquiries, 55 Broadway, Westminster, London SW1, dated April, 1972 (even the day of the month was blurred by the ink-fish), which says: "Although the identity of the passenger who pulled the emergency handle is unknown to us, the operator of the train in question was . . . ," etc.

Anybody familiar with the London Underground system can confirm that it is quite impossible for a passenger to see what is happening in front of the engine. Even the driver, who has a free view, has an emergency brake within reach, and trained reflexes, did not have time to act when Harold jumped. If we assume that the unknown passenger acted on a telepathic impulse, we must also assume that it was a precognitive impulse, anticipating the event by a couple of seconds to stop the train in time.

This is obviously a case which could be interpreted either in terms of telepathy combined with precognition, or as a "coincidental event." As already said, the two categories overlap—unless one is prepared to regard the former as subcategories of the latter. We shall return to this question in Part Four.

The next story is also one of a disaster averted—in less dramatic and more tortuous ways. It was told by Sir Alec

Guinness during a luncheon with mutual friends; he then kindly put it down in writing[6] at my request:

Saturday July 3rd 1971 was, for me, a quiet day of rehearsals ending with dinner with a friend and going to bed at 11:30 P.M. Before going to bed I set my two alarm clocks to wake me at 7:20 A.M. When working in London at a weekend it has been my habit to get up at 7:20 on the Sunday morning and leave my flat at 7:45 for the short walk to Westminster Cathedral for Mass at 8:00. (I have been a Catholic, of a sort, for about sixteen years.) On returning from Mass I would have a quick light breakfast and catch the 9:50 Portsmouth train, from Waterloo, to my home near Petersfield. On this particular night I remember I didn't sleep a great deal as I constantly woke up— perhaps each hour—with a tremendous sense of well-being and happiness, for no reason that I can put my finger on.

By habit and instinct I am a very punctual riser in the morning, and usually wake up two or three minutes before the alarm clock rings. On this particular morning I woke, glanced in the half light at the clock and thought "My God, I've overslept!" It appeared to me the clock said 7.40 (I didn't refer to the second clock). I rushed through washing and so on and hurried to the Cathedral. Very unexpectedly—in fact it had never happened before—I found a taxi at that early hour, so I thought I was at the Cathedral at 7:55. With time to spare I went to confession. When Mass started I thought the attendance was considerably larger than usual for eight o'clock. It was only when what was obviously going to be a rather tedious sermon, was under way that I glanced at my watch and realised I was at the 9:00 Mass instead of the 8:00. I went home, as usual, saw that both my alarm clocks were correct and decided to catch the 10:50 train instead of the 9:50. (My wife was away in Ireland so it made no difference what train I caught.) When I arrived at Waterloo at 10:30 there was an announcement that all trains on the Portsmouth line were delayed for an unspecified amount of time. An enquiry gave me the information that the 9:50 train had been derailed a few miles outside London. Subsequently I found out that it was the front coach of the train which had toppled on its side and that, although no one was killed, or even grievously injured, the occupants of that coach had been badly bruised and taken to hospital. My habit, when catching the 9:50 on a Sunday morning, had been to sit in the front compartment of the front coach because, when in Waterloo station, that coach was in the open air, away from the roofing of Waterloo and consequently with more light for reading and less likelihood of being crowded. . . .

In my reply to this letter I pointed out that he had not only overslept (by an hour and twenty minutes!) but had also misread the clock by an hour; had he not done so, he might have decided to skip mass and catch the ill-fated 9:50 train after all.

He wrote back that he also thought that his misreading of the clock was the oddest thing about the story—"particularly as there were two clocks, almost side by side."

If one opts for the ESP hypothesis—unconscious precognition—one must also assume that the unconscious cunningly persuaded the conscious self to misread the clock.

But usually "warnings" come in a simpler form, not infrequently as auditory hallucinations. The following account by an octogenarian former mine-worker (RERU case no. 2784) is typical of many others:

I was working in a coal mine north of Pittsburg, Kansas, at the age of 24. I asked the mine foreman for a job at a deep mine. The foreman said he had a room not being worked—the man had quit. If I would take it I would get a new one when it was worked out.

The rooms were each 200 ft. from the main tunnel, and the entries to each room were 400 ft. apart. I had no men working on either side, the others were further up the tunnel. One day before noon I pushed out to the entry a loaded car (1,800 to 2,000 pounds). A man driving a mule would hook the mule to the car and drive it away. As I had crawled back to work the driver yelled, "Kid—here's an empty for you." As I started out for the car I heard a voice "Stop." I sat there, I did not move, then I heard "Quick, go, go." I was scared. I crawled as fast as I could to the face of the room (the passage was 3 feet high) then through the cross cut (this is an opening between the rooms allowing air to circulate). I cannot describe the noise the falling rock made. The falling roof pushed the air with great force—my miner's lamp was put out. I could see nothing. The room next to mine being worked out, the rails had been removed so I had no way of knowing which way to go. The men who had heard this rock fall came then, and I could see by the light of their lamps the way out.

. . . My father who worked in the mine said later that hundreds of tons of rock had fallen. He had never seen so much rock come down. I never went back to that mine, nor did my father.

If it had not been for that voice "Stop" and a few seconds later "Quick, go, go," I would have been covered with that rockfall.

I am 5 ft. 11 in. tall—in a small 3 ft. space I heard the voice right over my head, not from a distance. I have never forgotten this and never will.

Another "warning" case came from a lady (RERU no. 467):

In London soon after the First War. There was a dense fog and all traffic had stopped—I was reading. Suddenly, I put down my book and ran into the street without waiting to put on a coat—it was November and bitterly cold. I had no idea why I was doing this. I ran on and came to a man who was dying. He had been gassed in the war.

The last "warning" case appeared, rather surprisingly, in the Personal View column of the *British Medical Journal*[7] —not usually given to printing this kind of stuff. The author, F. I. D. Konotey Ahulu, a physician in Accra, Ghana, related in his article various paranormal phenomena frequently encountered in his country. The concluding part of it read:

The following story, though not peculiarly African, concerns my own family. On Friday, 16 December 1949, I came home from Achimota School for five weeks' holiday. My brother Jerry had also just arrived home on the same day from the Presbyterian Secondary School. Though their school had eight weeks' break Jerry insisted he had just one week. "Don't be silly, I just heard you had eight weeks," I remarked. "I have one week," he simply replied. On Wednesday the 21st while we helped Mamma make cakes and doughnuts for Christmas, Jerry sat quietly in a corner rather unconcerned. Asked whether he wouldn't be the first to pounce on the finished product, he retorted, "I'm not going to eat this cake and neither are you." Strange remark from one who never played with his food. Mamma then commented that Jerry had been moody "these past few days." On the Friday, the 23rd, there was a students' football match three miles away at Somanya. He played at centre-forward while I was inside-left. Soon after half-time a flash of lightning cracked across the field grazing my forehead and my left hand—it didn't burn me, but it felt as if I had been sharply sprinkled with sand. I heard the whistle go, and to my right was Jerry lying on his back, his left hand across his chest, quite dead. The shock was quite indescribable. "A week ago he said he had just one week," I kept whispering, in a daze. We were in mourning at Christmas—how could we eat cakes?

I told this story to fellow students at Westminster Hospital. Most of the boys listened without comment, but one (who with two more clinical years to go had already chosen his speciality—psychiatry) had a ready answer for the phenomenon. "Quite simple," he said, "your brother was just accident-prone!"

So it seems twentieth century "scientific" man finds a reason for everything. My personal view is that *Melius est nescire centrum, quam non tenere circulum*—it is better not to know the centre than wander out of the circle (literally). I prefer Blaise

Pascal's rendering of the same idea: "The supreme achievement of reason it to realise that there is a limit to reason."

Poltergeists

The counterparts of the *deus ex machina* are the malicious gremlins and library imps responsible for mislaid references, vanished documents, treacherous picture hooks and other delinquent gadgets. An extreme form of this type of phenomena is the Poltergeists of folklore—malicious sprites specializing in knockings, rappings, explosive bangs; in moving objects through the air, throwing stones through walls and, in modern times, causing electric appliances to get out of control. However inane these reported manifestations are, the reports reveal a curiously consistent and specific pattern, which is quite different from the lurid tales of ghosts and apparitions. A few examples will illustrate this.

First, there is the famous episode which took place when, in March, 1909, Jung visited Freud in Vienna. At that time, as Ernest Jones reports in his biography,[8] "Jung's admiration for Freud and enthusiasm for his work were unbounded. His encounter with Freud he regarded as the high point of his life. . . ."

In the emotionally charged atmosphere of the meeting, Jung, a lifelong believer in ESP, brought this subject up. Freud, at that time, did not believe in it (though in his later years he did). Jung describes what followed:

While Freud was going on this way, I had a curious sensation. It was as if my diaphragm was made of iron and was becoming red-hot—a glowing vault. And at that moment there was such a loud report in the bookcase, which stood right next to us, that we both started up in alarm, fearing the thing was going to topple over us. I said to Freud: "There, that is an example of a so-called catalytic phenomenon."

"Oh come," he exclaimed. "That is sheer bosh."

"It is not," I replied. "You are mistaken, Herr Professor. And to prove my point I now predict that in a moment there will be another loud report!" Sure enough, no sooner had I said the words than the same detonation went off in the bookcase.

To this day I do not know what gave me this certainty. But I knew beyond all doubt that the report would come again. Freud only stared aghast at me. I do not know what was in his mind, or what his look meant. In any case, this incident aroused his mistrust of me, and I had the feeling that I had done something against him. I never afterwards discussed the incident with him.[9]

Unless one assumes that Jung had invented the whole story, or that he hid Christmas crackers in Freud's bookshelf which he detonated by remote control, one has to admit that the event was decidedly odd.

But the oddity did not stop there. When I met for the first time co-author Robert Harvie on March 2, 1972, in Professor Hardy's Institute at Oxford, he told me the following sequel, which he subsequently put down in writing. On an evening in the second week of February, he was sitting in his study with a girl friend, "expounding on synchronicity and the prima donna aspect of Jung's personality. I began to read to her from your book *The Roots of Coincidence* Jung's account of the bookcase episode. . . ."

He had got to where Jung's diaphragm was "becoming red-hot" when a rubber band, holding the lampshade of the ceiling light together, snapped with a startling crack. "My friend jumped. I continued to read aloud. At the words 'That is sheer bosh,' the lampshade collapsed to the floor. Consternation in friend and myself. . . . Knowing what was to come in the anecdote, I think I was the more disturbed of the two of us. . . ."

The story is slightly weakened by the fact that the lamp-shade, a cardboard affair "made of twenty flanged equilateral triangles" to look like a large crystal—an icosahedron, to be precise—had previously shown signs of decrepitude—the rubber bands that held it together had perished; from time to time one would snap and occasionally the whole contraption would then slide over the hanging bulb to the floor. Nevertheless, the timing of the first crack and the final collapse could not have been a more perfect example of synchronicity—with or without the Jungian implications of the term.

But the Poltergeist that Jung had let loose had not yet come to rest. A few weeks later an unknown reader, Miss Margaret Green, of London W1, wrote:

Reading your . . . book, *The Roots of Coincidence*, yesterday morning on the way to Cambridge by train, I came upon the story of the loud detonations in Freud's bookcase during his talk with Jung. Long ago I had known that there was a fundamental clash of temperamental forces between these two thinkers, and I was intrigued by the story.

On the way back in the train in the evening I had your book with me and the story of the detonations kept coming back, with amusement, into my mind. About twenty minutes before getting to Liverpool Street, there was suddenly a bang, like a bomb, and splinters of glass flew round the carriage and there was a jagged hole in the big window. My attention and that of the other two unknown people in the carriage was taken up by shaking glass off ourselves and each other, and it was not, I think, until this morning that, again with amusement, the coincidence occurred to me.

One of the greatest physicists of our century, the Nobel Laureate Wolfgang Pauli, seemed to have all his life a Poltergeist attached to his ebullient person; its activities were so persistent that his colleagues thought them worthy of a scientific name and called them the "Pauli Effect" (meant as a parody of the "Pauli Principle," one of the cornerstones of modern physics). George Gamow, himself an eminent physicist, gives the following description of the Pauli Effect.[10]

It is well known that theoretical physicists cannot handle experimental equipment; it breaks whenever they touch it. Pauli was such a good theoretical physicist that something usually broke in the lab whenever he merely stepped across the threshold. A mysterious event that did not seem at first to be connected with Pauli's presence once occurred in Professor J. Franck's laboratory in Göttingen. Early one afternoon, without apparent cause, a complicated apparatus for the study of atomic phenomena collapsed. Franck wrote about this to Pauli at his Zürich address and, after some delay, received an answer in an envelope with a Danish stamp. Pauli wrote that he had gone to visit Bohr [in Copenhagen] and at the time of the mishap in Franck's laboratory his train was stopped for a few minutes at the Göttingen railroad station. You may believe this anecdote or not, but there are many other observations concerning the reality of the Pauli Effect!

The same anecdote, slightly differing in detail, was sent to me by a reader who had not read Gamow.

Pauli cooperated with Jung on the latter's famous essay, "Synchronicity: An Acausal Connecting Principle,"[11] and accepted Jung's view that meaningful coincidences are manifestations of an acausal, i.e., extraphysical principle "equal in importance to physical causality." Pauli called it a "metaphysical" or "absolute order" of the cosmos which provides the background of physical phenomena—as Jung's archetypes of the collective unconscious provide the substratum of consciousness (and are thus, by definition, beyond its grasp).

Pauli died in 1958. Although a considerable number

among the pioneers of modern physics, including Einstein, showed a favorable attitude towards parapsychology, Pauli, in his writings, had taken a more explicit and courageous stand than most of them. Unfortunately I never met him; but I was curious to know whether the "Pauli Effect"—his accident-proneness or Poltergeist—had something to do with his belief in acausal forces in the universe. So I put this question to Professor Werner Heisenberg, the doyen of modern quantum-physicists, who had been a lifelong friend of Pauli's. Heisenberg wrote back:[12]

Pauli did indeed take Jung's reflections on synchronicity entirely seriously. . . . I must confess that I myself have never had the courage to venture in earnest into this field, if for no other reason than because so much of the literature about it is of course unreliable. On the other hand I would never claim that physics and chemistry exclude the possibility of such phenomena. . . . As for the "Pauli Effect," Pauli himself took it half seriously, but only half. I could of course tell you anecdotes about this effect, or particular cases which I have witnessed myself. . . .

All of which seems to confirm that spontaneous experiences of the "anecdotal" kind can have a profound effect on the mental outlook and scientific philosophy even of the giants of modern physics. But perhaps I should say, *particularly* on physicists, who, more than scholars in any other field, have been forced to recognize the limits of physical explanations—and the possibility of other levels of reality beyond physical causation.

Incidentally, Pauli not only had his private Poltergeist, but also an efficient library angel. In his middle fifties he worked very intensely on certain fundamental problems in subatomic physics related to symmetry, "parity" (between particles of left-handed and right-handed spin) and other similar phenomena, all of which could be visualized as reflections in a mirror. But the reflecting mirror was to him also a symbol of the symmetrical correspondence of nature and mind, of *psyche* and *physis*. He became obsessed with mirror images; during the day he worked on the symmetrical field equations which he and Heisenberg hoped (vainly, as it turned out) would provide a unified theory—a kind of "open sesame"—of the elementary particles of matter; at night he had vivid dreams, such as the following: "I was in a room with an unknown woman with whom I shared a great secret: we knew that the objects in the room were not real but only mirror images, and we suffered great anxiety because we were different from other people who did not have that knowledge."

Plato's cave echoing the frustrations of physics. . . . A colleague in Basel teased Pauli about his mirroring-complex. Pauli wrote back, reminding him of the story of Perseus and Medusa. The head of that hideous gorgon had the power of turning any person who looked at it into stone. But Perseus, averting his glance, watched the Medusa's mirror image reflected in Athena's shield, and thus was able to cut off the Gorgon's head. . . . Soon after this excursion into mythology, Pauli received a paper from his former pupil Max Delbrück, who had turned from physics to biology, about a variety of *Phycomycetes*, a light-sensitive, monocellular fungus, *mykes* being the Greek word for mushroom. Delbrück's paper greatly excited the excitable Pauli, because he considered it relevant to the relations of physics to biology, and indirectly to the mind-body problem. A few days later, he read an essay by the philosopher Paul Kerènyi, dedicated to Jung,

about, of all things, the significance of the Perseus legend. It appears that after the Medusa venture, Perseus founded the town of Mykenae, which owes its name to a Greek pun. For on that site Perseus dug up a mushroom; but he had to dig so deep that a brook sprung up from the earth which quenched his thirst. So they called the town Mykene after that mushroom. When I read that story I roared with laughter.[13]

And yet these weird convergences of mirror images, Delbrück's fungus, the petrifying effects of the Medusa (read nuclear physics), Perseus putting both mirror and mushroom to beneficial use—this whole tangled web is only a small detail in the cluster of coincidental events which Pauli encountered in critical periods of his life; the benevolent librarian compensating for the misdeeds of his Poltergeist.

Although the controversial phenomena to which this whimsical term refers, do not belong strictly to our subject, they have an indirect bearing on it. Before the introduction of scientific methods and strict controls into parapsychological research, reports on alleged Poltergeist phenomena could hardly be taken seriously. The situation has changed since trained researchers, equipped with electronic recording apparatus, have investigated a number of cases, and—well aware of the unreliability of eye witnesses, of their unconscious tendencies towards embellishment, hysteria, autosuggestion, and so forth—nevertheless concluded that there remained a residue of inexplicable factors. The best-documented episode is no doubt the so-called Rosenheim case of 1967–8. It is unique in that a series of spontaneous events, extending over a period of several months, were actually observed and recorded by several teams of experts, under conditions resembling a planned laboratory experiment.[14]

The scene of these events was the offices and adjacent private quarters of Dr. Sigmund Adam, a lawyer at 13/11 Königstrasse in the town of Rosenheim, Bavaria, near the Austrian border. It all started harmlessly enough with the telephone system (switchboard and three extensions) going haywire. Conversations kept breaking down, the counter registered calls that were never made, the bills rose steeply.

For four months—July–November, 1967—the firm of
Siemens and the Rosenheim telephone headquarters tried
to put things right, but to no avail. In October a completely
new installation was made by the Post Office with a sealed
counter, but the disturbances continued. Telephones being
what they are, the episode would hardly be worth recording
if Dr. Adam had not had the bright idea of filing a lawsuit
against persons unknown "on suspicion of fraud or em-
bezzlement." This brought the Criminal Investigation Department in, with the happy result that the subsequent events
were witnessed and recorded by several detective inspectors
and police officers.

By the middle of November the disturbances had spread
to the ceiling lights. The neon tubes (two in each office
room) kept going out, accompanied by a bang, and were
found to be twisted in their sockets by 90 degrees; when
replaced by electricians, the same thing happened again
after a short while. Ordinary light bulbs exploded although
they had not been switched on; the automatic fuses kept
blowing without apparent cause. The town electricity department could find no fault in the internal installations and
was thus led to assume that the cause of the disturbances
lay in the supply-net. They accordingly disconnected Dr.
Adam's premises from the main supply and connected it to
an independent emergency power unit. At the same time
they installed sealed automatic voltage-recorders and amp-
meters, which on inspection showed violent deflections,
mostly (but not always) coinciding with loud bangs which
were tape-recorded. In spite of all precautions, the disturbances continued unabated and took even more bizarre
forms. Hanging lights were observed to swing, pictures to
rotate round their hooks or to fall off the wall (one picture
rotating through 320 degrees was video-recorded). A heavy
filing cabinet weighing about four hundred pounds was
reported by CID Inspector Wendl to have moved away from

the wall, without apparent cause, "by 28 centimetres" (trust Germanic thoroughness even in facing Poltergeists).

By the beginning of December further reinforcements were called in—in addition to the engineers of the Siemens Works, the Electricity Board, the Telephone Board and the CID. One team was headed by Professor Hans Bender, who holds the Chair for Psychology and Border Areas of Psychology at the University of Freiburg. He soon established that the abnormal phenomena seemed to be focused on the person of an eighteen-year-old secretary apprentice, Miss Annemarie S. With two exceptions things happened only when she was at the office. This fitted well into the familiar pattern of alleged Poltergeist phenomena which nearly always seem to be centered on emotionally unstable adolescents or young people, laboring under some repressed conflict or intense stress. Annemarie was found to have a "transference relationship" with Dr. Adam (who is married, with a grown-up son at the office); in common parlance she had a crush on the boss. She was also caught, on a single occasion, by Inspector Wendl, running along a corridor and setting a lamp in swinging motion—which she afterwards denied. This again fitted the characteristic pattern of alleged Poltergeist media, frequently given to confabulation and cheating when the phenomena they expect fail to materialize. But it did not explain the neon lights, exploding bulbs, the deflections of the recording pens in the sealed counters (up to fifty amperes), the rotating pictures and the rest. So two more electronics experts were called in: Dr. F. Karger of the Max Planck Institute of Garshing, near Munich, and Dr. G. Zicha of the Technische Universität in Munich. Their report[14] occupies nineteen pages, including detailed diagrams of the circuitry and control apparatus, and photographs of the oscillograms produced by the sealed recording instruments. In a preamble to this paper the authors say:

If a technological problem poses difficulties which seem to involve basic principles, it is frequently passed on to the physicist. Our subsequent report indicates that occasionally a problem may turn up which compels even the physicist to admit, up to a point, the defeat of his attempts at a solution and explanation.

The conclusions of the report state:

(1) Although recorded with the facilities available to experimental physics, the events defied explanation in terms of current physical theories.

(2) The phenomena seemed to be the result of non-periodic forces of short duration.

(3) The phenomena do not seem to be caused by known electrodynamic forces.

(4) Not only "explosive" events were involved, but also complex motions (rotating pictures, curves described by the recording needle).

(5) These movements gave the impression of being under intelligent control and to have a tendency to evade investigation.[14]

Even more interesting are the speculative comments of the two physicists:

Contemporary physics knows four types of interactions: the "strong" interaction [nuclear forces]; the "weak" interaction [e.g., radioactive beta decay], electromagnetism and gravity. Our investigation definitely excludes electromagnetic interactions as the source of the observed paranormal phenomena; nor can the other three interactions conceivably be held responsible for them. It seems therefore that the psychokinetic phenomena observed in Rosenheim and elsewhere necessitate the assumption of a fifth type of interaction, even more conclusively than the phenomena of K-meson decay [one of the unsolved paradoxa of quantum physics]. Since these phenomena only appear in connection with a certain individual, we are faced with the unexpected situation that theoretical physics may be led to the discovery of new principles through the study of human faculties. It appears, then, that the phenomena which at first glance give the impression of childish pranks, may, after thorough investigation, open up fundamentally new problems of physics.

While the various teams were busy investigating, Annemarie S. developed strong hysterical symptoms, uttering piercing shrieks when another bulb went pop and suffering muscular spasms with partial paralysis. Professor Bender made the sensible suggestion that she should be dismissed in her own interest. This was done, and after her departure the phenomena in Dr. Adam's office came to an end.

But Annemarie's tribulations did not stop there. She became engaged to a laboratory technician who was also a dedicated bowler. She may have got jealous of his passion, or bored by it, because out of the fourteen occasions when she went with him to the bowling alley, the electronic system controlling the pins broke down eight times. As a result, the engagement broke down too, on the fiancé's initiative.

She was submitted to various psychological tests and therapeutic sessions by Bender and his assistants at Freiburg University. The results of these, and other, tests were published (without naming the subjects); the gist of the results was "emotional instability and infantility; strong irritability; ego-weakness; bursts of aggression, displaced towards substitute-objects; repression and projection, dissimulation and confabulation." The report ended on a Jungian note:

It appears to me, as a result of this investigation, that within a given personality structure as outlined above the frustration tension produced by these conflicts not only discharges itself in the usual forms of aggression but that psychokinesis in addition can function as an aggression-release mechanism. With regard to the problem of transformation of energetic impulses into psychokinetically-caused destruction it seems that in momentary regression magic-animistic attitudes and fantasies become dynamically active.[15]

This, of course, leaves the question open how "magic-animistic fantasies" can become dynamically so active as to make pictures rotate in front of a video camera—or cause an explosion in Freud's bookcase. If it be pure chance, then chance has to be redefined. If one postulates a "fifth interaction," then that interaction belongs to a universe of discourse not only beyond the causality of classical physics, but also beyond the acausal microphenomena of quantum physics.

As for cheating—Annemarie was caught once by Inspector Wendl setting a lamp in swinging motion. She may have cheated on other occasions—they all do, the problem-children and disturbed adolescents associated with these phenomena, often unable to distinguish fact from fantasy. If it were not so, the whole field would not be in such disrepute, and serious research into it would have started long ago to separate the facts from the fantasies. Annemarie may have manipulated objects within her reach when she had a bad day and the phenomena failed to materialize; but the bulk of the phenomena to which the technicians and engineers testified were physically not within her reach, and their control by her a physical impossibility.

The opposite of these aggressive manifestations seems to occur in cases where a person finds himself on the receiving end, as it were, of whatever energy-transfers may be involved. Thus Mr. Kirkpatrick (see above, p. 175) reports:

My son was at The Pilgrims' School in Winchester. As you may know this is a prep school which provides the choristers for the cathedral. The headmaster's two sons are identical twins and

were members of the school. One was a chorister. One afternoon, in the middle of choir practice, he let out a yell and
cried: "Somebody kicked me on the shin." At the moment when
he experienced the pain his brother was in fact kicked on the
shin badly and was brought back from the playing field and put
in the sick-bay.

The practical joker

In most of these case histories, regardless of how you
interpret them, there seems to be some purpose, or personal motivation, or emotional significance involved. But
as often as not one comes across bizarre coincidental events
which seem to have been contrived wantonly, without rhyme
or reason, by some practical joker behind the scenes. Thus
J. B. Priestley sent me the following anecdote (which he
subsequently included in a book of his own).[16] It will be
remembered that Priestley is married to Jacquetta Hawkes,
the archaeologist.

My wife brought three large coloured lithographs by Graham
Sutherland. When they arrived here from London she took
them up to her bedroom, to hang them up in the morning. They
were leaning against a chair and the one on the outside, facing
the room, was a lithograph of a grasshopper. When Jacquetta got
into bed that night, she felt some sort of twittering movement
going on, so she got out and pulled back the clothes. There was
a grasshopper in the bed. No grasshopper had been seen in that
room before, nor has been seen since. No grasshopper has ever
been seen at any other time in this house.[17]

Dame Rebecca West had a similar experience:

Once in the South of France I was writing a passage about a
girl finding a hedgehog in her garden, when a servant told me
to come out and see a hedgehog they had found in the garden.[18]

A third case of the same type: a South American biologist, Mr. Ricardo Ferreira, writes:

One day in 1961, when I was living in Rio de Janeiro, I read
over the lunch break Charles Darwin's description of the "railroad beetle." This is a fire-fly with two side-lanterns found by
Darwin during his stay in Rio. That same evening, as we sat on
our verandah facing Botafogo Bay, a "rail-road beetle" came
flying from the woods and fell on the verandah, to the delight of
our guests, M. and Mme. Moises Haissinsky from the Institut du
Radium of Paris. Never before had I seen such a creature, nor
have I seen another again.[19]

One is immediately reminded of the archetypal model
of this type of story—the rare, scarabaeid bettle flying into
Jung's window at the very moment when a patient tells
him her critical dream about a scarab.[20]

One of the funniest of the practical-joke type of stories I
owe to Robin Fedden of the National Trust, who sent me
the following extract from William Morris's *Journal of his
Tour in Iceland*, published in 1871. The passage (pp. 25–6)
is in the chapter headed Reykjavik:

And now wait and consider if it isn't lucky that a good joke
should not lack its sacred poet—Evans and I bought some
stores at the co-operative society in the Haymarket: they were
to pack them in two cases and send them to us, as they did; but
the day after came a message to say they had made a mistake,
and put a parcel not ours in one of the cases, instead of some
bologna sausage we had ordered, and which they then delivered.
I asked them to unpack the case and take their property away;
they said they would send the next day to do it; I agreed to that,
but told them that if they didn't come that day, to Iceland their
case would go with all that was in it, and that there we would
eat their parcel if it was good to eat or otherwise treat it as it
deserved. Well, they never came, and here was the case, with
the hidden and mysterious parcel in its bowels: many were the

speculations as to what it was, on the way; and most true it is that I suggested (as the wildest possible idea) fragrant Floriline and hairbrushes—now in went the chisel, and off came the lid: there was the side of bacon; there were the tins of preserved meat; there was the Liebig, the soup-squares, the cocoa, the preserved carrots and the peas and sage and onions—and here IT was—wrapped up first in shavings—then in brown paper, then in waterproof paper, then in more ditto, then in whitney-brown—and here IT is—four (was it) boxes of FRAGRANT FLORILINE, and two dozen bottles of Atkinson of Bond Street his scents, white violet, Frangipanni, Guard's Bouquet—what do I know? yea and moreover the scents were stowed in little boxes that had hairbrushes printed on them.

We looked at each other to see if we were drunk or dreaming, and then—to say we laughed—how does that describe the row we made; we were on the edge of the hayfield at the back of the house; the haymakers ran up and leaned on their rakes and looked at us amazed and half-frightened; man, woman and child ran out from their houses, to see what was toward; but all shame or care had left us and there we rolled about and roared, till nature refused to help us any longer—then came the inevitable regrets of the time it would take before my friends could know it, and that I should not be by to see their faces change; for how was I to keep it out of my letters?

People, names and places

Among the commonest "coincidental" experiences are thinking or dreaming of a person with whom one has lost touch a long time ago—and the next day receiving a letter from, or bumping into, that person. Some of these cases obviously belong to the category of classical ESP. Others are so trivial that the skeptic can justifiably invoke the argument from selective memory—to wit, that there are innumerable instances in your life when you thought of Uncle Toby in Australia and did *not* get a letter from him—

and those instances you don't remember. Yet there are some cases of the "encounter" type so peculiar that the explanation by telepathy breaks down, and the memory-argument wears thin. The following episode I owe to Dr. Letitia Fairfield, C.B.E.:[21]

In October, 1928, I set out on a tour of the U.S.A., mainly to visit Child Guidance Clinics and other—then novel—arrangements for the psychiatric treatment of offenders. My first port of call was Montreal and there I contacted my only friend in Canada, a Dr. Lydia Henry who had been head of a woman's college in London until she married a Canadian.

A few days after arrival I went to lunch at her flat, which was across the street from a small park.

After lunch Dr. Henry asked me if I had any other friends in Canada. I said not exactly, I had an acquaintance, a gymnastic teacher whom I would like to see again, but I had quite lost touch and I didn't even know what province she lived in. The reason for wanting to see her again was her interesting obstetrical history. She had married at 39, had a baby at 41 and a second at 48, a few years ago.

My hostess was much interested as she and I had both been advisers to women's gymnastic colleges and had had a lot of trouble with antifeminist cranks who maintained that physical exercises and sports defeminised women, destroyed their sex life, ensured agonising labours and sickly children. Now my nice acquaintance "Mrs. Brown" had produced strong evidence to the contrary.

During our chat I had noticed that the foliage in the park was a glowing crimson and I moved over to the window to admire. Suddenly round the corner came Mrs. Brown herself with the younger child in a push-cart! Dr. Henry sent me flying down to the street to invite her up. She could not come, but was able to assure me that she was well, that her confinements had been easy and her children unusually sturdy.

Here is quite a constellation of coincidences. I had only 10 days in Canada, so it was a fairly narrow chance that we should meet at all. It was a still narrower chance that Mary Brown should be passing a house in which I was only staying for a couple of hours. Surely a million to one that I should look out of the window to admire the sumacs at the precise moment of her passing. Give another million for the fact that I was talking about her at that moment.

There was certainly no emotional drive to set this chain of coincidences in motion, only a mild curiosity to see a woman with an unusual obstetrical history on the part of myself and my hostess. I should perhaps add that my hostess had also married near 40, but her confinement (quite recent) had been very difficult and her child delicate.

The next case I owe to a friend of mine, Dr. James Durham. I should perhaps point out that Dr. Durham in our frequent arguments has always maintained a skeptical attitude towards parapsychology.

In the spring of this year [1972] there was a new receptionist at my rooms. I had not hired her and knew nothing about her. The girl was obviously a Central European and I had vaguely assumed that she was Swiss.

One day, some patient having failed to turn up, I had nothing to do. She made some coffee. We chatted, and it turned out she came from Prague. I asked her if she knew a beer-hall in the street called Thunovská on the Little Side (the Malostrana)—a place called the King of Brabant of which I was fond. She had lived quite nearby, and the King of Brabant had been her "local" (respectable girls, or at any rate girl students, are not averse from beer in Prague.) We spoke of no other such place; in fact I would not know the name of any other beer-hall in Prague, except one in U. Kalice.

While we were talking about this place the door-bell rang. We assumed it was the patient at last, and she went to the door. I heard some conversation which was indistinct but at the same time oddly sharp and abrupt: and then someone being shown into the waiting room. Then the receptionist came running into my room, quite pale and uneasy-looking. She said: "I don't know what's happening, it's the landlady of the King of Brabant. What's going on, I don't understand it—the landlady of the King of Brabant in Prague, do you understand? She's here in the waiting-room."

I could see she wasn't joking, but at first it went through my mind that she had gone off her head (I hardly knew her, and the previous receptionist had been markedly eccentric to say the least). But it was the landlady of the King of Brabant. I then remembered having told this lady and her husband, who had been very hospitable, that in the unlikely event of their ever coming to London they should look me up. This was one of those invitations one freely offers, in remote places on brief acquaintance to people who seem in the last degree unlikely ever to be in a position to take one up on them, and whom one never sees again in the ordinary way of things. This one seemed particularly unlikely at the time because Czechs were by then not able as a rule to travel abroad, and there was not the slightest reason to suppose that this lady in particular would have any reason, let alone excuse, to do so. I had not thought of her in the interval, so far as I remember.

The next, rather involved, episode contains a whole traffic jam of coincidences. It comes from the Rev. Dr. Norman J. Cockburn of New Malden, Surrey. I have slightly condensed his typewritten account:*

On May 19, 1967, I received a phone-call from two Canadians, friends of my cousin in Ontario, on a short trip to this country.

I gladly agreed to their request that I "show them over the City" and about an hour later met them at their London hotel and took them by bus to the front of St. Paul's Cathedral. Before going in, I suggested that we all have a light snack at one of the neighbouring tourist restaurants. It was during the meal that three items of conversation apparently emerged spon-

---

* It was originally addressed to Mrs. Rosalind Heywood.

taneously and became items connected with an enigmatic succession of three coincidences.

My friends, whom I had met for the first time, were Beth and Bill Purves of Toronto. Conversation began by their asking me how far out did I live. I explained that New Malden was a little over ten miles out from the centre of London and that it was "built up" area all that way out. Then I remarked that only a few days previously, one of my neighbours, Mrs. Widdup, when calling had remarked that she had never in her life been "in St. Paul's Cathedral." I expressed surprise at such a thing happening when one was only "ten miles away."

The waitress came and gave the menu card. As I checked over it, to help them I suggested that, being Canadians, they would enjoy the fruit salad. This was agreed and they said, "You've been in Canada, Norman. Where have you stayed apart from visits to you Cousin Nellie and her husband?" I replied that I had stayed with a Presbyterian Minister friend, Stuart Johnston of Lynwood Crescent, Montreal.

As the meal neared its end, Beth Purves said, "It's very good of you finding time at such short notice to take us around. But today was practically the only day that we could fix, as we're off to Northern Ireland. Bill has old friends there. You don't happen to know a place called Green Island?" "Why, yes," I replied, "I stay there with a close friend and his family, when I am over there. His name is Jim McDonald and he lives in Green Island."

They left the restaurant and then the following events occurred:

After taking them round St. Paul's, I finished by getting them to stand on the exact spot where Churchill's body lay in State at his funeral. When moving away, we brushed two ladies, one of whom lifted her head and said, "I thought I recognised your voice, Dr. Cockburn. I'm paying my first visit to St. Paul's Cathedral!" It was Mrs. Widdup of New Malden.

After leaving the Cathedral, they went to the nearby Tourist Information Office:

We crossed the road, I took my friends to the desk where two visitors were just leaving after getting attention. They were Jim McDonald and his wife from Green Island!

The afternoon moved on and the last visit was the Tower of London. After spending nearly an hour there, I said, "Now just let me take you to the Traitor's Gate before we leave." We reached it, a very large party of Canadian tourists were being guided around. Suddenly, their leader, a Minister, exclaimed, "Well, Norman, how amazing meeting you here." It was Stuart Johnston of Montreal, Canada!

The next incident is a nice miraculet which every motorist will delight in. It happened to Michael Meyer, the translator and biographer of Ibsen (letter of 8.11.72):

This May, early one morning, a lorry ground along the side of my car parked in the street and caused over £100-worth of damage, and drove off without leaving any details. Some workmen on a scaffolding had seen it and said that a passer-by had stopped the driver and apparently taken details. A day later I found an unsigned note, evidently from this passer-by, giving me the number of the lorry and the owners' name and address; the bottom of the piece of paper had been torn off, as though the writer had signed it but then decided against involving himself further (which I later found to have been the case). These owners, when contacted by my insurers, refused to acknowledge that any such accident had occurred and my insurers said that unless we could produce the witness we might not be able to claim. A few days later, I was playing cricket at Hurlingham and a member of the opposing team, a man named Fitzgerald whom I had played cricket with during the war but had not met since, said: "Your car's had a nasty crack." When I began to tell him about it, he interrupted: "I know. I was the man who stopped the driver and put the details on your windscreen." The result was that we were able to reclaim from the owners (I think the final bill was £115). That I think is an amazing coincidence; what on earth can the odds have been against my meeting that witness under circumstances which could enable him to identify me as the owner of that car? If it had been at a party he would never have known; nor would he have if there had not fortunately been space around the actual playing pitch for us to park our cars, as seldom happens at cricket matches.

Note that Michael Meyer had lost touch with Mr. Fitzgerald since the war; that Mr. Fitzgerald had no idea of Meyer's present address, nor that the damaged car was his car.

The following terse account from the RERU file (no. 1493) involves an encounter of a quite different type:

In 1941 I travelled out to India by troopship and spent three days in Cape Town with a school friend, B— Y—.

We were both commissioned at the same time in February 1942, and had a small party in Mhow, India.

We parted and never met again, but in November 1943, I was walking at Tamma on the Burma border with Assam and had chosen to walk along an unfrequented river bank.

I literally strumbled into the grave of B— Y—, who was killed in action while serving with the 5th Malsett Light Infantry. He had been buried a month earlier (by "Elephant Bill," a friend of my father's).

The next equally terse report from a Major General (RERU file no. 1057) reads like a variation on the theme of the previous one:

Without praying for it, problems that have long baffled one are sometimes solved all of a sudden. For example, for 50 years I tried every clue I could think of in order to trace a collateral forebear. Just over two years ago I found myself within two miles of her gave in New Zealand—I had no idea she had emigrated to N.Z.—staying with people who knew a great deal about her.

In the last two cases there was an element of personal involvement with people, culminating in a chance encounter at a specific locale—their burial place. The next account, too, is of an involvement with a dead person, focused on particular localities. It comes from Dr. Fairfield (see above, p. 204):

Early in 1942 or '43, when I was in charge of the medical services for the A.T.S., an army car called to take me to Luton Hoo, a great country house outside Bedford where a woman's service detachment was having minor difficulties. On the way out I picked up a book from my hall table which had just come from the Times Book Club. I had put it on my library list as the reviews were very good and the subject (*The Letters of Lady Louisa Stuart, c.* 1780) was the sort of undemanding history I much enjoyed. No other reason. On the way I discovered that Luton Hoo was the birth-place of Lady Louisa! It was of course full of traces of her.

My evening engagement was at a house in Gloucester Place, W.1, of which I knew nothing. A Catholic society had been lent rooms here to replace bombed premises and this was our first meeting there. It turned out to be the house in which Lady Louisa had spent her last years and died.

Late that evening I was rung up by a lady I knew only slightly and who had never rung me up before. A charity we were both interested in—nothing to do with the Gloucester Place organisation—had encountered a sudden crisis. She was the sister of the then Marquis of Bute and on enquiry admitted to being Lady Louisa's nearest living relative—her great-great-grandniece, in fact.

Lady Louisa's charming ghost then slipped away. I have never heard from her since!

A further variation on the theme of places or dwellings involved with people—also by Michael Meyer:

A year or two ago, I found myself talking to an elderly Swedish lady at a dinner at the Swedish Embassy here named Countess Bismarck, widow of the (I think) grandson of the old man. Her husband had been in the German Embassy in London under Ribbentrop, and it turned out that my house, 17 Stanhope Terrace, had been theirs. Some months later, a taxi driver who had just brought me here said as we drew up: "17 Stanhope Terrace. I used to work here." He, it transpired, had been on the staff of the Bismarcks. To meet two quite separate people who had previously lived in the same house as oneself seems remarkable.

The next sad anecdote I have culled from André Malraux's *Antimémoires*. In a conversation I had once brought up the subject of coincidences, and Malraux had replied in a dry, flat voice: "Coincidence is the language of destiny." He has certainly been haunted by tragic coincidences: his brother was killed in the last war; the brother's widow, who became his second wife, was killed as the result of a train accident; his two sons were killed in a car accident. . . .

Malraux, though not a native of Alsace, was deeply involved with that region. His last novel, *Les Noyers d'Altenbourg*, had Alsace as its background. In the last stages of the war he fought there:

I was called upon by the Alsatians to command the Alsace-Lorraine Brigade, and I fought the battles of Dannemarie a few days after the death of my second wife in a clinique in the Avenue Alsace-Lorraine in Brieve. My third wife lived then in the rue Alsace-Lorraine in Toulouse. Let it pass. There are many streets of that name in France. . . .[22]

A cluster of nebulae

One need not be a professional gambler to believe in Kammerer's "Law of the Series." Most languages have a phrase or proverb for it—*Das Gesetz der Serie* is a cliché in German. One could in fact lump together all coincidental cases in this part as a "clustering" or "converging" of events which are meaningfully related but causally unrelated. Moreover, once the series has started, it tends to continue ("it never rains but it pours"); some people become coincidence-prone, as others become accident-prone. Selective memory may again play a part in this; but one would have to stretch the argument to inordinate length to account, for instance, for the well-known phenomenon mentioned in the following letter by a practicing physician:[23]

I have read your letter in *New Scientist* 26.10.72. In the medical profession we have a law called "the law of repeating"—it goes like this:

If, during a surgery or out-patient session a rare and unusual case turns up—one can guarantee that a similar case will turn up as the 2nd or 3rd patient—or perhaps later during that session.

Similarly, I often find that if a person phones me, i.e., Donnell —then another patient with that name will be seen during the session. This phenomenon recurs many times.

In a similar vein, another correspondent wrote:[24]

Your letter in the *New Scientist* (26th October) has reminded me of what has long been in the background of my mind as an unsolved puzzle. Unfortunately I have no definite data, and am no longer in touch with the people who mentioned the facts to me, but the problem may perhaps give a pointer to fields to explore for improbable chance coincidences.

A previous dentist of mine commented on the queer way in which he would have a run of cases (difficult extractions, for example) of the same type, after, perhaps, having had nothing like that for months.

A friend, practising along the lines of the Bates system of natural eye exercises, similarly said she had runs of patients with the same type of eye trouble, quite unconnected with each other.

A typewriter supplier and repairer also noticed that either machines of the same make would come in one after the other for repair (at other times hardly at all) or else it would be the same thing had gone wrong with machines of different makes.

The manager at a small hardware shop said he had sudden runs on particular goods for which he couldn't account, since there had been no advertising or other publicity for them. Sudden runs on electric light bulbs could perhaps be accounted for by sudden changes in temperature, which do affect bulbs, but the other items were a puzzle.

All the above comments were spontaneously made and not the result of specific questioning. There is, of course, the superstition that things come in threes, but none of the people above mentioned that.

In September, 1972, I met Axel Firsoff, the astronomer and author, at an ESP congress (of the Parapsychological Association) in Edinburgh. After his return to his home in Somerset he wrote:

To begin with coincidences, that car ESP 48D was extraordinary. I don't remember ever seeing a car with "ESP" before. And why should it have been parked bang in front of my coach door on this particular occasion? But this is not quite the end of the story. About 3 weeks ago I had a peculiar dream about a small island, which, to judge by basaltic rocks and a hot spring, was somewhere in Iceland.* In the dream I was not directly aware

* Iceland again! (cf. pp. 172, 202.)

of the name of the islet, but the word *Katrineholm* was clearly present in my mind. I decided to check this up, and wrote to Magnus Magnusson about it. However, he says that there is no islet of this name in Iceland. This is not particularly surprising, inasmuch as the name is un-Icelandic in form.

On the way back from Edinburgh I broke the journey in London, and next morning at breakfast found myself facing a pleasant middle-aged gent. After a becoming silence we fell to talking, and it transpired that he was a Swedish artist, who was either a native of or had just come from *Katrineholm*, which is not an island, but a small town in central Sweden. I may have passed through it by train about 36 years ago, but I was not consciously aware of its existence.

Coincidence or precognition? Some of the coincidences may be due to the kind of association that exists in the popular mind between fine weather and full moon—the moon is not noticeable when the sky is overcast. But this is not quite enough. We are here in an interpersonal domain, but there may be an impersonal "general" mind, where coincidence could be shaped. Thus there may be some justification for the widespread belief in omens.[25]

The mathematician Warren Weaver, an expert on the theory of probability, reported, among others, the following improbable story:

My next-door neighbour, Mr. George D. Bryson, was making a business trip some years ago from St. Louis to New York. Since this involved weekend travel and he was in no hurry, since he had never been in Louisville, Kentucky, since he was interested in seeing the town, and since his train went through Louisville, he asked the conductor, after he had boarded the train, whether he might have a stopover at Louisville.

This was possible, and on arrival at Louisville he inquired at the station for the leading hotel. He accordingly went to the Brown Hotel and registered. And then, just as a lark, he stepped up to the mail desk and asked if there was any mail for him.

The girl calmly handed him a letter addressed to "Mr. George D. Bryson, Room 307," that being the number of the room to which he had just been assigned.

It turned out that the preceding resident of Room 307 was another George D. Bryson, who was associated with an insurance company in Montreal but came originally from North Carolina. The two Mr. Brysons eventually met, so each could pinch the other to be sure he was real.[26]

And as we are at names, why should I receive on the same day two readers' letters, on different subjects, one from Mr. V. G. Rivlin in Greenford, Middlesex, the other from Miss Lilly Rivlin in New York? And a few days later, a letter from Professor Stephen Rose, and another one from a Miss Rose? And what unknown agency plays the clustering game with numbers—such as in the following example, which I owe to Professor Hans Zeisl of the University of Chicago Law School:

My grandparents on my mother's side lived in Gablonz, Mozart-gasse 23; we lived in Vienna at Rossauerlaende 23; our law office at Gonzagagasse 23; my mother at Alserstrasse 23, Tuer [flat] 23, and so it went. One spring, my mother was about to leave for a trip to Southern France with a friend of hers and asked me to bring her "something to read." A friend, who owned a bookstore, recommended Ilya Ehrenburg's *Die Liebe der Jeanne Ney*: "It is just out." I bought it without looking at it. My mother wrote at intervals. When she approached Monte Carlo she wrote, "You know I am not the gambling type, but I am tempted to put a little money on our number 23." Of course, I encouraged her. The next letter came from Monte Carlo: "We arrived last night and before falling asleep I read some more in *The Love of Jeanne Ney*. There I came upon a passage where (whoever it was) played roulette and won—on number 23. That settles it: tomorrow I am going to put some chips on 23." One day later, another letter arrived: "23 came out on my

second try." The win was confirmed by my mother's travelling
companion.[27]

It is amusing to note that Professor Weaver and Professor Zeisl both deny that there is anything special about
coincidences and believe (in Zeisl's words) that "the simple
manifestations of the *Gesetz der Serie* can be derived from
classical probability theory. That randomly spaced events
tend to concentrate in clusters is more probable than that
they come in even intervals." Does that make the encounter
of the two Brysons, or Mamma Zeisl's adventures, any less
improbable? And why do people who "do not believe in
coincidences" love to tell stories about their coincidences?
Could it be that inside each hardened skeptic there is a
superstitious old wife crying to be let out?

In 1970, while I was working on the biography of Paul
Kammerer,* the Austrian biologist who wrote *The Law of
the Series*, dealing with coincidences, a whole series of
coincidences seemed to descend on me—like a meteor
shower on a summer night. It was as if Kammerer's amiable
ghost were beckoning with a malicious grin: "I told you
so." I shall relate only a single episode, which occurred at
the very beginning of my research, and for which there is
complete documentary evidence.

Kammerer committed suicide in 1926, at the age of
forty-five. The obituaries mentioned that he had left a
daughter, then eighteen, and that was all I knew about her,
except that her first name was Lacerta.† Fortunately I
knew a very efficient research worker in Austria who, over
a number of years, had done occasional jobs for me. She

* *The Case of the Midwife Toad.*

† Kammerer was very fond of lizards—*lacertae*—and named his daughter
after them.

is now married, but her maiden name—which is relevant to what follows—was Herta Buresch.

In February, 1970, I asked Herta, née Buresch, to try to discover the whereabouts of Kammerer's daughter—provided she was still alive. Her inquiries at various town halls, record offices and parish registers—which in Austria form an almost impenetrable labyrinth—yielded no results, except the fact that in 1935 Lacerta Kammerer had renounced the Roman Catholic faith. After that there was no trace of her. However, Herta Buresch had managed to discover an address where the Kammerer family had once lived: 239 Auhofstrasse in Hietzing, a prosperous suburb of Vienna. With little hope but much curiosity she took a taxi and went there. On the next day (February 12, 1970) she wrote to me:

. . . Auhofstrasse 239 is a Hapsburg-yellow villa, completely cut off from its surroundings by tall hedges, iron gates and a curving drive. There is no bell and no sign at the gate. I was hanging around, uncertain what to do next and thereby attracted the attention of an aged crone, peering through a window from a house across the road. From her I learnt that the "old Baroness" [Kammerer's widow] had died around 1954, and that the daughter had long before that emigrated to America or Australia. The villa is now inhabited by an old lady, a crazy paintress, who has lived in the back wing for the last forty or fifty years. She is never seen, receives no visitors, and the gates are never opened. There was a letter-box with some mail in it, so she must be emptying it from time to time.

This looked pretty hopeless; but Herta's informant then remembered that after the death of Kammerer's widow, a solicitor had appeared on the scene to deal with the estate, and she also remembered his name—Dr. Schweighofer. There were only three law firms of that name in the Vienna

telephone book, so it was not difficult to trace the right one.
Through him I was able to contact Lacerta Kammerer, who
lives in Australia; she gave me invaluable help in writing
her father's biography.

In my very first letter to her, dated March 2, 1970, I
inquired, among other things, about "the crazy old paintress" at Auhofstrasse 239—without going into detail about
Herta Buresch's exploits or mentioning her maiden name,
which of course would have been quite irrelevant. Lacerta
Kammerer answered by return of mail, on March 6. I
quote from her letter:

The lady of Auhofstrasse 239 whom you mention in your
letter is probably Herta? Buresch, née Bitterlich, or her sister
Liesl. I remember both well. . . .

In my next letter I asked her what the question mark
meant.

She replied that she was not sure whether the old lady
was Herta Buresch or Liesl Buresch.

The other Herta Buresch has no relatives in Vienna.

Yet this was, as I said, only the overture to the Kammerer
series.

Down and across

Crosswords are a favorite playground of library angels—
or dictionary imps. Addicts are familiar with what one
might call "the echo-phenomenon": you find a rare word
in a crossword which is unfamiliar or unknown to you and
in the next few days it keeps cropping up in newspapers and
books; or vice versa: you are preoccupied with an idea and
find it the next day reflected in the magic grid. When I
started on this chapter I was much preoccupied with the

"clustering effect"; sure enough, during the first week of my labors, *The Times* crossword no. 12,427 carried this obliging light: *2 down:* "Close-packed groups of many desirous characters (8)." "Clusters" of course (a hundred vile lusters).

Crosswords appearing on the same day in different papers sometimes also display a "convergence effect." On May 19, *The Times* had *1 across:* "What the purchaser of unseasoned timber gets? (3, 4)"; and the *Daily Telepraph: 18 across:* "Harsh treatment for unseasoned timber (3, 4)." Solution of both, "Raw deal." *The Times* Diary commented: "our crossword editor, Edmund Akenhead, avowed that he had not known the like in more than six years at his post." Yet only a week later, on May 26, it happened again. *The Times* has: "No hedgehopping priest (3, 5)," and the *Financial Times*: "Parson operating on a lofty plane 3, 5)." Solution: "Sky pilot."

In terms of classical ESP, we would have to assume telepathic links between the compilers of these tortuous conundrums. But in other cases we would also have to assume precognition. Mr. Adrian Bell is not only an eminent writer, but also the doyen of *The Times* team of ten crossword compilers. He spends about twelve hours on each puzzle and does one a week. Two days before the Soviet spy George Blake made his sensational escape from Wormwood Scrubs gaol by means of a car which was waiting for him in a narrow lane outside, called Artillery Row, *The Times* published a crossword composed by Adrian Bell. The solution of *4 down* was "Gaol," and the solution of *27 across* was "Artillery Row." Special Branch detectives interviewed Mr. Bell, but he had no clue as to what made him invent that clue.

The most remarkable cluster of coincidences—or echoes —appeared in the *Daily Telegraph*'s crossword columns immediately preceding the allied invasion of Europe—D-

Day, June 6, 1944. The codewords referring to various operations were perhaps the best-kept secrets of the war. The codename for the entire invasion plan was *Overlord*. For the naval operations: *Neptune*. The two Normandy beaches chosen for landing the American task force were referred to as *Utah* and *Omaha*. And the artificial harbors that were to be placed in position off the beaches were called *Mulberry*.

The first codeword appeared in the solution of crossword 5,775 in the *Daily Telegraph* of May 3: UTAH. The second on May 23: OMAHA. The third on May 31: MULBERRY. The fourth and fifth—the principal codewords—*both* appeared on June 2, four days before D-Day: NEPTUNE and OVERLORD.*

MI5 was called in to investigate. The crosswords had been composed by Mr. Leonard Sidney Dawe, a schoolmaster who lived in Leatherhead, Surrey. He had been the *Daily Telegraph*'s senior crossword compiler for more than twenty years. He had not known that the words he used were codewords, and had not the foggiest idea how they had come into his head.

The little book

The last anecdote in this collection I have recorded in an earlier, autobiographical book.[28] I am quoting it again because it was instrumental in changing my attitude towards ESP, long before I became acquainted with the work of Rhine and his school.

---

* The clues had been: "One of the U.S.," "Red Indian on the Missouri," "This bush is a centre for nursery revolutions," "Britannia and he hold the same thing," ". . . But some big-wig like this has stolen some of it at times"—in that order. The last clue becomes a little less mystifying in the light of the preceding one: "Not apparently very high class land"—solution: "common."

In 1937, during the Spanish Civil War, I was imprisoned for three months by the Franco regime as a suspected spy and threatened with execution. (I was saved by the International Red Cross which negotiated my exchange against a hostage held by the Republicans.) In such situations one tends to look for metaphysical comforts, and one day I suddenly remembered a certain episode in Thomas Mann's novel *The Buddenbrooks*. One of the characters, Consul Thomas Buddenbrook, though only in his forties, knows that he is about to die. He was never given to religious speculations, but now he falls under the spell of a "little book"—which for years had stood unread in his library—in which it is explained that death is not final, merely a transition to another, impersonal kind of existence, a reunion with cosmic oneness. ". . . There clung to his senses a profound intoxication, a strange, sweet, vague allurement . . . he was no longer prevented from grasping eternity. . . ."

Remembering that passage gave me just the comfort I needed. The "little book" to which Consul Buddenbrook owes his revelation is Schopenhauer's essay *Uber den Tod und sein Verhältnis zur Unzerstörbarkeit unseres Wesens an sich—On Death and its Relation to the Indestructibility of our Essential Selves*.

The day after I was set free, I wrote Thomas Mann a letter in which I thanked him for the comfort that I had derived from that passage, explaining the circumstances under which I had remembered it. I had not met him before; it was the first fan letter I had ever written. It was dated from the Rock Hotel, Gibraltar, May 16 or 17, 1937. The title of Schopenhauer's essay was expressly mentioned in my letter.

Thomas Mann's answer reached me a few days later in London. It was a handwritten letter, which was lost, together with all my manuscripts and files, during my flight from occupied France in 1940. I cannot, of course, remember its actual text, but its content was not easy to forget. Mann explained that he had read the Schopenhauer essay in 1897 or '98, while he was writing *The Buddenbrooks*, and had never wanted to read it again because he did not want to weaken its original strong impact. The day before, however, sitting in his garden, he felt a sudden impulse to read the essay once more after nearly forty years. He went indoors to fetch the volume from the library; at that moment there was a ring at the door and the postman handed him my letter.

Since Thomas Mann's letter was lost, there is no direct evidence for this episode. But indirect evidence is provided by the fact that I published this story in *The Invisible Writing* in 1954, when Mann was still alive. I could not have dared to do so if it had not been veridical.

There is a sequel to it which fits neatly into the pattern. I mentioned the episode in an interview with John Clare, who published it in *The Times* of February 7, 1972. On the same date a reader (Mr. Walter Bluhm, London WC1) wrote to me:

Last night I went to my book case and took out the BUDDEN-BROOKS in order to find the passage relating to the "little book"—I had recently recovered from a heart attack. I could not find the reference and mentioned it to my wife who loved the BUDDENBROOKS when Oberprimanerin in Berlin. She told me the "little book" was ascribed to Schopenhauer but she had never read it. This morning I read John Clare's interview in THE TIMES. Where can I find the "little book"?

References to Part Three

1. Wong, R., St. Albans, Herts. Letter dated October 30, 1972.
2. London and New York, 1971.
3. Letter dated April 4, 1972.

4. Maurois, André, *The Life of Sir Alexander Fleming*, trans. Gerard Hopkins (London 1959) p. 127.

5. London and New York, 1972.

6. Letter dated May 2, 1972.

7. *British Medical Journal*, April 5, 1969.

8. *Sigmund Freud*, Vol. II (London 1953–7), p. 37.

9. Jung, C. G., *Memories, Dreams, Reflections*, ed. A. Jaffé (London 1963) p. 152.

10. Gamow, G., *Thirty Years That Shook Physics* (New York 1966), p. 64.

11. "Synchronizität als ein Prinzip akausaler Zusammenhänge" in Jung-Pauli, *Naturerklärung und Psyche. Studien aus dem C. G. Jung-Institut, Zürich*, IV, 1952.

12. Letter dated October 24, 1972.

13. Quoted from the transcript of a tape-recorded dialogue with Professor Hans Bender, University of Freiburg, April 30, 1957 (unpublished).

14. Hans Bender, "Der Rosenheimer Spuk—ein Fall spontaner Psychokinese" in *Zeitschrift fuer Parapsychologie und Grenzgebiete der Psychologie*, Band XI, no. 2, pp. 104–12 (1968).

F. Karger and G. Zicha, "Physikalische Untersuchung des Spukfalles in Rosenheim, 1967," in *Zeitschrift fuer Parapsychologie und Grenzgebiete der Psychologie*, Band XI, no. 2, pp. 113–31 (1968), Francke Verlag, Bern and Munich.

Hans Bender, "An Investigation of 'Poltergeist' Occurrences in *Proceedings of the Parapsychological Association*, no. 5, pp. 31–3 (1968).

F. Karger and G. Zicha, "Physical Investigation of Psychokinetic Phenomena in Rosenheim, Germany, 1967" in *Proc. of the PA*, no. 5, pp. 33–5 (1968).

Hans Bender, "New Developments in Poltergeist Research" in *Proc. of the PA*, no. 6, pp. 81–7 (1969).

Dr. H. Resch in *Grenzgebeite der Wissenschaft*, no. 2 (1968); no. 3 (1968); no. 1 (1969); no. 2 (1969).

Extracts from Resch, translated in the *J. of Paraphysics*, vol. 2, no. 4 (1968); vol. 3, no. 1 (1969); vol. 3, no. 2 (1969); vol. 3, no. 3 (1969); vol. 3, no. 4 (1969); vol. 3, no. 5 (1969); vol. 4, no. 1 (1960).

15. Mischo, John, "Personality Structure of Psychokinetic Mediums," *Proc. of the P.A.*, no. 5, p. 36 (1968).

16. *Over the High Wall* (London 1972).

17. Letter dated February 7, 1972.

18. Letter, summer 1972—undated.

19. Letter dated October 25, 1972.

20. Jung, C. G., *The Structure and Dynamics of the Psyche, Collected Works*, Vol. VIII, trans. R. F. C. Hull (London 1960), p. 438.

21. Letter, autumn 1972—undated.

22. Malraux, André, *Antimémoires* (Paris 1967), pp. 18–19.

23. Finch, Dr. Bernard E., London NW11.

24. Whiteman, Miss W. E., London W2.

25. Letter dated September 17, 1972.

26. Weaver, Warren, *Lady Luck and the Theory of Probability* (New York 1963), pp. 282–3.

27. Letter dated August 23, 1972.

28. *The Invisible Writing* (London and New York 1954), p. 452.

PART FOUR

Speculations on problems beyond our present understanding

ARTHUR KOESTLER

We have to learn to live with problems beyond our present understanding, and not impulsively to deny either the existence or the reality of such problems.
                                        SIR JOHN ECCLES

CONVERGENCES AND CLUSTERINGS

While working through the vast amount of anecdotal material of which the previous part represents a selection, certain patterns began to emerge, although they frequently overlapped or combined in individual cases.

Some of these patterns or leitmotifs are reflected in the subheadings. Thus in the "*library*" cases ("Eckerman," "Penicillin," "Buddenbrooks"), cross-connections are established in unexpected ways—as if magnetic lines of force were converging in semantic space.

In the *deus ex machina* type of episode we have a seemingly providential interposition just in the nick of time, to solve a problem (pulping Tarzan), avert a disaster (the emergency brake) or fulfill a premonition (lightning on the football field). We note in passing that the interposition occurs indiscriminately on tragic as on trivial occasions—whether "a hero perish or a sparrow fall."

In the "*Poltergeist*" cases (Freud's bookcase, Harvie's lampshade, Rosenheim), emotional tensions coincide with gross physical events—again regardless of whether the effect is dramatic or grotesque.

Among the most frequent convergence-phenomena are unlikely *encounters* not explainable by classical ESP: Michael Meyer's cricket partner witnessing the accident to his car; Dr. Cockburn's visitors from Canada; the landlady of the "King of Brabant," etc. The "encounters" may even focus on a dead person, as in Dr. Fairfield's triple involvement on a single day with Lady Louisa Stewart. Or they may involve an animal: Jung's scarab, Mrs. Priestley's grasshopper, Dame Rebecca's hedgehog.

Less frequent but equally striking are cases focused on *habitations*: Ribbentrop, Malraux. Worst of all, from the point of view of rational minds, are the clusterings of such conceptual symbols as *names and numbers*. The invasion of codewords in the crosswords could conceivably be explained by a strong telepathic effect generated by a vital secret shared by thousands of anxious men. But what conceivable agency, causal or acausal, would produce the cluster of coincidental events in the book-pulping case? Intellectual decency demands that somewhere we should draw the line between *significant* coincidences, which we suspect to contain some hidden factor, and *trivial* coincidences, due to pure chance alone.

But there's the rub—which Hardy and Harvie have rubbed in so energetically in their highly original series of experiments. They show not only the practical impossibility of drawing the line between "hits" due to telepathy, and those due to pure chance; they also cast doubt on the "purity" of chance itself. Thus there are two steps involved; the first, an experiment in conventional telepathy, with the added refinement of a great mass of people acting as "senders" to twenty "receivers" curtained off in their midst; the second, a mock experiment which is no longer concerned with the nature of ESP but with the nature of chance. The fiendish set-up of the second experiment makes one feel that it was designed by the Devil's Advocate—the devil being intent on destroying man's belief in his extrasensory powers.

Yet the outcome is wholly unexpected. First, a significant number of curtained subjects seem to enter into telepathic communication with each other regardless of the "target" displayed on the platform—a sort of cross-country ESP, it seems. *Quantitatively*, these cross-country hits, and also the "direct hits," are moderately impressive, but the *quality* of the correspondences is astounding.

Thus the first round looks like a victory for the ESP camp. Yet in the second round the Devil's Advocate succeeds in proving that chance alone, based on meticulous randomizing procedures, is capable of producing results which more or less approximate those produced in the original experiment. But that is not the end of it. The results of the mock experiments in themselves are so improbable that all we can say is that the enigmatic clustering or synchronicity effect has spread from the domain of ESP into the domain of "pure chance." Spencer Brown and Alister Hardy foreshadowed such a possibility in the 1950s; and Harvie's further mock experiments (pp. 141 et seq.) point in the same direction—of "harmonies that may resonate from the otherwise surd digits of random-number tables."

As the authors repeatedly emphasize, a single series of experiments, even if it involves two hundred people and lasts a whole week, is not sufficient evidence to prove what we are tentatively suggesting: that there is a basic flaw or inadequacy in the current concepts of chance and randomness, which calls for some additional hypothesis to account for the spontaneous emergence of order from disorder—perhaps more or less on the lines of Pauli's acausal principle. But we can at least modestly include the Caxton Hall experiment as a particularly strong and well-documented "case" in our "anecdotal evidence." We have seen certain patterns emerging from the material, which can be classified according to recurrent themes, such as library cases, dwellings, encounters and so on; to these we may now add another category: "*para-randomness*." Number lore is an old parlor game—and so is "thought reading";

but a strictly empirical approach to both can, as has been seen, produce unexpected results.

Although these different categories of coincidences represent a motley collection, there is a common element shared by all of them, a general tendency which defies definition, but invites metaphors such as "convergence," "clusterings," "resonances," "synchronizations," or what have you. It looks as if the acausal factor postulated by Pauli and Jung were guided by E. M. Forster's motto: "Only connect. . . ." One might tentatively call it the "convergence effect."

Whether one believes that some highly improbable meaningful coincidences are manifestations of some such unknown principle operating beyond physical causality, or are produced by that immortal monkey at the typewriter, is ultimately a matter of inclination and temperament; the point I shall try to make is that *no amount of scientific knowledge can help a person to decide which of these alternative beliefs is more reasonable or nearer to the truth.* I have found to my surprise that the majority of my acquaintances—among whom scientists predominate—are inclined towards the first alternative, although some are reluctant to admit it, for fear of ridicule, even to themselves. But perhaps this is less surprising than it appears because scientists—and physicists in particular—are more intensively aware than the layman of the fact that *the principle of causality is no longer applicable to modern atomic physics.* Furthermore, scientists know that no amount of sophisticated play with the theory of probability can get one over its basic paradox—the logical indecency contained in the statement that a lot of totally indeterminate and unpredictable individual events can lead to an exactly determined and predictable collective result. Robert Harvie (pp. 132f.) mentioned a classic example of this: radioactive decay. I shall return to it later; but first I must forestall a possible misunderstanding.

The mystery of probability theory is *why* it works; but nobody in his right mind would deny *that* it works. It is built into the very foundations of theoretical physics and biology; without it the edifice of modern science would collapse. Moreover, classical parapsychology of the Rhine school became scientifically respectable because the theory of probability clearly indicated that the experimental results could not be explained by chance alone.

But when we turn from laboratory experiments, involving long series of trials, to single coincidental events, the theory of probability is no longer of much help and can be put to insidious use by emotionally biassed skeptics. A few examples will indicate the uses and abuses of probability calculus.

The first two guests arrive at a cocktail party; what is the probability that they should have the same birthday (month and day, regardless of year)? Obviously 1 in 365. As the room begins to fill with more people, the chances that any two among them should have matching birthdays gradually improve. The calculus shows, rather surprisingly, that with 22 people in the room the odds of at least 2 having the same birthday are about even; and with 50 people in the room the probability is 0.97—that is, approaching 100 per cent certainty.*

This classic teaser is frequently used by skeptics as a proof that we should not attribute any special significance

* The formula for the probability p of at least one match among n persons is:

$$p = 1 - \frac{365 \times 364 \times 363 \times 362 \dots (365-n+1)}{365n}$$

to coincidences, because the oddities of the probability calculus are sufficient to explain them. This is no doubt true for trivial examples of this type. Though at first sight rather startling, its triviality becomes at once apparent if we imagine a roulette wheel with 365 slots, on which the croupier throws 50 little balls at the same time. Without complicated calculations, intuition tells us to expect that at least one pair of the 50 balls will land in the same slot. And if Lloyd's were asked for an insurance against such accidental collisions, they would promptly refuse.

Similar considerations apply to what is known among statistical mathematicians as the "small world problem." If two strangers meet on an airplane, the chances of their discovering they have an acquaintance in common is, by the same reasoning, much greater than we ordinarily assume. On p. 205 I quoted Dr. Durham's story about his new receptionist from Prague. But I omitted the last paragraph of his letter which said:

Within the next few weeks the same receptionist, on a holiday in Austria, met an old friend of mine, completely by chance, who was on a holiday from Australia; *and* met another girl, a South African friend of mine whom in the ordinary way one would not have expected her to meet—just by chance.

The reason why I omitted this paragraph was that it seemed to me to fall into the "small world" category, and could be dismissed as trivial. There are only a limited number of holiday resorts in Austria which are frequented by the category of young women who would be likely to belong to Dr. Durham's circle of acquaintances. And although the double coincidence involved three girls from three different continents, which conveys a high degree of improbability, the skeptic would be justified in replying that

the theory of probability predicts the occurrence of improbable sequences in any long series of random events.

The longest series recorded in Monte Carlo is red
coming up twenty-eight times in succession. Weaver[1] has
calculated that the probability of this happening is, in
round figures 1 in 270 million. But in Monte Carlo there
are several tables in daily use, each making an average of
500 coups a day; a simple calculation shows that an un-
interrupted series of twenty-eight reds should occur on the
average once in a century; and since the wheels have been
turning for seventy years, there is nothing to get excited
about. All you have to do is to stay for a hundred years in
the sunny climate of Monte Carlo and you can be practically
certain to have a run of twenty-eight reds.

But now reverse the situation. A gambling casino opens
in Brighton with a license valid for a single Bank Holiday
and limited to twenty-eight coups on a single table. All
twenty-eight produce red. In this case you are entitled to
think that either there is a fault in the wheel or that you
have witnessed a spectacular manifestation of the "clustering effect," with odds of 270 million against it. For in this
case the succession of twenty-eight reds represents a discrete event—a single episode on a single occasion, and cannot be trivialized by referring to the millions of runs when
they did *not* occur. The same calculus of probabilities which
reduces the Monte Carlo series to triviality turns the Brighton series into a miracle.

This leads to the related subject of selective attention or
selective memory. There is a widespread belief that the full
moon always coincides with good weather. But we only
notice the full moon when there is a cloudless sky. Or take
this example: on June 24, 1970, *The Times* carried a news
item under the heading "Elementary, my dear Wilson." It
reported that Mr. Harold Wilson had taken a lease on a

house in Vincent Square, Westminster, where he has two close neighbors: a Mr. Sherlock and a Mr. Holmes! Countless Mr. Wilsons—or Mr. Watsons—have countless neighbors who are *not* called either Sherlock or Holmes; but these cases do not receive attention; hence, by the laws of probability. . . .

This argument is reasonable as far as it goes; but it can be stretched to unreasonable lengths. Mr. Kirkpatrick (p. 175) reads a passage from Goethe's conversations with Eckermann; he switches on his radio, which happens to be tuned in to a German station, and hears the same passage being read. Thomas Mann feels an impulse to re-read the "little book" after forty years, when the postman knocks with a letter concerning the little book. When Annemarie S. is in a tense state, the neon lights explode. In these, and the majority of other cases in the previous part, to invoke probability theory or selective memory means not to explain phenomena, but to explain them away. When you put a kettle on the fire, there is, within the probability laws of thermodynamics, an infinitesimally small theoretical possibility that the water will freeze rather than boil. But as Eddington remarked, we should never believe that such a thing happened by chance, and would be justified in looking for an explanation beyond the known principles of science.

This brings us back to the question raised earlier on: where to draw the line between trivial coincidences which can be explained by probability theory, selective attention, or the "small world" argument, and that other category of experiences which prompt us to follow Eddington's advice? However, we find the same dilemma reflected in many episodes in the history of science, where the validity of empirical induction appeared in a dubious light. To mention one example: Kepler's curiosity was aroused by the apparent coincidences between the motions of the tides and the positions of the moon; he was thus led to believe that there was a hidden principle involved in this convergence and postulated (eighty years before Newton) the principle of universal gravity.* It was laughed off even by Galileo as an occult fancy, and Kepler soon dropped the idea and suggested instead that the sun acted on the planets by means of its magnetic force. (Magnetism was an established phenomenon, gravity a harebrained idea.)

Yet in spite of these historical consolations, the dilemma of "where to draw the line" is a decidedly awkward one. We are moving in a borderland shrouded in fog which blurs the frontier between chance and design, between coincidences which appear to us meaningful in a numinous way, and others which are merely an insult to the laws of probability. The psychological effect of this uncertainty is an ambivalent condition, alternating between opposite attitudes. In periods of "coincidence-proneness" one tends to suspect even trivial events of being part of a design; while other periods pass under the sign of the ink-fish, obliterating the view.

Another related difficulty mentioned earlier on derives from the fact that some of these coincidental events give the impression of being purposefully arranged or have some emotional relevance, while others are just impish or whimsical. A theologian may regard the unknown tube-passenger's pulling of the emergency handle as an act of Divine Providence—but what prompted Providence to put the grasshopper in Mrs. Priestley's bed? We have never heard it suggested that Providence has a sense of humor.

Let us go back for a moment to Sir Ronald Fisher's famous tea-tasting experiment quoted by Harvie (pp. 135f.). We remember that the lady passed the ordeal with flying

* In the Preface to his *Astronomia Nova*, published in 1609.

colors: she correctly identified the method of pouring for all eight cups, with odds against chance of one in seventy. But now let us assume that immediately after the test the lady has to rush off because she promised to have a cup of tea with a friend, and on her way is run over by a bus; so the experiment cannot be repeated and is reduced in status to an isolated episode. Was it a fluke, or were the lady's taste buds endowed with some special faculty? After a while the eyewitnesses no longer remember what exactly had happened, and it is more convenient to assume that they were deluded.

But assume that a second lady comes along, raises the same claim and passes the same test. Now, probability theory tells us that the odds against this happening by chance are $70 \times 70 = 4{,}900$ to 1. At this stage even the most conservative physiologist will admit that there may be an unknown factor at work which might be worth investigating. At which point should this change of attitude occur? When the odds are 100 to 1, 1,000 to 1, 2,500 to 1? As a rule, scientific researchers accept a much lower probability value to rule out chance. In a routine experiment, odds of 50 or 100 to 1 that the phenomenon is due to something other than chance would be considered quite satisfactory. The ESP experiments of Rhine, Soal, Schmidt, et al. have produced much higher probability ratios—in some experimental series they were of astronomical magnitudes— but are still not universally accepted. And Hardy's and Harvie's disturbing "control" experiments will no doubt provoke even stronger resistances. To say it again: in view of the paradoxa and ambiguities of the theory of probability, which occupies a strategic key position in the controversy, contemporary science can no longer be relied on to decide for us which attitude to adopt in these matters, which quantitative or other criteria to apply to the evidence, and which interpretation to put on it.

G. Spencer Brown, who was among the first to question the validity of our concept of randomness, has proposed an amusing thought-experiment as a corollary to Fisher's teacup test:[2]

Let us suppose we have an old car, and that on one occasion when we are unable to start the engine Mr. X is in the car. If our attention were drawn to this conjunction of events we should probably say that they "had nothing to do with one another," that they just "chanced" to be coincidental and that their correlation was "not significant" (p. 43).

But suppose that during the next week the car started willingly on the three occasions when Mr. X wasn't there, and refused to start on the three occasions when he was in it. "Of course we should admit that it might still very well be chance, but we should have begun to feel that it might also very well not be" (p. 44).

To verify our suspicions, we follow scientific routine and repeat the experiment. "So, if we try to start the car again with Mr. X inside and it still does not start, but starts perfectly well without him, we shall say our suspicions were *justified*, and this curious association of data is not chance after all" (pp. 44-5). But note that this verdict is *retroactive*, so to speak; it applies not only to the latest test, "in that all our previous associations of Mr. X with the car's not starting, although previously called chance associations, are now reclassified as not chance. The unreal becomes real, and Mr. X was guilty all the time" (p. 45).

But suddenly the voodoo is lifted: the car starts or refuses to start regardless of whether Mr. X is in it or not:

After a few observations we begin to suspect that we might, after all, have been wrong about Mr. X; and later, when more observations have "reduced" the original data to "insignificance," we assume that we were in fact wrong, and reclassify

the observations of the past accordingly. The real becomes
unreal, and we apologise to Mr. X (p. 45).

But this is not the end of the parable. The change of
heart will only occur if the "Mr. X effect" ceases after a
relatively short time, before our conviction of his guilt has
hardened to a degree where it becomes irreversible. If the
lifting of the curse occurs *after* that point is reached, we
shall no longer be willing to exonerate Mr. X and revert to
the chance hypothesis; we shall say instead that Mr. X has
now lost the evil power which in the past he undoubtedly
possessed. And this attitude would indeed be considered
legitimate in all statistically based sciences after, say, a
hundred successive manifestations of that power. If we
replace the words "evil power" with "psi faculty," then we
arrive at precisely the attitude which parapsychologists take
towards experimental subjects who start with high scores
of successful hits, and then suddenly or gradually go into
decline through fatigue or boredom. It is difficult to see on
what scientific grounds some hostile critics have taken exception to this standard method of procedure.

There is yet another lesson to be drawn from these
illustrations. Intuitively, we are more inclined to attribute
the successful tea-guesses to chance than the recurrences of
car starts and non-starts—in spite of the fact that in the first
case some physiological explanation might offer an alternative to the chance hypothesis, whereas in the second case
the only alternative hypothesis we could fall back on would
be black magic. However, a car has incomparably greater
personal significance for us than a cup of tea, and any
coincidence connected with the car will thus appear to us
as something much more remarkable and puzzling. The
point is that the importance we attach to coincidences depends mainly on their objective improbability, but partly
also on their subjective impact. Other people's coincidences

are never as fascinating as one's own. This should make us beware of seeing mysteries where a trivial explanation will do. But that is no justification for wearing blinkers.

The results of this discussion of the uses and abuses of the theory of probability can be summed up in a simple metaphor. Unless a person belongs to the moneyed classes, the chances are that all the pearly ornaments he will ever see worn by his female acquaintances will be cultured pearls or made of paste. Yet if he were to draw the conclusion that natural pearls do not exist except as a myth, we would consider him rather foolish and ignorant of scientific method.

ORDER FROM DISORDER

In *The Roots of Coincidence* I tried to make the point that the unthinkable phenomena of parapsychology appear somewhat less preposterous in the light of the unthinkable propositions of modern quantum physics. This argument is not new, and enlightened physicists are quite willing to concede it; yet it has not yet penetrated into the consciousness of the wider public, simply because quantum physics is an esoteric discipline beyond the grasp of the educated layman.

But the argument can also be extended into the past and applied to classical schoolbook physics. To mention an obvious example: from the point of view of naïve common sense, the type of action-at-a-distance which we call telepathy appears no more mysterious (and perhaps even less so) than that other action-at-a-distance which we call gravitational attraction. As Professor David Bohm reminds us:

To emphasise the seriousness of the problem, let us note that a steel cable having the diameter of the earth would not be strong enough to hold the earth in its orbit around the sun. Yet the gravitational force that holds the earth in its orbit is transmitted across 93,000,000 miles of space without any traces of a material medium in which these forces might be carried.[3]

Telepathy, on the other hand, could conceivably involve only small energy transfers—a kind of mental walkie-talkie

—and a small miracle is easier to accept than a big one. No wonder that Galileo dismissed the notion of universal gravity as pure mysticism and contrary to the laws of nature—which required that a body which acts on another body must be in physical contact with it. And Newton himself vehemently rejected the concept of gravity *unless* there existed some interstellar medium—either material or spiritual—which transmitted it. In a letter to Bentley he wrote:

That one body may act upon another, at a distance, through a vacuum, without the mediation of anything else by and through which their action and force may be conveyed from one to another, is to me so great an absurdity that no man who has . . . a competent faculty of thinking can ever fall into it.[4]

As I was reading again, after many years, this tortured passage, I was reminded of a science editor's remark to me: "ESP is a pain in the neck. I would be happier without it; but it is there." Newton must have felt the same pain at the thought of gravity pulling immense stellar objects with ubiquitous ghost fingers. If we no longer feel that pain, it is only because we use the term mindlessly. To live with a paradox is like being married to a shrew: after a while you no longer hear her nagging and settle down in comfortable resignation.

Thus even classical physics could only make progress at the price of insulting common sense and operating with concepts previously considered unscientific. Twentieth-century physics had to repeat both offenses in even more brutal ways. An excellent textbook for American college students contains this warning:

The physicist of the early twentieth century who lived through the development of modern physics found it a magical but a terrible time. It seemed full of paradox: things were both waves and particles, waves of no substance at all, particles without definite paths through space.[5]

In those first, magical decades of the century, Einstein, de Broglie and Schrödinger among them dematerialized matter like the conjuror who makes the lady vanish from the curtained box on the stage. Heisenberg replaced determinism with the principle of indeterminacy, and causality with probability. Dirac postulated holes in space stuffed with electrons of *negative mass*. Thomson made a single particle go through two holes in a screen at the same time—which, Sir Cyril Burt commented, is more than a ghost can do. Photons—packets of light devoid of mass—were observed in the process of giving virgin birth to twin particles endowed with solid mass; Feynman made time flow backward on his diagrams. To paraphrase an old saying: inside the atom is where things happen that don't. Yet these were not crank theories: each of the physicists whom I mentioned, received a Nobel prize for his contribution to the surrealistic panorama which modern physics has substituted for the tangible world.

The astronomers were also having a gay time. The Big Bang versus Continuous Creation controversy would have delighted medieval theologians. Some radio astronomers claim that they can detect background noises which may have originated with the pristine Bang of Creation. More recently the universe became pockmarked with so-called Black Holes. The term was coined by John A. Wheeler, Joseph Henry Professor of Physics at Princeton. It refers to hypothetical locations in the universe into which the mass of a burnt-out star which has suffered gravitational collapse is sucked at the speed of light, to be annihilated and vanish from our universe into the blue yonder. "For an object comparable to the mass of the sun," Wheeler writes, "this time [of the collapse] is less than a millisecond." The regions where these apocalyptic events are taking place are referred to as "singularities" in the continuum; here, according to the equations of General Relativity, the curvature of space becomes infinite, time is frozen and the laws of physics are suspended. The universe is turning out to be a very odd place indeed, and we no longer need ghosts to make our hair stand on end.

At the time of writing, a Black Hole has been tentatively located in the constellation of Cygnus and some astrophysicists suspect that there is a Black Hole at the center of our galaxy. One may naïvely ask where the matter that has vanished in the Black Hole "goes." Wheeler has an answer to that: it might emerge somewhere in another universe, located in superspace.

The stage on which the space of the universe moves is certainly not space itself. Nobody can be a stage for himself; he has to have a larger arena in which to move. The arena in which space does its changing is not even the space-time of Einstein, for space-time is the history of space changing with time. The arena must be a larger object: *superspace*. . . . It is not endowed with three or four dimensions—it's endowed with an *infinite* number of dimensions. Any single point in superspace represents an entire, three-dimensional world; nearby points represent slightly different three-dimensional worlds.[6]

Wheeler's colleagues have given the concept of superspace a quite favorable reception. Why not? The stranger the data which the radio telescopes and bubble chambers extracted from the world of the infinitely large and infinitely small, the stranger the explanations had to be which attempt to account for them. Superspace (or hyperspace) has been an old standby of science fiction, together with the notion of parallel universes and Dunne's multi-dimensional time. Gradually they are acquiring academic respectability.

Biology too is in the process of discovering that the mind-body continuum, which constitutes the inner universe of living organisms, manifests some very odd phenomena.

Twenty years ago, Sir John Eccles created quite a stir when he proposed that the exercise of conscious volition—a dirty word in behavioristic psychology—could, by affecting a single neuron, trigger off changes of activity in large areas of the cortical network. Since then, other researchers have shown that mental volition, assisted by various types of biofeedback apparatus, can influence the activities of the autonomic nervous system, produce changes in pulse rate, blood-pressure, and, most striking of all, it can bring on the alpha-wave rhythm of the brain. Nobody as yet can tell to what new insights the new techniques of biocybernetics will lead us. Willis Harman of the Stanford Research Institute recently wrote:

There are many signs that man may be undertaking a systematic exploration of the vast, imperfectly known universe of his own being, a step as epochal as his construction of a science of the galaxies.[7]

Even a cursory glance at these revolutionary trends in modern science is sufficient to show that the strictly deterministic, mechanistic world view, which is still dominant in sociology, the behavioral sciences and among educated laymen, has in fact no longer a leg left to stand on; it has become a Victorian anachronism. The nineteenth-century clockwork model of the universe is in shambles, and since the concept of matter itself has been dematerialized by the physicists, materialism can no longer claim to be a scientific philosophy.

As a side-effect of this philosophical upheaval, one can observe a curiously reciprocal development in the "exact" sciences on the one hand, and in parapsychology on the other. For the last fifty years, our leading physicists have been engaged in ruthlessly discarding previously sacrosanct "laws of nature" (or "rules of logic"), and replacing them with obscure mental constructs whose quasi-mystical implications are hidden in technical jargon and mathematical formalism. If Galileo were alive, he would certainly accuse them of "dabbling in occult fancies." At the same time he might have looked with a benevolent eye at the parapsychologists' increasing reliance on statistical method, rigorous controls, mechanical gadgets and electronic computers. Thus the climate in the two camps of post-materialistic physics and post-spiritualistic parapsychology seems to have been changing in opposite directions. Rhine's statistically minded successors have sometimes been accused of drab pedantry, while Einstein's successors were accused of flirting with ghosts in the guise of particles which have no mass, nor weight, nor any precise location in space.

There may be some significance in these convergent trends, yet one must be careful in drawing conclusions. The time for physics and parapsychology to fall happily into each other's arms is not yet. What they have in common are the negative attributes I mentioned earlier on: both defy common sense, and both defy laws previously considered sacrosanct. Both are provocative and iconoclastic. And, to say it once more, the baffling paradoxa produced by one make the baffling paradoxa of the other appear a little less preposterous. If whole stars can vanish into Black Holes, may there not also be singularities in the continuum which produce Poltergeists? At any rate, it is encouraging to know that if the parapsychologist is out on a limb, the physicist is out on a tightrope.

This may explain the fact that a number of eminent physicists, from Einstein downward, have shown an inclination to flirt with parapsychology—as witnessed by the list of past presidents of the British Society for Psychical Research; and, as in other subversive movements, the number of fellow-travelers exceeds by far that of card-carrying members. Thus, for instance, the discoverer of the electron, Sir Joseph J. Thomson, was one of the earliest members of the Society. Why should physicists in particular show this proneness to infection by the ESP virus? The answer is hinted at in the autobiographical writings and metaphysical speculations of some of the greatest among them. The dominant chord that echoes through them is a pervasive feeling of frustration, caused by the realization that science can elucidate only certain aspects, or levels, of reality, while the ultimate questions must always elude its grasp—vanishing into infinite regress like images reflected in a hall of mirrors. This resigned agnosticism leads either into a spiritual desert—Schrödinger, in his middle age, gave up physics in disgust—or, more often, it leads to a new open-mindedness, a sophisticated kind of innocence on a higher turn of the spiral.

These are subjective reactions. But our impatient minds are asking for more than that—for objective data and explanatory theories which would point the way to the ultimate fusion of science and parascience. There has been no shortage of such theories. The earlier ones were crude efforts to provide physical explanations for telepathy by radio waves or other known forms of radiation. They were naïve attempts at dressing the wolf in sheep's clothing, and inevitably failed. With the advent of modern quantum theory, however, these efforts became considerably more sophisticated. They were inspired by the discovery of types of elementary particles and types of processes never dreamt of before. Thus the discovery of the elusive particle called the neutrino* inspired astronomers, mathematicians and physicists to propose hypothetical explanations for parapsycho-

---

* Its existence was predicted by Wolfgang Pauli several years before it was actually found.

logical phenomena. Neutrinos are particles of cosmic origin, devoid of physical attributes (mass, weight, charge, magnetic field) traversing the earth (and our bodies) in swarms of billions at the speed of light. Because of this lack of attributes they are not stopped by other particles except in the rare case of a direct collision—which is the reason why it took so long to detect their existence. This led the late Adrian Dobbs, a brilliant mathematician, to put forward an elaborate theory in which hypothetical "psytrons" with properties somewhat similar to the neutrino's, were regarded as the carriers of ESP phenomena, capable of impinging directly on neurons in the percipient's brain. Other examples are the theory of the physicist Martin Ruderfer, postulating a neutrino-sea interacting with the nervous system, and the astronomer Axel Firsoff's suggestion of extrasensory communication by *mindons*, neutrino-like particles of an all-pervasive "mind-stuff." (And why not, one may ask, if Nobel laureate Dirac postulates a cosmic ocean of bubbles in space filled with things of negative mass?) These theories were of great ingenuity, but they could neither be proved nor disproved, which deprived them of scientific value. Like many similar efforts, they give the impression of improvised bridges across an abyss, supported by ad hoc hypotheses. One cannot help feeling that these imaginative constructions are stimulating but premature, and that they are marred by what Whitehead called "misplaced concreteness." To put it differently, parapsychology should not try to force physics into a shot-gun marriage, thus hoping to make herself into an honest woman.

A more modest yet promising approach is to be on the alert for new developments in the "official" sciences which point to certain affinities with parapsychological research. These pointers may be implicit rather than explicit, mere hints indicating analogies of limited applicability—convergent trends rather than premature shortcuts—yet they are worth a brief discussion.

In the first place, the phenomena of parapsychology imply that in certain circumstances mind has control over matter—which nineteenth-century science regarded as nonsense. Today, even conservative biologists can no longer afford that rigid attitude; they have at least to admit the evidence that hypnotic suggestion can cause physiological changes, and that biofeedback can mediate voluntary control of autonomous functions.

But, more surprisingly, it is again quantum physics which has led to a revolutionary reappraisal of the mind-body problem. Sir James Jeans's oft-quoted epigram "the universe begins to look more like a great thought than a great machine"[8] was not inspired by mysticism, but by one of the fundamental principles of quantum theory, the Principle of Complementarity. Put into plain language, it states that the elementary constituents of the universe, such as electrons and photons, are Janus-faced entities which under certain conditions behave like hard grains of matter, under other conditions like waves in a non-material medium. These two descriptions are mutually contradictory, yet the physicist needs them both, and is thus forced to treat them as if they were complementary, in peaceful coexistence. Heisenberg was apparently the first to realize that the complementarity of graininess and waviness provided a "very neat" analogy to the Cartesian dualism of matter and mind. "Atoms are not *things*," he wrote in his autobiography. "When we get down to the atomic level, the objective world in space and time no longer exists."[9] *Mutatis mutandis*, the contents of mental experience—ideas, images, memories—also exist outside the objective framework of space, time and substance, yet are somehow linked to the material brain—as the wave-character of the light-photon is somehow linked to its graininess.

Eugene Wigner (another Nobel laureate) carried the analogy a step further. He pointed out that a century ago it was regarded as a dogma that matter can influence the motion of light but light cannot directly influence the motion of matter. Today we know better: witness the polite, automatic opening and shutting of doors at airports and department stores operated by photoelectric cells. Similarly, Wigner says, some scientists hold that

the motion of matter (in the broadest sense of the word) is not influenced by consciousness, even though consciousness is obviously influenced by the motion of matter. . . . It seems more likely, however, that this view is incorrect, and that living matter is actually influenced by what it influences: consciousness. The description of this phenomenon clearly needs incorporation into our laws of nature of concepts which are foreign to the present laws of physics. . . .[10]

Elsewhere, he argues even more radically that "consciousness modifies the usual laws of physics," since "we do not know of any phenomenon in which one object is influenced by another without exerting influence thereupon."[11]

One of the difficulties which bedeviled quantum theory from its beginnings was the inevitable interference of the observer with the process observed, which led into insoluble paradoxes. Von Neumann (greatest of modern mathematicians) thought that these could only be resolved by regarding any definite statement about the process observed as valid only for the observer who makes it: "the conception of objective reality . . . has thus evaporated."[12] To talk about what the electron was "really doing" without stating what the observer was doing, became meaningless, for the electron's doings were *indeterminate* and thus could not be objectively defined, only approximately described in terms of probabilities; but this description had to include the observer, otherwise it became empty. Commenting on these developments, Ludwik Bass recently wrote: "The deepest philosophical implications of quantum theory are connected with the need for the explicit introduction of events occurring in the consciousness of an observer into the description of the . . . process."[13] David Bohm, in a symposium on *Quantum Theory and Beyond*,[14] sums up the situation by rejecting "any kind of description which [considers] the 'observer' and the 'observed system' as separately existent."

Now this, as many leading physicists are aware, is an attitude with certain similarities to Vedantism—which teaches that the object perceived cannot be separated from the mind of the perceiver; that the observer and the thing observed constitute a single, indivisible, fluid reality: I am thou and thou art I.

One might conclude, with Dr. Good, writing in that brilliant anthology *The Scientist Speculates*, that "the physicist's psi function [i.e., Schrödinger's basic wave equation of the electron] is mysterious enough to provoke the conjecture that it may in some sense explain features of the mind. Perhaps the psi of quantum physics depends on the psi of the parapsychologists."[15] Henry Margenau, Professor of Physics at Yale, arrived at exactly the same conclusion: "Interestingly and perhaps amusingly, the physicist's psi . . . has a certain abstractness and vagueness of interpretation in common with the parapsychologist's psi."[16]

Thus it is no exaggeration to say that there is an esoteric, "mentalistic" trend running through the fantastic world of quantum physics—which ranges from veiled hints to frankly mystical statements by men like Einstein ("God does not play dice with the universe"), Pauli, Eddington,

Jeans, Wigner, Bohm, Margenau, Pascal Jordan, Fred Hoyle and so on—all eminent in their profession. Jeans's epigram, already quoted, that the universe looks more like a thought than a machine, was a sober, factual summary of this trend.

A second analogy between recent developments in science and parascience is provided by the increasingly *holistic* trend in the former—based on the insight that the whole is as necessary for the understanding of its parts as the part is for the understanding of the whole. In biology this trend is again obvious (I shall return to it later); in physics it is fairly recent and fraught with revolutionary implications.

The physicist of the eighteenth and nineteenth centuries believed in the dictum of that great astronomer, Laplace, that a superior intelligence, given a complete description of the atoms in a single grain of sand, could deduce therefrom the state of the whole universe and the entire course of its future. Today the situation is virtually reversed. The wave-function describing a free electron traveling through space is, theoretically, spread out over the whole universe, and the amplitude of the wave in a given region is merely a measure of the probability that the electron will be found in that region. As Professor Northrop put it in his introduction to Heisenberg's *Physics and Philosophy*:[17]

Heisenberg shows also that the including of the experimental apparatus and even of the eye of the observing scientist in the physical system which is the object of the knower's knowledge does not help, since, if quantum mechanics be correct, the states of all objects have to be defined in principle by recourse to the concept of probability. Consequently, only if the whole universe is included in the object of scientific knowledge can the qualifying condition "for an isolated system" be satisfied. . . .

And Heisenberg himself: "The system which is treated by the methods of quantum mechanics is in fact a part of a much bigger system (eventually the whole world. . . .)"[18] Or, a physicist of the younger generation, Dr. F. Capra: "What we call an isolated particle is in reality the product of its interaction with its surroundings. It is therefore impossible to separate any part of the universe from the rest."[19]

This statement can be applied not only to the microworld of quantum physics, but also to the familiar large-sized objects of everyday life. The inertia of all terrestrial objects is, according to the so-called Mach's Principle, determined by the total mass of the universe around us. The flattening of the earth's poles, according to General Relativity, must be explainable either in terms of the earth's rotation *or* by the influence of the daily rotation of the firmament around us. And the same applies to the swinging of Foucault's pendulum, to the Coriolis force which affects the course of jet planes, and to centrifugal—i.e., inertial—forces in general. To quote Professor Margenau again:

Inertia is not intrinsic in the body at all; it is induced by the circumstance that the body is surrounded by the whole universe. It is for this reason that a force is needed to accelerate an object. . . . We know of no physical effect conveying this action; very few people worry about a physical agency transmitting it. As far as I can see, Mach's principle is as mysterious as your unexplained psychic phenomena, and its formulation seems to me almost as obscure.[20]

I shall try the reader's patience with three more brief illustrations of quantum lore—known as the Einstein–Podolski–Rosen, or E.P.R., paradox; the paradox of "Schrödinger's cat"; and the paradox of the "Pauli–Verbot" or Pauli's Exclusion.

The first has often been compared to telepathy or psychokinesis in the quantum realm; but it is rather involved, so I must tell it in a simplified way. We bounce two electrons off each other; they will fly away in different directions.

But because of their previous interaction, observing electron A enables me to make precise statements about electron B *without interfering with it*; and even to influence its behavior within the limits of its indeterminacy. The controversy about the interpretation of the E.P.R. paradox has been going on since 1933 when Einstein proposed it, and is still happily continuing in the technical journals.

"Schrödinger's cat" needs a word of introduction. Classical logic was ruled by the principle *tertium non datur*—"the excluded third" (or "excluded middle"). If a statement has any meaning at all, it must either be true, or its negation must be true: "the chair is here" or "the chair is not here" excludes a third possibility. But in quantum theory (and in new types of symbolic logic) this is no longer the case. Heisenberg gives the example of an atom which may be in the left half of a box or in the right half of the box in a state of indecision: "But the term 'not decided' is by no means equivalent to the term 'not known.' 'Not known' would mean that the atom is 'really' left or right, only we do not know where it is. But 'not decided' indicates a different situation."[21] This "different situation" arises as a consequence of the atom's indeterminateness, and can only be described by a multi-leveled logic which accepts "degrees of truth" and readmits the excluded third. But supposing we have a cat in a cage with a vial of cyanide. So long as the atom stays in the right half of the box, all is well. But when it enters the left half of the box, it will trigger a sensitive mechanism which breaks the vial and thus kills the cat. After this experiment has continued for a while, is the cat dead or alive?

It must be one or the other—or so we would think. But according to a standard . . . interpretation of the mathematics of quantum mechanics, the cat at the end of the hour is in a limbo state, with a fifty-fifty chance of being alive and a fifty-fifty chance of being dead.[22]

The cat's existence or nonexistence is not subject to a multi-tiered logic. The paradox was proposed in a different version by Schrödinger in 1935 and is still going strong.* Its value as an analogy lies in showing how acausal micro-events ruled—or rather, set free—by the indeterminacy principle, could trigger off dramatic events in our own macro-world. Professor Michael Polanyi has invented a nicer variation of it:

There is a story of a dog-owner who prided himself on the perfect training of his pet. Whenever he called: "Here! will you come or not!" the dog invariably either came or not. That is exactly how electrons behave when controlled by probability.[23]

My third and last example is the Pauli Exclusion principle—which says, roughly speaking, that any one of the "planetary orbits" inside an atom can only be occupied by one electron at a time. If it were not so, chaos would result; but why is it so? The answer—or rather, absence of an answer—is again best described in a passage (compressed) from Margenau:†

Most of the organising actions that occur in nature are brought about by the Pauli Principle, which is simply a principle of symmetry, a formal mathematical characteristic of the equations which in the end regulate phenomena in nature. Almost miraculously it calls into being the forces which bind atoms into molecules and molecules into crystals. The impenetrability of matter, its very stability, can be directly traced to the Pauli Exclusion Principle. Now, this principle has no dynamic aspect to it at all. It acts like a force though it is not a force. We cannot speak of it as doing anything by mechanical action.

* It actually referred to the indeterminacy in radioactive decay, but the principle is the same.

† Quoted at greater length in *The Roots of Coincidence*, p. 89.

No, it is a very general and elusive thing; a mathematical symmetry imposed upon the basic equations of nature.[24]

We remember Pauli's obsession with symmetry and mirror images. It turned out to yield one of the fundamental principles in physics. But if we ask for the cause which makes nature obey it—there is no cause to answer.

A German proverb says: "*Alle Vergleiche hinken*"—all analogies limp. Some may even hobble along with a wooden leg or an artificial joint. One must bear this warning in mind whenever the temptation arises to regard an analogy as a proof—to jump to the conclusion that if neutrinos exist, then ghosts must exist.

On the other hand, it seems perfectly legitimate, and even imperative, to assimilate into our habits of thought the lessons which modern physics has taught us, and to incorporate them into our world-view. Relativity and quantum theory are transforming man's image of the universe around him more radically than the Copernican revolution had done, but the general public is slow in becoming aware of the change. The dogmas and taboos of nineteenth-century science relating to the concepts of space, time, matter and energy, contained within a rigid framework of causality and determinism, still dominate the habits of thought of the average educated person who prides himself on a "rational" outlook. He thus feels compelled to deny the existence of phenomena which in his view contradict the laws of nature—unaware that those laws have long been overthrown.

Let us now take another look at the main categories of parapsychological research in the light of modern physics. The most common ESP phenomena, both in folklore and in the laboratory, are telepathy and clairvoyance. Both

imply action-at-a-distance, "without the mediation of anything else"—we remember Newton's words, dismissing the
concept as an absurdity; and he would no doubt reject as
an even greater absurdity the modern interpretation of
gravity as a result of curved and warped space. The analogy
limps, of course, because gravity, whatever it is, can be
quantified and works in a reliable and predictable way—
which telepathy does not. But the basic conceptual difficulty
is shared by both, and is further shared by the notion of
electromagnetic waves traveling through a vacuum, without
any substance to carry them—ripples that spread not in
water, nor in air, nor in a piano-string, but in nothingness.
Imagine Newton resurrected and invited to watch a tele-
vision program showing a football match played in Mexico
and transmitted by satellite. The engineer appointed to explain to Sir Isaac how and why the thing works would get
tied up in knots, like a schoolboy who has not learnt his
lesson properly—until the Visitor, tired of his evasions,
would utter the verdict that the figures on the screen were a
product, not of science, but of magic. Insofar as understanding is concerned, are we in a much better position
than Newton? The anthropomorphic notion of "forces" has
now been replaced by the more noncommittal term "fields"
—electromagnetic fields, gravitational fields, etc. This does
not help in the least our efforts at comprehending what
"really" happens inside the box and outside in the (nonex-
istent) "ether"; yet the semantic sleight-of-hand is justified
because, once more, the theories *work*—reliably, predict-
ably, repeatably. There is nothing to prevent the parapsychologist from postulating his own psi-field, or "psycho-
magnetic" field. But he cannot provide his own equivalents
of Maxwell's and Einstein's field equations, nor any guarantee that his field will do what is expected of it—and so
for the time being it will be a rather barren field, with here

and there a few stalks of corn among the weeds. But a priori he is quite entitled to create his field, and cultivate it as best he can, for there is sufficient evidence to justify his belief that the phenomena are worth investigating.

The third category of classic ESP phenomena, precognition, including premonitory dreams, seems to have an even higher degree of incredibility than telepathy and clairvoyance. Yet one must again bear in mind that the physicist's concept of Time is radically different today from what it was under Queen Victoria's reign. Fred Hoyle, England's leading astronomer, has put the matter in his usual provocative way:

You're stuck with a grotesque and absurd illusion . . . the idea of time as an ever-rolling stream. . . . There's one thing quite certain in this business: the idea of time as a steady progression from past to future is wrong. I know very well we feel this way about it subjectively. But we're the victims of a confidence trick.*

On the macrocosmic scale of very large distances and high speeds, the paradoxa of Relativity play havoc with our earthly notions of time. On the microcosmic scale they do the same. Feynman's positrons are pellets of antimatter which are assumed to travel for short distances backwards in time, yet leave tracks observable on photographic plates. At present it is an open question whether there exist galaxies composed entirely of antimatter,† and whether in such galaxies time would flow in a direction opposite to ours. In

---

* Fred Hoyle, *October the First is Too Late* (London 1966). This is a work of science fiction, but the author's introduction reassures the reader that "the discussions of the significance of time are intended to be quite serious."

† i.e., atoms in which the electric charges of their constituents are the reverse of those in "ordinary" matter.

some laboratories an active search is going on for hypothetical "tachyons"—particles of cosmic origin which are supposed to fly faster than light and consequently, according to orthodox Relativity theory, in a reversed time direction. They would thus carry information from the future into our present, as light and x-rays from distant galaxies carry information from the remote past of the universe into our now and here. In the light of these developments, we can no longer exclude on a priori grounds the theoretical possibility of precognitive phenomena, such as, for instance, those produced in the Soal–Shackleton experiments. The logical paradox that predicting a future event may prevent or distort it is circumvented by the indeterminateness of the future in modern physics and the probabilistic nature of all forecasts.

The situation is different, however, when we turn to the fourth category of parapsychological phenomena, psychokinesis, or PK for short. Helmut Schmidt's experiments at Duke University, with the beta-ray emission of a radioactive substance, could still be accommodated within the framework of quantum physics, because that PK influence, whatever it is, would operate on the micro-scale of the atomic world, triggering a process which in itself is undetermined— one unknown entity impinging on another. But when we move up to the macro-scale—e.g., the dice-throwing experiments—the energies required to make the dice roll in a given direction or show a pre-selected face, are of a much higher order of magnitude, where quantum indeterminism no longer applies.* And when we get to Poltergeist-type phenomena, such as the explosions in Freud's bookcase and other "convergence effects," analogies with specific aspects of modern physics can no longer be found; but we still have

---

* A notable exception is apparently the dice experiments by Jan Forwald evaluated in terms of quantum mechanics by Evan Harris Walker.[25]

those general affinities which have been discussed in previous pages. Why should we shrink mentally from Jung–Pauli's synchronicity concept as an "acausal connecting principle" when physicists calmly accept the same Pauli's acausal Exclusion Principle as a cornerstone of modern science? Why should we be shocked by Jung's claim that acausal connections might be "of equal importance in the universe to physical causation," when the laws of probability which lend order to the universe are the prime example of such acausal connections? And could it be that telepathy, clairvoyance, precognition, psychokinesis and meaningful coincidences are merely *different manifestations, under different conditions, of the same universal principle?* This is the question which Alister Hardy raised in the opening pages of this book, and to which we must return at the end of the journey.

The idea of connections beyond physical causality did not, of course, originate with Jung and Pauli; its immediate ancestry can be traced back partly to Schopenhauer and partly to the Austrian biologist Paul Kammerer. Schopenhauer wrote:

Coincidence is the simultaneous occurrence of causally unconnected events. . . . If we visualise each causal chain progressing in time as a meridian on the globe, then we may represent simultaneous events by the parallel circles of latitude. . . . All the events in a man's life would accordingly stand in two fundamentally different connections.*

As for Kammerer, he published in 1919 his book *Das Gesetz der Serie*[26] (which put an end to his academic career).

* Schopenhauer's ideas and the history of the classic forerunners of the synchronicity concept are treated at greater length in *The Roots of Coincidence.*

His concept of Seriality referred to the recurrence of meaningfully, but not causally, connected events. He too, like Jung, kept a log-book of coincidences—he regarded them as the tips of the icebergs which happened to catch our eyes among the ubiquitous manifestations of Seriality. And he, too, compared the acausal factor to universal gravity—although the latter acts indiscriminately on matter, whereas the hypothetical factor correlates by affinity, or a kind of selective resonance. "We thus arrive," he wrote, "at the image of a world mosaic or cosmic kaleidoscope, which, in spite of constant shufflings and rearrangements, also takes care of bringing like and like together."

This could almost be taken as a comment on Harvie's randomizing experiments. But in fact the idea can be followed all the way back to the Pythagorean Harmony of the Spheres, and the Hypocratic's "sympathy of all things": "there is one common flow, one common breathing, all things are in sympathy." The doctrine that everything in the universe hangs together, partly by mechanical causes but mainly by hidden affinities which also account for apparent coincidences, was not only the foundation of primitive magic, of astrology and alchemy; it runs as a leitmotif through the teachings of Taoism, of the Neoplatonists and the philosophers of the early Renaissance. It was neatly formulated among many others by Pico della Mirandola, *anno Domini* 1550:

Firstly there is the unity in things whereby each thing is at one with itself, consists of itself, and coheres with itself. Secondly, there is the unity whereby one creature is united with the others and all parts of the world constitute one world.[27]

Compare this with the modern physicist's statement (p. 252): "It is impossible to separate any part of the universe from the rest." The dominant aspect in both quotations, separated by four centuries, is a holistic view of the universe which transcends physical causality. The scientific revolution of the seventeenth century put a temporary end to this type of thinking and proclaimed mechanical causality as the absolute ruler of matter and mind. By historical standards, this rule did not last too long: after three centuries of it, we are witnessing a swing of the pendulum in the opposite direction. The twin tyranny of mechanical causality and strict determinism has come to an end; the universe has acquired a new look, which seems to reflect some ancient, archetypal intuitions of unity-in-diversity, on a higher turn of the spiral. Mach's principle (p. 252) has become an integral part of modern physics, even though it has an odor of mysticism. For it implies not only that the universe at large influences local events, but also that local events have an influence, however small, on the universe at large. As Whitehead has put it, rather dramatically: "Any local agitation shakes the whole universe. The distant effects are minute, but they are there. . . . There is no possibility of a detached, self-contained existence."[28] Everything hangs together; no atom is an island; microcosm reflects macrocosm, and is reflected by it.

In biology, too, as briefly mentioned before, there is a search for new principles—or, perhaps, a revival of earlier insights—which would provide a more satisfactory approach to the creative aspects of evolution than Neo-Darwinism, for all its historical merits, has been able to provide. Jacques Monod's *Chance and Necessity* may turn out to be the swan-song of a somewhat presumptuous generation of biologists who claimed that chance mutations preserved by natural selection provide the *complete* explanation of the emergence of higher forms of life, and its complex, purposive forms of behavior. Here is a typical passage from Monod's book that in 1971 created such a stir:

. . . Chance alone is at the source of every innovation, of all creation in the biosphere. Pure chance, absolutely free but blind, at the very root of the stupendous edifice of evolution: this central concept of modern biology is no longer one among other possible or even conceivable hypotheses. It is today the *sole* conceivable hypothesis, the only one that squares with observed and tested fact. And nothing warrants the supposition—or the hope—that on this score our position is likely ever to be revised.[29]

One might think it is the voice of Moses on Mount Sinai rather than of a geneticist at the Institut Pasteur.* In spite of his naïve assertion that the theory he defends is, so to speak, guaranteed to last for eternity, there are today a growing number of eminent biologists who have come to realize that chance mutations may provide part of the explanation, but not the whole explanation, and perhaps not even an important part of it. "I have come to believe," Hardy said in his Gifford lectures, "that this present-day view of evolution is inadequate." The arguments of the critics are varied, but they all share the conviction that an essential part of the picture is missing.

This discontent with the mechanistic interpretation of evolution is indirectly connected with the progressive emancipation of biology from the stranglehold of certain principles of classical physics, epitomized in the famous Second Law of Thermodynamics. Enunciated by the German physicist Clausius in 1850, it said: Heat cannot of itself pass from a colder to a hotter body. This laconic, lapidary and apparently self-evident statement was to have momentous

---

* Malicious French critics have accused him of preaching "Monod-theism."

repercussions in physics, cosmology and philosophy. For it seemed to imply that the universe is running down like a mechanical clock which must eventually come to a stop because its energy is being slowly but inexorably dissipated through friction into heat and thus into the random motion of molecules; by this process, the universe, too, must finally dissolve into a single, amorphous bubble of gas of uniform temperature—the cosmic *Wärmetod*. Only during the last few decades have biologists begun to realize that the Second Law applies only to "closed systems" which are perfectly isolated from their environment. But no completely isolated systems are known even in inanimate nature; and all living organisms are "open systems" which absorb energy and matter from their environment. Instead of "*running down*" like a mechanical toy which, once wound up, disperses its energy through friction, the living organism is all the time "*building up*" more complex chemical structures from the substances on which it feeds, more complex patterns of energy from the energies it absorbs, and more complex forms of knowledge and behavior from the information conveyed by its senses.*

A similar "building up" tendency is manifested in the evolution of organisms towards an optimal realization of the potentials of living matter and living minds—a universal tendency towards "spontaneously developing states of greater heterogeneity and complexity."[31] Evolution proceeds from unity to diversity, and thence to higher forms of unity-in-diversity, creating order out of disorder, designing patterns where none existed before. This ubiquitous creative principle is as fundamental to life as its antagonist, the Second Law of Thermodynamics, is to inanimate matter. Aristotle called it the "formal (or formative) cause"—as

* cf. Schrödinger's famous dictum: "what the organism feeds on is negative entropy."[30]

distinct from the "effective cause" which corresponds to mechanical causation. Galen, and after him Kepler, called it the "*facultas formatrix*"; it is reflected in Spinoza's pantheism, and carries echoes of Goethe's "*Gestaltung*" and Bergson's *élan vital*. After its temporary eclipse during the reign of the neo-Darwinian orthodoxy, it is once more gaining ascendancy in more sophisticated versions. The German biologist Woltereck coined the term "anamorphosis" for nature's tendency to create higher forms of life; von Bertalanffy, one of the pioneers of this modern revival, adopted the term as a contrast to "morpholysis"—the disintegration of anorganic matter; L. L. Whyte called it the "morphic principle," or "the fundamental principle of the development of pattern."* It is related to Schrödinger's concept of "negative entropy" (the reversal of this dissipation of energy), which in its turn is related to what I have called elsewhere the "Integrative Tendency."†

What all these tentative formulations have in common is that they regard the morphic, or formative, or Integrative Tendency, Nature's striving towards creating order out of disorder, cosmos out of chaos, as an ultimate and irreducible principle, to be considered as equal in importance to mechanical causation, and *complementary to it in the sense that wave-function and particle-effect are complementary in quantum theory*. The phenomena of parapsychology, including the convergence or clustering effects, would then appear as the highest manifestation of the Integrative

* "Two major contrasted tendencies are evident in natural processes, towards local order and towards uniformity or general 'disorder.' The first is displayed in all processes where a region of order tends to differentiate itself from a less ordered environment. This is seen in crystallisation, in chemical combination, and in most organic processes. The second tendency is displayed in the processes of radiation and diffusion, and leads towards a uniformity of thermal 'disorder.' The two tendencies normally work in opposed directions."[32]

† See *The Ghost in the Machine*, and for a condensed version, *The Roots of Coincidence*.

Tendency, although their *modus operandi* is at present unknown, and may or may not be beyond the faculties of comprehension of our species.

It is interesting to note that speculations on these lines are very much "in the air" among contemporary physicists and biologists. The following excerpt may serve as an example; it is quoted from a letter by F. D. Peat, a physicist at the National Research Council of Canada, to the Editor of the *Journal of the Society for Psychical Research*, published in the correspondence columns of that journal.[33]

The scientific observation of recurring classes of events leads one to recognise a functional relationship of one event in terms of the parameters and coordinates of the other. Such functional relationships form many of the phenomenological laws of classical physics. In many cases the search for such a functional relationship is the result of some theoretical suggestion; however in certain cases the theoretical explanation follows some time later. (Take for example the explanation of the classical gas laws in terms of the kinetic theory of gases, or of Kepler's laws of planetary motion in terms of Newtonian gravity.)

Even in the case of relationships for which a theoretical basis had not been found, the assumption of causal relationship was normally made: the assumption, that is, that a chain of cause and effect involving material bodies in material interaction connects the two events. The question remains as to whether it is possible for functional relationships to exist in the absence of a causal chain linking them.

An answer to the above must begin with a qualification; modern quantum physics, in Bohr's interpretation, has shown that the classical idea of an isolated system or body removed from all external influences may not be maintained. That is, all systems are subject to interactions of varying strength, arising from all other systems. The majority of these interactions may be dismissed as contingencies giving rise to small "random" effects of fluctuations; that is, while all systems are strictly causally linked, the majority of such causal chains may be dismissed as negligible contingencies. The systems will be said to be causally linked if there exists a definite strong causal chain connecting them, while all other contingencies are small.

The causal relationship defined above is the Effective Cause of Aristotle and it will be recalled that he distinguished four classes of cause, amongst which were Effective and Formative cause. The latter cause deals with relationships between parts of a system *imposed by the form or structure of the system as a whole* [my italics].

I would like to suggest that the notion of the Formative Cause, and the use of Formative Cause with Effective Cause in a complementary description of a process, may be of great value in science, although somewhat neglected. Further I would suggest that processes exist for which no simple Effective Causal explanation suffices; such processes may better be described in terms of Formative Cause. It will be realised that many competing schools of psychiatry and psychology are essentially taking sides, in favour of Formative or Effective cause. It would be better if such explanations could be taken as complementing one another. The explanation by effective cause ran into difficulties with the advent of Newtonian Relativity since "causes" which propagated across empty space were postulated. With the advent of General Relativity it was realised that an explanation based within Formative Cause was more appropriate. Again, in the case of classical electro-magnetic behaviour a complementary description exists in the form of Wheeler and Feynman's "Action-at-a-distance theory" or Maxwell's theory of the electromagnetic field.

In certain cases therefore, relationships between the parts of a system may arise as a result of the properties of the whole; and in such cases the argument by formative cause is appropriate and not "a less obvious form of causality." It may be gratuitous to point out that in such cases experiments and their interpretation in terms of Effective Cause may not be the most efficient way of obtaining understanding of the particular phenomena. In addition, the inference should be clear that phenomena involving perception, personal reactions and experiences, and in particular psi phenomena, should be questioned in the complementary light of formative cause as well as effective cause.*

The somewhat obscure reference to psychology in the letter invokes yet another complementarity. Conscious reasoning is essentially governed by logic and causality, by the rule of the effective cause; unconscious mentation is irrational and symbolic, closer to the "formative cause." Thus we get: unconscious processes are related to conscious processes in the mind as the acausal factor is related to the causal factor in nature.

Another speculative suggestion was made by a reader, Mr. Chester M. Gray, formerly on the Australian Atomic Energy Commission. After advocating a pilot survey of coincidental events, which might "throw up indications of significant patterns," he continues:

I have been tempted to enunciate a "theorem" which would run something like this: "World lines† which have intersected have an enhanced probability of intersecting again."

In areas of high probability this is manifestly true, and the causality component is obvious—as for instance the probability of successive encounters of individuals who habitually travel in the same train, but there seems to be a spectrum of types of encounter coincidence in which the discernible causality component dwindles to the point of extinction—and yet "way-out" encounter coincidence events continue to occur, which seems to me to sustain a case for believing the probability of re-encounter to be enhanced far beyond mathematical probability.[34]

* To avoid semantic confusion, it should be borne in mind that the meaning of the term "causality" (in physics and in general parlance) is restricted to Aristotle's "effective cause" and does not apply to his "formative cause."

† "World lines" in Relativity Theory are tracks of processes in the four-dimensional space-time continuum. Thus the world-line of a planet is a spiral wound around the "arrow of time."

THE "HIDDEN VARIABLES"

In their stimulating book *Mathematics and the Imagination*,[35] Edward Kasner and James R. Newman made some pertinent remarks on the new look of physics. (The passages they quote are from C. G. Darwin's Presidential Address to the British Association, 1938):

Instead of serving as an expedient, as a substitute for natural laws as yet unrevealed, statistical inference has come in time to supplant them almost completely. This signifies a change in the interpretation of physical reality comparable in intellectual importance to the Renaissance. With this in mind contemporary physicists often refer to the Renaissance of Modern Physics. . . .

The old materialistic dogmatism seemed to foreclose further metaphysical speculations about the nature of reality and was "comfortable and complete." It had the "compelling power of the old logic." The outlines of the world were hard and fast, and the mysteries of the universe, its apparent uncertainties, were confessions of our own incompetence, our own limitations. When we said that the fall of a penny was determined by chance, "we regarded this confession of uncertainty as due to our own ignorance, and not the uncertainties of nature."

But the new physics and the new logic have changed our outlook as profoundly as they have changed our basic distinction between matter and energy. "We start prejudiced against probability, grudging it as a makeshift, and in favour of causality," and we end convinced that the outlines of the world are "not hard, but fuzzy. . . . The uncertainties of the world we now ascribe not to the uncertainties of our thoughts, but rather to the character of the world around us." (pp. 254–6.)

The "fuzziness" is of course caused by the indeterminacy of subatomic events. Some eminent physicists, among them Einstein, de Broglie and Bohm, were unwilling to accept this state of affairs and assumed that there must be a substratum beyond and beneath the subatomic world which determines those apparently indeterminate processes. This was called the theory of "hidden variables"—of causal factors, inaccessible to our laboratory instruments, which "secretly" enforce the laws of probability. However, the hidden variable theory has been abandoned even by its staunchest supporters, like Bohm, because it led into blatant self-contradictions—whereas the non-causal probabilistic view was self-consistent once you came to terms with its paradoxical nature.

Although the "hidden variables" were unacceptable to physics, they were and still are a fertile field of metaphysical, or paraphysical, theorizing. Theologians proposed that Divine Destiny might work from within the causality-gaps of the subatomic world ("the god of the gaps"). Niels Bohr and Sir John Eccles, Nobel laureates in physics and physiology, were among those who proposed that the quantum indeterminacy of "critically poised" neurons in the brain made room for free will as a possibility acceptable to science, while Eccles went further and included ESP and PK phenomena in his theory. Among more recent writers, E. H. Walker of the Ballistic Research Laboratories, Aberdeen, Maryland, has developed an ingenious quantum-mechanical theory in which the "hidden variables" are identified with consciousness as "non-physical, but real entities," independent of space and time, and "connected to the physical

world by means of the quantum mechanical wave function."
This theory also includes parapsychological phenomena;
but it involves advanced mathematics and is altogether too
technical to be discussed in detail.[36]

Among the many riddles of the universe, one of the most
fundamental to science and philosophy turns out to be the
question of how the laws of probability can translate this
fuzzy world of micro-events into the solid world of everyday
experience. The translation is supposed to be done by the
law of large numbers, but this law, like Pauli's Exclusion
Principle, is devoid of any physical support; it hangs so to
speak in the air. In his book on the theory of probability,
Weaver gives some striking examples which illustrate the
point.[37] The statistics of the New York Department of
Health show that in 1955 the average number of dogs biting
people reported per day was 75.3; in 1956, 73.6; in 1957,
73.5; in 1958, 74.5; in 1959, 72.4. A similar statistical
reliability was shown by cavalry horses administering fatal
kicks to soldiers in the German army of the last century;
they were apparently guided by the so-called Poisson equation of probability theory. Murderers in England and Wales,
however different in character and motives, displayed the
same respect for the law of statistics: since the end of the
first World War, the average number of murders over
successive decades was: 1920–29, 3.84 per million of the
population; 1930–39, 3.27 per million; 1940–49, 3.92 per
million; 1950–59, 3.3 per million; 1960–69, approximately
3.5 per million.

These bizarre examples may sharpen our appreciation of
the mysterious nature of probability. Von Neumann called
it black magic; paraphrasing Churchill, we may call it a
mystery wrapped in an enigma. When we discuss it in
terms of cavalry horses or the roulette wheel, we are mildly

puzzled or amused, but we may also get some intimations of its philosophical impact, and its relevance to the problem of chance and design. In physics, the role of the unpredictable dogs producing predictable statistics is played by the unpredictable behavior of micro-entities like radioactive atoms producing exactly predictable overall results. As Harvie explained earlier on (pp. 132–3), the point in time at which a radioactive atom will disintegrate is totally unpredictable, both theoretically and experimentally. It does not depend on the atom's past history, nor on its present environment; as Bohm says, "it does not have any causes"; it is "*completely arbitrary* in the sense that it has no relationship whatever to anything else that exists in the world or that ever has existed."[38] And yet it *does* have a hidden relationship with the rest of the world, because the "half-life period" of any grain of a radioactive substance (the time required for half of the totality of atoms in the grain to disintegrate) is precisely fixed and predictable. The half-life of uranium is four and a half thousand million years. The half-life of radium A is 3.825 days. The half-life of thorium C is 60.5 minutes. And so on, down to millionths of a second. There are fluctuations: somewhere along the road there may be an excess of deceased atoms over the predicted mean, or a deficit. But it will soon be put right. How is this done, since the individual disintegrations are uncaused and physically uninfluenced by what goes on in the rest of the grain? How do the dogs of New York know when to stop biting, and when to make up the daily quota? How do the murderers of England and Wales know to stop at four victims per million? It may seem that I am laboring the point, but this question is indeed at the center of the whole problem of chance and design. Since the chains of events which lead to each individual murder, or atomic decay, are ostensibly unconnected with each other, we must either assume that the fulfillment of the statistical prediction is itself due to blind coincidence, or else we are driven to opt for some alternative hypothesis on the lines discussed in previous sections, such as Jung-Pauli's acausal connecting principle or the convergence effect. On this hypothesis, *individual coincidences—acausal clusterings—would be the reciprocal of the equally acausal smoothing-out effect of the law of large numbers*: the first operating by bunching world-lines together, the second by straightening them out. Both create order from disorder, in opposite ways: the exact timing of thorium C decay to a half-life of 60.5 minutes seems to be marshaled by a military commander; the surrealistic patterns of coincidence seem to be designed by an artist. Both appear to us equally miraculous in the sense of St. Augustine's definition: "The Miracle occurs not in contradiction to Nature, but in contradiction to what we know about nature."

The experiments of Spencer Brown, Hardy and Harvie seem to indicate a vast area of ignorance at the very core of the current notions of chance and randomness. The hidden variables of some formative principle seem to invade even the sober realm of random tables—as they invaded Stewart Kauffman's random networks (pp. 160–3). It looks as if the speculations in these pages could be summed up in a single sentence, paraphrasing Spinoza: "Nature abhors randomness."

A few years ago, Alister Hardy, pursuing the same line of thought, said in his Gifford lectures: "Let me say that if some of this apparent card-guessing and dice-influencing work should in fact turn out to be something very different, it will not, I believe, have been a wasted effort; it will have provided a wonderful mine of material for the study of a very remarkable new principle."[39]

That new principle, as we are well aware, is a contemporary restatement of a conception which can be traced all the way back to the Pythagoreans. How it works we do not know; but we know that it cannot work within the frame of mechanical causality any more than the quantum phenomena can be fitted into it. It could be that it is related to the physicist's causality gaps; it could be that the roots of coincidence sprout from those gaps. To try to explain by it how the grasshopper got into Mrs. Priestley's bed would be a grotesque exercise in misplaced concreteness. It could also be that an explanation lies altogether beyond the reach of our traditional categories of thought, and the language into which we project them. Our leading physicists keep pointing out that words like time, space, matter, energy, causality, have changed their meaning and become snares for thought—language can stand as a screen between the mind and reality. As John Weightman[40] wrote in a different context, but reflecting our own perplexities:

I understand that I don't really understand what I have the illusion of understanding, since all language is no more than a mirage of comprehensibility above a sea of unknowing.

References to part four

1. Weaver, Warren, *Lady Luck and the Theory of Probability* (New York 1963).

2. Spencer Brown, G., *Probability and Scientific Inference* (London 1957).

3. *Causality and Chance in Modern Physics* (London 1957), pp. 43f.

4. Third letter to Bentley, *Opera Omnia*, IV (London 1779–85), p. 380.

5. *Physics*, Physical Science Study Committee (Boston 1960), p. 610.

6. Wheeler, John A., quoted by Laurence B. Chase, "The Black Hole of the Universe" in *University, A Princeton Quarterly* (Summer 1972).

7. Quoted in M. Karlins and L. M. Andrews, *Biofeedback* (Philadelphia and New York 1972), p. 17.

8. *The Mysterious Universe* (Cambridge 1937), p. 122.

9. *Der Teil und das Ganze* (München 1969), p. 51.

10. In *The Logic of Personal Knowledge—Essays Presented to Michael Polanyi*, ed. Marjorie Grene (London 1958), p. 232.

11. In *The Scientist Speculates*, ed. I. J. Good (London 1962), pp. 294–6.

12. Quoted by Wigner, P., in *The Logic of Personal Knowledge*, p. 237. See note 10, Part IV.

13. *Hermathena, A Dublin University Review*, no. cxii, p. 57 (1971).

14. Ed. Ted Bastin (Cambridge 1972).

15. Good, I. J., in *The Scientist Speculates*. See note 11, Part IV.

16. In *Science and ESP*, ed. J. R. Smythies (London 1967), p. 219.

17. Northrop, F. S. C., in W. Heisenberg, *Physics and Philosophy* (London 1959), pp. 29–30.

18. Ibid., p. 153.

19. *Main Currents in Modern Thought* (New York, September–October 1972).

20. In *Science and ESP*, p. 218. See note 16, Part IV.

21. Heisenberg, W., *Physics and Philosophy* (London 1959), p. 158.

22. Hoffman, Banesh, with the collaboration of Helen Dukas, *Albert Einstein—Creator and Rebel* (New York 1972), p. 198.

23. Polanyi, M., *Personal Knowledge* (London 1958), p. 21.

24. Margenau, H., in *Science and ESP*, p. 218. See note 16, Part IV.

25. Walker, Evan Harris, "Foundations of Paraphysical and Parapsychological Phenomena." To appear in the *J. for the Study of Consciousness* (1973).

26. *Das Gesetz der Serie* (Deutsche Verlags-Anstalt, Stuttgart-Berlin, 1919).

27. della Mirandola, Pico, *Opera Omnia* (Basel 1557), p. 40.

28. Whitehead, A. N., *Nature and Life* (Cambridge 1934), p. 181.

29. *Chance and Necessity* (New York and London 1971).

30. Schrödinger, Erwin, *What is Life?* (Cambridge 1944).

31. Herrick, C. J., *The Evolution of Human Nature* (New York 1961), p. 51.

32. Whyte, L. L., *The Unitary Principle in Physics and Biology* (London 1949), p. 35.

33. Vol. 46, no. 754, December 1972.

34. Letter dated Oct. 5, 1972.

35. London 1949.

36. See note 25, Part IV.

37. *Lady Luck and the Theory of Probability*. See note 1, Part IV.

38. Italics in the original. David Bohm, *Causalty and Chance in Modern Physics* (London 1957), p. 87.

39. *The Living Stream* (London 1965).

40. Book review in *The Observer*, January 21, 1973, p. 34.

APPENDIX I

(a) Details of randomizing procedure adopted to produce the large control experiments

The control-group responses were selected by the following procedures. The responses from the experiments were stored in ninety envelopes each containing the twenty responses from the different experiments. These envelopes were first of all shuffled by hand and then put into ten piles of nine envelopes apiece. These ten piles were now labeled with the digits 0 to 9, and by referring to random-number tables the envelopes were redistributed into five new piles—four of twenty envelopes, and one of ten. Thus the first lot of twenty would be selected by taking envelopes from piles 0 to 9 in the order in which the digits appear in the tables. For example, the first twenty digits in the tables are 3, 8, 8, 4, 0, 2, 2, 3, 6, 2, 7, 0, 2, 3, 6, 1, 2, 3, 0, 7. So the first lot of twenty envelopes would be made up by taking an envelope from pile 3, two from pile 8, one from pile 4, and so forth until the twentieth envelope taken from pile 7.

The twenty envelopes are now arranged in four rows of five, replicating the original formation of the cubicles (see Figure 2). The responses are taken from their envelopes, and we now have twenty piles of twenty responses—400 responses in all which after just one more operation will yield twenty control groups. If we were to look at the top layer of the present ensemble of twenty piles, we would see that all the responses are from cubicle *a*, and also that in some cases the responses originate from the same individual.

This is because there will inevitably be more than one envelope from one of the sequences of ten experiments, in which the same individuals took part, in the original series. Thus in the first ensemble of twenty we have the responses from experiments 80, 78, 73, 111, 115, 119, 9, 70, 30, 107, 41, 49, 48, 123, 11, 20, 13, 19, 12, 109. The same group of subjects took part in experiments 11, 13, 19, 12; another group took part in experiments 41, 49, 48; another in numbers 73, 78, 80; another in 107 and 109; and finally yet another in 111, 115 and 119.

The response piles from these experiments are now cut, like a pack of cards, at an arbitrary point, again by reference to random-number tables. We end up with a twenty-layered ensemble, each layer of which comprises twenty responses originating from different individuals on different occasions. And now, *voilà*, we have twenty control groups.

The layers of the ensemble are now peeled off one by one, and those responses within a control group which are appreciably similar to one another are recorded and their positions relative to one another within the array of four rows of five noted.

This procedure was repeated for three of the lots of twenty randomly selected envelopes. The responses from the remaining thirty envelopes were amalgamated in the following way. First of all the pile of twenty was treated in the same way as the three previous lots—ending up with an ensemble of twenty control groups. The responses from the ten remaining envelopes were now shuffled by hand. Ten of these 200 responses were then shuffled into each of the twenty piles of the ensemble. The resulting piles of thirty responses were cut by reference to random-number tables, and the similar responses within each control group recorded as before. The method of sampling which we used to draw out the random groups of responses for the controls is known as "sampling without replacement." An alternative method of drawing out responses, "sampling with replacement," could also have been used. Using the latter method, a response, after it had been selected, is put back into the pool of responses before the next draw. Thus on each draw, each response has an equal chance of being selected and the size of the pool never diminishes. In this way one can continue to draw samples to infinity; so sampling is from an infinite population of responses. In sampling without replacement the size of the pool decreases after each draw. It may be thought that this method would lead to an overestimation of the number of coincidences—that as the pool from which the responses are drawn becomes smaller the probability of finding similar responses becomes larger. However, this is not so. It can be shown that when the size of the sample is small in comparision to the size of the population, then sampling from a finite population (i.e., without replacement) gives as accurate an estimate as sampling with replacement (i.e., from an infinite population). A proof of the equivalence of these two methods of sampling may be found in most standard works on probability and statistics.* Where the sample size is 20 and the population size is 1,800, one can be quite confident that the method of sampling used gives as unbiased an estimate of the population mean as sampling with replacement.

(b) Further consideration of the adjacent coincidences

The number of different ways of selecting two adjacent cells in a four-by-five array is 31. But the total number of com-

---

* e.g., Mosteller, Rourke, Thomas, *Probability with Statistical Applications* (Reading, Mass. 1970).

binations of two cells (adjacent and non-adjacent) from twenty cells is 190.

If the coincident thoughts were to occur in random positions in the array, we would then expect that over a long series of experiments—each with twenty subjects—the proportion of coincident thoughts occurring in adjacent positions would be equivalent to 31/190 of the total number of coincidences.

Thus in the original series of 90 experiments, where 328 coincident thoughts were found, the number which could be expected to occur in adjacent positions, *if the distribution is random*, is 31/190 of 328 = 54. Against this theoretical number of adjacent coincidences we found that 98 of the 328 coincident thoughts in the original experiments were actually adjacent. In the 90 mock experiments we found that 67 of the 321 coincidences were adjacent, whereas the expected theoretical number would be $31/190 \times 321 = 52$. It would appear then that the coincident thoughts in the original experiments occurred in adjacent positions to a far greater extent than would be expected from a random distribution of similar responses within the array. Are there indeed a significantly greater number of adjacent coincidences in the original experiments than in the mock experiments? To test whether this was the case, a χ^2 test to determine the significance of the difference between the original and mock experiments was carried out. This gave a value of $\chi^2 = 6.34$, for which p is less than .01. The coincidences in the original experiments therefore occur in adjacent positions to a significantly greater extent than in the mock experiments, and the odds against this difference having arisen by chance alone are about 100 to 1. So in addition to the coming together in time of similar thoughts, there seems to be, in the original experiments at least, an inexplicable spatial clustering of similar responses.

APPENDIX II

A note on the formula used in Part Two

The probability distribution of a discrete random variable may be approximated by means of the standard normal distribution for a continuous random variable. For binomial experiments the probability of an observed deviation from mean expectation may be obtained by transformation of the observed deviation into a standard deviate, or "Critical Ratio." The probability associated with a given Critical Ratio may be obtained by reference to tables of the standard normal distribution.

For binomial experiments such as those described in Part Two the Critical Ratio is obtained by dividing the observed deviation by the standard deviation.

$$\text{Thus, C.R.} = \frac{X - np}{\sqrt{npq}}$$

where n = number of trials, p = probability of success on a single trial, q = probability of non-success, and X is the observed matching score.

So, for example, in the first experiment with pseudo-random digits (p. 148)

$$\text{C.R.} = \frac{2{,}364 - 24{,}800 \times 1/10}{\sqrt{24{,}800 \times 1/10 \times 9/10}}$$
$$= -2.41$$

Reference to tables shows that a Critical Ratio of 2.41 has an associated probability of .016.

The level of significance of an observed deviation of 116 (either positive or negative) is therefore p = .016.

APPENDIX III

Catalogue of responses at the Caxton Hall telepathy experiments

A complete list of all the responses (i.e., individual thoughts) expressed either in drawings or in words by those taking part as "percipients" in the Caxton Hall "telepathy" experiments except those in which symbols were used as "targets." Against each item is shown the number of the experiment in which it occurred, together with the letter indicating in which cubicle the particular "percipient" was situated; for example, in the first item shown, "ACCIDENT, people taken to hospital, 100*b*" indicates that the response occurred in experiment 100, cubicle *b*. Where an idea occurred as an alternative to another one in the same response, each would be listed as a half, thus: "ACORN, 103*s*½," or if there were three ideas in the same response, each would be shown as "APPLE 116*s*⅓."

ACCIDENT, people taken to hospital, 100*b*
ACE OF HEARTS, 15*q*
ACORN, 103*s*½, 126*i*½
AERIAL VIEW, 118*i*
AEROPLANE (or s) or AIRCRAFT, 14*t*, 16*c*, 22*q*, 29*q*, 30*n*, 60*f*, 64*b*, 64*e*, 69*n*, 79*f*, 80*l*, 114*e*, 126*b*, 130*d*
   flying towards one, 83*i*
   aircraft in blue sky or clouds, 7*c*, 16*p*½, 30*s*, 139*b*
   aircraft—space—earth below, 119*j*

old-fashioned aircraft, 60*c*, 114*s*
   approaching airfield, 129*h*½
   looking down from height over sea and mountains, 87*f*
   flying over mountains, 119*k*
AFRICA, MAP? 90
AFRICAN SCENE,
   hut and natives, 8*l*
AIR, 126*l*½
   connected with, planes? clouds?, 60*h*
AIR LINER, with gangway steps and bus, 135*b*
AIRSHIP, 79*a*½, 107*r*

ALLIGATORS, 79*i*

AMAZEMENT, 21*b*

AMERICA, 8*a*½

ANIMAL, 10*t*, 29*p*, 84*b*, 104*a*½,
105*b*, 116*m*
(bear?) in woodland scene, 28*n*
furry, 120*i*
large animals, head with horns,
122*j*
farm (cow or goat), 1*q*
four-legged, 94*l*
small animal, 137*a*½
small animal with long snout,
137*f*

ANIMAL LIFE, or Nature, 59*h*

ANIMALS, 8*q*
possibly at zoo, 40*s*, 68*e*
with curly horns, outdoors, 30*d*
in fields, 7*p*
animals feeding, 38*e*
in snowstorm, 58*a*
litter of baby animals at play,
140*e*

ANTELOPE, 74*j*

ANTS, 8*a*½

APPLE, 2*j*, 12*p*, 21*i*, 22*r*, 41*s*, 52*f*,
63*f*, 71*f*, 73*o*, 81*h*, 102*m*,
116*l*, 116*s*½, 117*n*½
green sour, 105*c*
(or orange) segment or peel,
133*b*

APPLE TREE, 1*s*, 83*c*

ARCH, or magnet, 43*o*

ARCHWAY, 10*h*½
stone, 61*r*

ARMADILLO, 135*c*

ARMCHAIR,
facing right, 104*c*, 127*r*
facing right with tongs, 8*h*½
facing left, 15*n*, 15*o*

ARMOUR, 6*h*½

ARMY marching, 27*r*, 90*d*
—soldiers or children, 105*m*

ARROW,
going into water, 23*d*
piercing bullseye, 124*j*

ATHLETE, 5*r*

ATOMIC explosion or mushroom,
38*o*

BABY, 5*k*½, 73*e*

BALL, 14*f*, 32*g*, 103*f*, 114*f*½
beach, 71*g*
child's, 41*k*

BALLET,
dancing, 110*s*
scene, 19*a*

BALLOON (or s), 27*j*½, 52*j*½, 79*a*½
with gondola, 90*e*, 130*n*, 139*j*
with scenery below, 108*c*
toy balloons, 51*q*½, 117*l*
red, 107*q*

BALUSTRADE, 50*b*

BANANAS,
bunch of, 84*d*, 104*q*
and grapes, 117*k*

BAND, marching, 18*r*

BARREL, 91*h*

BASKET, 133*j*½
wastepaper, 115*l*
of flowers, 131*h*
shopping, 93*i*
wicker or lobster pot, 132*i*

BAT, 80*g*½

BATHING HUTS along beach, 70*c*

BATTLE FIELD,
with soldiers, 73*p*
scene with guns and violent
figures, 38*j*

BEACH, 49*n*½
lonely, with sand dunes, 120*k*

BEADS, string of, 127*q*

BEAR, 106*s*

BED or BEDSTEAD, 32*k*, 33*p*, 40*h*,
116*o*½, 134*g*
cover, 137*j*½

BEEHIVE with bees, 19*c*

BELL-SHAPED OBJECTS (bells, um-
brella, toadstool), 136*b*

BELLS in tower, 50*c*½

INDEX

About the Authors

Sir Alister Hardy, a native of England and a graduate of Oxford University, was elected a Fellow of the Royal Society in 1940 and knighted in 1957. He served on the "Discovery" expedition to the Antarctic (1925–27), has held professorships of sociology at the Universities of Hull (1928–41), Aberdeen (1942–45) and Oxford (1946–63), and now directs the Religious Experience Research Unit at Oxford. His books include *The Open Sea, Great Waters, The Living Stream* and *The Divine Flame*.

Robert Harvie was born in 1946 at Malvern, England. Before taking a degree in psychology at the University of London, he worked as a journalist and as a community worker with the nomadic Irish caravan dwellers in Britain. He is now conducting research in parapsychology at the Religious Experience Research Unit at Oxford.

Arthur Koestler was born in 1905 in Budapest. Though he studied science and psychology in Vienna, at the age of twenty he became a foreign correspondent and worked for various European newspapers in the Middle East, Paris, Berlin, Russia and Spain. During the Spanish Civil War, which he covered from the Republican side, he was captured and imprisoned for several months by the Nationalists, but was exchanged after international protest. In 1939–40 he was interned in a French detention camp. After his release, due to British government intervention, he joined the French Foreign Legion, subsequently escaped to England and joined the British Army.

Like many other intellectuals in the thirties, Koestler saw in the Soviet experiment the only hope and alternative to fascism. He became a member of the Communist Party in 1931, but left it in disillusionment during the Moscow purges in 1938. His earlier books were mainly concerned with these experiences, either in autobiographical form or in essays or political novels. Among the latter, *Darkness at Noon* has been translated into thirty-three languages.

After World War II, Mr. Koestler became a British citizen, and all his books since 1940 have been written in English. He now lives in London, but he frequently lectures at American universities, and was a Fellow at the Center for Advanced Study in the Behavioral Sciences at Stanford in 1964–65.

In 1968 Mr. Koestler received the Sonning Prize at the University of Copenhagen for his contributions to European culture. His works are now being republished in a collected edition of twenty volumes.

VINTAGE WORKS OF SCIENCE
AND PSYCHOLOGY